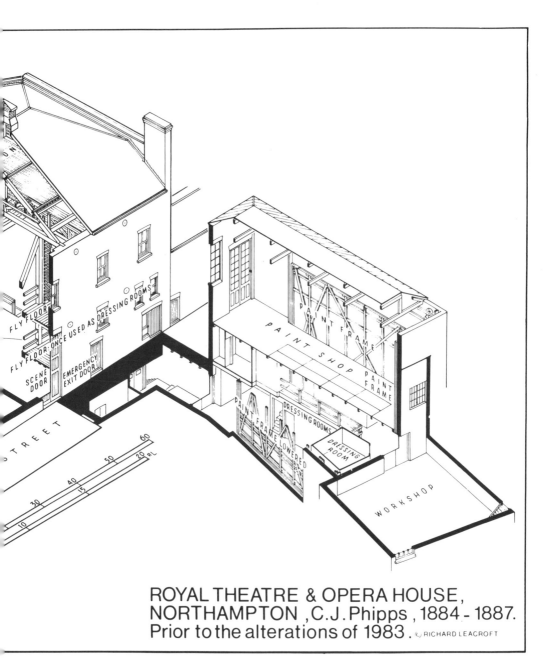

FLY FLOOR
FLY FLOOR: ONCE USED AS DRESSING ROOMS
SCENE DOOR
EMERGENCY EXIT DOOR
STREET
60
50
20 P.L.
40
15
30
10

PAINT FRAME
PAINT SHOP
PAINT FRAME
PAINT FRAME LOWERED
DRESSING ROOMS
DRESSING ROOM
WORKSHOP

ROYAL THEATRE & OPERA HOUSE,
NORTHAMPTON ,C.J.Phipps , 1884 - 1887.
Prior to the alterations of 1983 . © RICHARD LEACROFT

Repertory at The Royal

Sixty-Five Years of Theatre
in Northampton 1927–92

Subscription Copy No. *110*
This copy was subscribed for by

Alan Brown

to whom sincere thanks are expressed

Richard Foulkes

Richard Foulkes

Interior of Royal Theatre, Northampton from a drawing by Osborne Robinson. (*Adventure in Repertory*)

Repertory at The Royal

Sixty-Five Years of Theatre in Northampton 1927–92

Richard Foulkes

Foreword by Nigel Hawthorne

Northampton Repertory Players Ltd.
Sponsored by Barclaycard

To the memory of
Louis Norman Warwick d. 8 April 1989
and of
George Whitfield Dakin Foulkes d. 1 April 1989

First published 1992 by
The Northampton Repertory Players
Guildhall Road
Northampton NN1 1EA

ISBN 0 9505442 1 3

Printed by Woolnough Bookbinding
Church Street, Irthlingborough, Northants.
Typeset by EMS Photosetters, Thorpe Bay, Essex

Contents

Illustrations

Photographers are credited by name where known. The contributions of Bryan Douglas are gratefully acknowledged, as are those of Alan Burman, the Central Photographic Unit, University of Leicester and Lionel Hamilton.

vii

Foreword

THE Royal Theatre will always have a very special place in my affections. I came to it first in the mid-1950s, after a long spell of understudying in the West End, to appear in a creaking old farce called *The Sport Of Kings*. Although the critic of the *Chronicle and Echo* at the time thought I was too inexperienced to play the role – I found out subsequently that she was still at school – I was asked to remain with the company for the princely sum of, if I remember correctly, £12 a week. I was to stay there for eighteen months, and return again some five or six years later for a briefer stint.

Inevitably, Tom Osborne Robinson was the designer on both occasions. His influence was not only in the settings and costumes with which we worked, but in the very building itself. Each year on 23 April, Shakespeare's birthday, we would gather round the bard's bust at the back of the stalls and toast him in cheap, sweet sherry. This little ceremony was a small indication of the tradition Tom Robinson had built up during his years at Northampton. He loved every brick, every cornice, every strip of wallpaper – every inch of that theatre. I shall never forget that, on being told that a chandelier had crashed, like the one in *The Phantom of the Opera*, into the audience, his concern was for the chandelier which he treasured rather than for anybody who might have been killed or injured down below. As it transpired this, his favourite chandelier, was intact, it was another that had bitten the dust, and no one was hurt.

Such was Tom's care for artistic detail, that to be in a period play invoked a lesson in period movement and gesture from the great man himself. Mary Kenton told me that she was playing Titania in *A Midsummer Night's Dream* when, during the dress rehearsal, Tom leapt up from the audience, crossed the stage, regardless of the action, and stuck a large feather in her hand.

To me and to many others, Northampton Rep and Tom Robinson were synonymous. I went to see him a few weeks before he died. He was suffering from cancer and much reduced in size, and yet, curled up on a Regency chaise-longue, there was a style about his reclining position and a feeling for the period elegance it evoked which he could not help but project. He was a great character – flamboyant but very gentle. I see him now striding round the town like some nobleman of the Italian renaissance, big-bellied, big-nosed and bearded, glancing up at his favourite pieces of architecture as though he had fashioned them all himself and would guard them with his life.

Nigel Hawthorne C.B.E.

Prologue

IN March 1966 I purchased a copy of Aubrey Dyas's *Adventure in Repertory Northampton Repertory Theatre - 1927-48* in a secondhand bookshop in Swansea. Seven years later I was appointed to a job at the University Centre, Northampton. My head of department was Professor Henry Arthur Jones, a namesake of the Victorian dramatist and himself a theatre enthusiast. The first play I saw at the Royal Theatre was Simon Gray's *Butley* . . . the principal character in which is a lecturer in English Literature. Amongst my own students at the University Centre was the irrepressible Elizabeth Robinson, who promptly introduced me to her brother-in-law, the legendary Tom Osborne Robinson, who extended his friendship to me. Within months of my arrival I attended a meeting of the Northampton Literature Group - presided over by Anne Tibble, sprightly doyen of Clare scholars - at which Lou Warwick discoursed on his current theatre history project, *Theatre Un-Royal*. From Lou I learnt that Dr. Ernest Reynolds, whose book *Early Victorian Drama* had ignited my interest in the subject, was a native of the town and I lost no time in making his acquaintance. The next year Sir Gyles Isham of Lamport Hall, an idolised Hamlet for the Oxford University Dramatic Society and Hal at the opening of the Shakespeare Memorial Theatre in 1932, lectured at my first theatre summer school.

Rather to my surprise Northampton had proved to be an extraordinarily rich and propitious place for a theatre historian to settle in. My only tinge of regret was that if anything it was too well provided for - with the likes of Aubrey Dyas, Lou Warwick and Ernest Reynolds there seemed to be little scope left for me. And so for the next fifteen years I concentrated on my interest in the Victorian theatre with only minor diversions into the local scene. Then in January 1989 Lou Warwick invited me to visit him. He spoke, with courage and frankness, of his terminal illness and asked me if I would take over his projected history of the Northampton Repertory Players from 1927 to the present. This I was both sad and glad to do . . . sad at the occasion, glad that I could set Lou's mind at rest that the work would be done.

I duly received Lou's extensive collection of material - nearly thirty bulging ring-files, programmes, news-cuttings, board minutes and numerous taped interviews. One frustration for me was that Lou extended the journalist's principle of not disclosing his sources to his theatrical research, but in any case it was inevitable that my book would be very different from one by Lou.

Considering the importance of the repertory movement in the history of the twentieth-century theatre books on specific companies are few in number and confined mainly to the pioneers, Manchester, Liverpool and Birmingham. In his foreword to *Adventure in Repertory* J. B. Priestley wrote of the interest "of a repertory venture in a town that is neither very large nor very rich – a fairly average sort of place". Priestley discounted as "mistaken" the view that "A History of a Repertory Theatre in Northampton may seem of no great matter, except to people living in that town and its neighbourhood". Indeed the story of the repertory movement can only be told through individual examples and the interaction between specific local factors and national trends has proved to be the most fascinating aspect of my research.

Priestley regretted Dyas's omission of "frank details of the financial background" and I have endeavoured to rectify this, since economics are inseparable from art in the theatre. Aubrey Dyas's discretion about some of the more controversial incidents in the period covered by his book highlights the problems for an historian dealing with the recent past. I have sought to give a fair evaluation of the achievements of all concerned with the Northampton Repertory Players right up-to-date.

My requests for information have received positive responses on all fronts. Greta and Nigel Warwick have availed me of all Lou's material. The current staff of the Royal Theatre have afforded me every assistance: Michael Napier Brown, Anthony Radford, David Newland, Norma Dunville and Julie Martell, who has literally ensured that no door has remained closed to me. Anthony Radford shouldered the tasks involved in getting the book printed and masterminded its promotion. Alwyn Hargrave, chairman of the board, has been resolutely supportive throughout. Tony Parker and Alan Claridge of Northamptonshire County Council have made their records available to me. Alan Maskell has provided information for Northampton Borough Council.

I am grateful to the staff of the Northamptonshire County Record Office and the Local Collection in Northampton Public Library (Miss Arnold).

I have enjoyed lively and informative conversations with Henry Bird and the late Freda Jackson, Bryan Douglas, Maurice and Alison Dunmore, Eric and Margaret Roberts, Arnold Peters, Mrs. Irene Peake and Rose Walding to whom Aubrey Dyas was similarly indebted back in 1947. Lionel Hamilton has been a tower of strength encouraging the project, enlisting the support of former members of the company and giving unstintingly from his vast repository of personal knowledge. My other acknowledgements include John Bennett, Doris Broad, Alan Burman, David Cheshire, John Cunningham, Helen Flach, Lavinia Gibbs, Mrs. J. Harding, the late Victor Hatley, John Perkins, John Rochfort, George Rowell, Reginald Salberg and Kate Wills.

Without the help of Betty Elliott and Marjorie Jenkinson my progress would have been significantly slower. Betty sifted through Lou's files and analysed company casting; Marjorie spent hours at the microfilm viewer acquiring reviews of productions and other press material.

The publication of the book has been resourced by the generosity of Barclaycard and the subscriptions of Lou Warwick's patrons.

As with all my writing projects I have been dependent upon Pat Perkins for producing a clear typescript from an often chaotic manuscript through which she unerringly found her way. I am grateful to the University of Leicester for granting me study leave, in part to enable me to complete this book.

To my family I am indebted for their tolerance and the care with which they have picked their way through my study, the floor of which has almost disappeared under the piles of papers resting there in an order intelligible only to me. Above all to my wife Christine who has given me support, encouragement and understanding and has shared this venture with me chapter by chapter.

Richard Foulkes
University Centre, Northampton

CHAPTER ONE

Prelude

IN 1973–4 the Christmas–New Year production at Northampton's Royal Theatre was *Chu Chin Chow*. The talented cast included Oz Clarke, Bernice Stegers, Henry Knowles (as Ali Baba), Marjorie Bland and Julian Fellowes. Oscar Asche's "Musical Tale of the East" provided ample opportunities for Osborne Robinson (assisted by Alan Miller Bunford) as scenic designer: palaces, markets and of course Abu Hassan's Cave. The high point of Frederic Norton's musical score was "The Cobbler's Song". The programme included a synopsis of the plot with its Chinese merchants, slave girls, robbers and the unfortunate Kasim Baba whose body is cut into four pieces, which are later sewn together by the cobbler Hassan. Despite a generous measure of intrigue and the aforementioned dismemberment, by the fall of the curtain "The lovers are married and everyone lives happily ever after."

Chu Chin Chow was the outstanding popular theatrical entertainment of the First World War. It opened at His Majesty's Theatre in London on 31 August 1916 where it ran for 2,238 performances and was seen by over 2,800,000 people. Its success lay in the escapism which it provided not only for combatants home on leave from the front, but also for the bereaved and the population at large. Essentially during the 1914–18 war the theatre was a means of distraction from the horrors of an unprecedented military conflict and its consequences at home. Audiences did not attend theatres to confront let alone comprehend the reality of their everyday lives.

At the beginning of the next decade (popularly dubbed the "Gay Twenties") this impulse towards escapism continued to find expression in the theatre, for example, in C. B. Cochran's extravagant revues and musical comedies such as *The Naughty Princess* and *Irene*, but the conclusion of the record breaking run of *Chu Chin Chow* in 1921 seemed to signal a change in mood. A woman who had attended the opening performance with her son booked two tickets (double prices were charged) for the last explaining to Oscar Asche:

> "My son and I were at the first night . . . Whenever he came home on leave he came to see the play . . . my son was killed in France in the last week of the war, but I shall sit in one stall and my son's cap will be in the other. I think he will be there, too . . ."[1]

1

Chu Chin Chow Christmas 1973. (Royal Theatre Collection)

The way was open for J. M. Barrie's *Mary Rose* (1920), Somerset Maugham's *Home and Beauty* (1923) and R. C. Sherriff's *Journey's End* (1928), all of which in their very different ways explored the experiences and effects of the recent war. 1921 saw the first performance of G. B. Shaw's *Heartbreak House* – his "fantasia in the Russian manner on English themes" – and he completed his "Metabiological Pentateuch" *Back to Methuselah* in the same year. *Saint Joan* followed in 1923. Noel Coward emerged as an *enfant terrible* with *The Vortex* (1924). A new inventiveness was apparent in classic revivals ranging from Nigel Playfair's rediscovery of Restoration Comedy at the Lyric Theatre, Hammersmith to Barry Jackson's modern-dress Shakespeare in Birmingham and London. From overseas came Sean O'Casey, Eugene O'Neill, Elmer Rice and Karel Capek, the Czech dramatist, whose own plays (*R.U.R.*) and collaborations with his artist brother Josef (*The Insect Play*) excited international interest.

Such were the dramatic forces operating on the metropolitan stage. But what of Northampton? Though only seventy miles from the capital, and served by a railway line which put London theatres within accessible reach, this county town, internationally famous for shoe-manufacture, was hardly at the forefront of artistic taste. Northampton's two theatres were the Royal Theatre and Opera

House in Guildhall Road and the New Theatre in Abington Street. Of these the senior was the Royal Theatre, the enchantingly intimate creation of the prolific theatre architect C. J. Phipps, which had opened in 1884 with Edward Compton's Comedy Company in *Twelfth Night*.[2] By the 1920s the Royal Theatre was in the sole ownership of the aging Milton Bode, who resided in Reading. The New Theatre had been built in 1912 to the design of another prolific theatre architect, W. G. Sprague.[3] It had been constructed by the Northampton Theatre Syndicate, headed by Alderman John Brown, Mayor of Northampton in 1908 and proprietor of the Garibaldi public house in Bailiff Street. A large (capacity 2,000) and ornate theatre the New was not initially licensed for straight plays, but only for variety shows of various kinds. The Watch Committee's decision in May 1918 to extend the New Theatre's licence to straight plays inevitably had serious implications for its rival establishment, the Royal.

What the Royal and the New Theatres had in common was that they were both touring houses. The development of the railway network in the second half of the nineteenth century had exercised a significant influence upon provincial theatres. Locally based stock companies were progressively replaced by managements which simply bought in such travelling productions as were available. London stars made personal appearances at the first-rank touring dates in the large cities (Birmingham, Manchester and so on), but towns like Northampton were generally restricted to second and third range companies in London successes and others (such as Frank Benson's) whose orbit was confined to the provinces. On Sundays the railroads of the nation were populated by actors shuttling (with their scenery and costumes) from one venue to another, catching glimpses of former colleagues across the platforms at Crewe station. As a system the touring theatre was not without its merits – it brought a range of entertainment even to small towns, ensuring some worthwhile weeks amongst the dross. What it failed to do was to enable a given town to develop a theatrical flavour of its own and from its inception the repertory movement was designed to counter that shortcoming. By the 1920s the touring theatre was facing stern competition from the cinema, which by means of a compact canister of film could ensure the same quality of entertainment in a remote mining town in Wales as in the West End of London.

What then was the nature of the product which would arrive at (a) Northampton railway station on a Sunday evening to be presented to the town's theatre-goers during the ensuing week? Posters, programmes and press cuttings provide the basic information, but in the case of the Royal Theatre more revealing evidence is available in a handsomely bound accounts book covering the period 1920–3.[4] This volume, which has survived use as a stage property, bears eloquent testimony to the languishing fortunes of a small touring theatre, charting the nightly takings not only for the box office, but also for programmes and chocolates, alongside the outgoings to the theatre's own permanent staff, advertising, postage, gas, water and electricity charges, not forgetting the deeply resented entertainment tax first imposed in May 1916.

The terms under which touring companies were contracted were on a sliding scale, based on a given company's potential at the box office. Thus a top company (*Chu Chin Chow* 18 October 1920) could command 70 per cent of the box office revenue. The D'Oyly Carte Opera Company was guaranteed two-thirds of box office income and the Carl Rosa Opera Company increased its share from 65 per cent to 70 per cent over the period. Sometimes the percentage was graduated (as with Frank Benson in March 1920) the visiting company receiving 50 per cent of the first £200, 55 per cent of the next £250 and 60 per cent of anything above that. The percentage share of other companies reflected their lowlier status. Thus several so-called "Repertory Companies" (whose claim to the title rested merely on the fact that they presented several plays in a week) settled for 47½ per cent (the Cecile Barclay and Robert Lister Repertory Company in May 1921) or even as low as 40 per cent (the Ann Welfitt and Cecil Gray Repertory Theatre in June 1921).

Seat prices were also graduated with top attractions (*Chu Chin Chow*, D'Oyly Carte) charging 5s. 3d. for the dress circle, middle-ranking shows 4s. 9d. and most straight plays 3s.. Seats elsewhere in the theatre were on the same differential. Inevitably takings fluctuated widely. The D'Oyly Carte Opera Company received £481 8s. and the theatre £241 4s. for the week of 27 September 1920, and in the following month (18 October 1920) the *Chu Chin Chow* company £502 6s. 4d. and the theatre £215 5s. 8d.. At the other end of the scale the Barclay–Lister Company garnered only £22 12s. 8d. for the week of 23 May 1921 leaving the theatre with £25 0s. 5d.. Once nightly performances were the norm (with usually just one matinee on a Saturday) but occasionally companies resorted to twice nightly. In the case of Welfitt-Gray (20 June 1921) this was to little avail producing £20 2s. 7d. for the company and £30 3s. 10d. for the theatre, with takings on the first house on Tuesday amounting to all of £1 4s. 5d..

The Royal Theatre's own expenses also fluctuated (extra casual staff were brought in for large-scale productions: a big bill might fall fortuitously in a poor week), but for the aforementioned *Chu Chin Chow* and D'Oyly Carte a week's outgoings just exceeded £200; for Barclay–Lister they were down to £68. Milton Bode drew regular subventions and substantial orders of whisky (apparently for his own consumption) passed through the theatre books. The annual balances, calculated at the end of June, indicate that a modest provincial theatre was no crock of gold: £568 profit in 1920; £42 loss in 1921; £272 profit in 1922; and £202 profit in 1923.

The discerning playgoer of Northampton would have found little to attract him to the Royal Theatre in these years. Much earlier in his career, at the age of thirty-eight, Milton Bode had concluded that "'the playgoer, and especially the

4

provincial playgoer, would rather laugh than weep.' What is more he [Bode] does not think that the means by which laughter is provoked should be too elegant or subtle. Broad fun . . . is the saleable commodity" (*Era* 2.2.1901). As his network of provincial theatres waxed and waned Bode's commercial principles remained static. There were exceptions: that doughty Shakespearean Frank Benson brought his company to the town in March 1920 (total takings a creditable £460 3s. 7d.) and again during the difficult pre-Christmas period from 11 December 1922. During that week theatre enthusiasts, who were not too preoccupied with the approaching festivities, could see seven different Shakespeare plays (six evenings and a Saturday matinee). No doubt seasonal distractions accounted for the modest take of £162 8s. 6d.. The Charles Doran Shakespearean Company (14 March 1921) offered an equally large repertoire and drew tolerably good attendances (£297 3s. 11d.). A rare personal appearance by a – albeit somewhat faded – star occurred in October 1922 when Mrs. Patrick Campbell played Ibsen's *Hedda Gabler* for the full week (£259 6s. 1d.). In the following week (23 October) John Gay's *The Beggar's Opera*, which was enjoying a record-breaking (1,463 performances) run at Nigel Playfair's Lyric Theatre, Hammersmith, attracted sizable audiences (£348 4s. 5d.).

Most of the self-styled "Repertory Companies" that visited Northampton had only a spurious claim to the title. The Welfitt–Gray Company did indeed offer a repertoire of plays, with such lurid titles as *Toys of Fate* and *A Remembered Kiss*, both of them advertised as "For Adults Only" (June 1920). Somewhat more authentic was the Rex Gerard Repertory Company which stayed in the town for five (twice nightly) weeks in May and June 1922, but the high points of their repertoire amounted to nothing more than revivals of the Tom Robertson plays from the 1860s *David Garrick* and *Caste*.

Northampton audiences did have the opportunity to sample the artistic fare of the country's premier repertory company. During the week of 25 October 1920 Barry Jackson's Birmingham Repertory Company performed John Drinkwater's *Abraham Lincoln*, generally considered to be the dramatist's best work. With its purpose-built theatre in Station Street and the security of Jackson's own personal fortune behind it the Birmingham Rep was able to extend its operations beyond its home city.[5] The company returned to Northampton in April 1922 with a repertoire consisting of *The Romantic Young Lady* (adapted by Harley Granville-Barker from the Spanish dramatist Martinez-Sierra), Oscar Wilde's *The Importance of Being Earnest*, an adaptation of Emile Zola's *Thérèse Raquin* and Shaw's *Getting Married*, all of which had been performed in Birmingham in the 1921 season. Unquestionably this was the most substantial dramatic fare ever laid before the playgoers of Northampton. With receipts of £233 18s. the response was at least not discouraging.

In March 1923 the Birmingham Repertory Company was back for four weeks with a programme of six plays: *The Importance of Being Earnest* again, St. John

Hankin's *The Return of the Prodigal*, Harold Chapin's *The New Morality*, A. A. Milne's *The Romantic Age*, R. B. Sheridan's *The Rivals* and *Advertising April* by Herbert Farjeon and Horace Horsnell – all, save *The Rivals*, recently staged in Birmingham. The company included Eric H. Messiter, Grosvenor North, Osmund Willson, Clifford Marquand and Elsie Irving who, having appeared in Northampton in 1922, were welcomed back as old friends. Newcomers included Frances Doble, Yvette Pienne and Joyce Corfield.

The most important and influential organ of the local press – the *Northampton Independent* – rejoiced in the return of the Birmingham company: "Rarely has a touring company met with such a rapturous reception from the discriminating Northampton playgoers as was accorded the members of the Birmingham Repertory Company this week, when they opened a four week season at the Opera House" (*NI* 10.3.1923). The *Independent* referred to "full houses" for *The Romantic Age* on the Monday (when Rotary Club members were present), Tuesday and Wednesday of the first week, but the evidence of the account book scarcely corroborates this claim, the takings being only £21 16s. 1d., £21 9s. 9d. and £22 10s. 2d. respectively. If those houses were indeed full, many members of the audience must have been expressing their appreciation for complimentary tickets as well as for the quality of the performance. In fact the weekly takings for the Birmingham Repertory Company were £184 1s. 2d., £140 11s. 7d., £185 5s., and £98 18s. 7d..

Clearly the key words were "the discriminating Northampton playgoers", amongst whom W. H. Holloway, the editor of the *Independent* numbered himself. Holloway was Northampton-born and served his journalistic apprenticeship on the long-established *Northampton Mercury* under the editorship of S. S. Campion, who as an alderman also played an active part in local life. In 1905 Holloway and his fellow journalist W. W. Cockbill founded the *Northampton Independent*, an illustrated weekly news magazine devoted to local topics. As Holloway's obituary in his own publication observed:

> Over the years, the "Independent" now became identified with an almost continuous succession of campaigns for the improvement and development of Northampton's civic, social and industrial resources and amenities. (*NI* 15.11.57)

During the First World War Holloway, using the *Independent* as his mouthpiece, raised £100,000 for war charities; he helped to found and was commissioned in the Northampton Volunteer Training Corps (the equivalent of the Home Guard) for which he was awarded the O.B.E.. In addition to his journalism Holloway wrote an illustrated account of the battle of Naseby, a guide to the Washington country and *Northamptonshire and the Great War*.

Holloway's enthusiasm for the theatre was not confined to his seat in the

6

auditorium of the Royal Theatre. In 1925 he masterminded the Northampton Pageant, galvanising hundreds of local people into action as performers and thousands more into enthusiasm as spectators. The begetter of the modern pageant was Louis N. Parker, who wrote (and helped to stage) elaborate costume dramas for Herbert Beerbohm Tree at His Majesty's Theatre in London, where one of his most successful ventures *Drake* was presented in 1912. Parker's grandson Anthony, who upheld the family tradition into the 1950s, claimed "the Historical Pageant as we know it was originated by my grandfather . . . in 1905 [at] Sherborne Castle in Dorset".[6] To the Parkers the essence of a true pageant was the re-enactment of (a series of) historical events preferably in their original setting.

In June 1923 the *Northampton Independent* carried an account of the Harrow Pageant, which had been opened by Prince Henry. The article proclaimed a characteristic Holloway injunction "Northampton Please Copy" (*NI* 30.6.1923). The workings of Holloway's mind were as intricate as they were ingenious. In the same year James Manfield, of the prominent Northampton shoe-manufacturers, was having difficulty in disposing of the extensive family property. Holloway launched a campaign to turn the local magnate's residence into a hospital for crippled children. Even though James Manfield donated the property funds were needed for the fitting out and running of the new hospital. Local philanthropy and Holloway's advocacy of a pageant went hand-in-hand. Holloway became (with Mrs. J. Astbury) joint honorary organising secretary of the carnival and pageant and set about enlisting all shades of local opinion to support the venture.

Patrons included the Marquess and Marchioness of Exeter, the Marquis and Marchioness of Northampton, Earl and Countess Spencer, Sir Mervyn and Lady Manningham-Buller, Sir Hereward and Lady Wake, Sir Thomas and Lady Fermor-Hesketh, the artistic Elwes family and leading shoe-manufacturers Sir James Crockett, the Manfields, W. T. Sears, together with civic dignitaries and representatives of churches (most denominations) and schools.

In addition to his organising role Holloway wrote much of the pageant, which consisted of eight episodes "that best lend themselves to spectacular effect . . . from the wealth of historic incidents in Northampton's richly storied past", beginning with "The Discovery of Northampton (Hamtune) by the Saxons AD 900" via Thomas à Becket, Queen Eleanor and Queen Elizabeth I to Queen Victoria's visit to the town in 1844. The pageant master was J. T. Savage and prominent amongst the participants were many teachers (headmaster W. C. C. Cooke and P. B. Baskcomb from the Northampton Town and County School) and clergymen. The Northampton Amateur Operatic Society gave its support and the directors of the New and Royal Theatres loaned properties. The pageant drew huge crowds to Abington Park for the performances on 25, 26 and 27 June, which also attracted favourable attention in the national press. Furthermore the pageant raised £4,340 for the Manfield Hospital (after the deduction of £1,500 expenses).[7]

Programme cover for the Northampton Pageant 1925. (*NI* 20.6.1925)

With Holloway the successful completion of one campaign generally led on to the next. Thus C. O'Brien Donaghey, who had produced the congregation of the Roman Catholic Cathedral in "The Passing of Eleanor" section of the pageant, recalled nearly half a century later:

> Inspired by the tremendous success of the Northampton Historic Pageant of 1925, a success due to the almost universal co-operative effort of the citizens, I was certain that better fare than "The Face at the Window" and a make-shift pantomime at Christmas would be appreciated and supported by the City [*sic*], with its Repertory Theatre on the pattern of the Birmingham Rep. . . .[8]

Coincidentally 1925 had seen another development which was to be conducive to this end – Milton Bode disposed of the Royal Theatre to the Northampton Theatre Syndicate, now headed by the founder's son, architect John Brown. Although some anxiety was expressed about the theatrical monopoly thereby created, Holloway welcomed the outcome:

> It is a refreshing reflection that the Northampton Opera House was started by Northampton initiative. Now, after many long years, it is restored to a local gentleman, in whose hands we feel certain its continued success is assured. (*NI* 31.1.1925)

Finding no immediate response in support of this aspiration early in 1926 Holloway penned a forthright editorial "Is Northampton's Dramatic Taste Declining?" (*NI* 30.1.1926). He condemned much of the "dramatic fare now being offered at the N.O.H." as "an insult to the intelligence and dramatic taste of Northampton playgoers". He claimed that "slowly but surely Northampton is being 'black-listed' by leading producers" and he appealed to the public to support the lead then being taken by the management in restoring the quality of entertainment on offer.

The Northampton Theatre Syndicate's initiative took the form of inviting Alfred and Sidney Barnard and N. Carter Slaughter "to produce a series of plays by our greatest dramatists" (*NI* 27.3.1926). The Barnards and Slaughter already ran a repertory company at the Elephant Theatre, London where "their productions upon the same lines as those of the 'Old Vic' . . . have been rewarded with rapturous ovations". The season commenced at the end of March 1926 with Walter Howard's Lyceum success *Seven Days' Leave*, which was followed by another London hit *Leah Kleschna* by C. M. S. McLellan. Hardly the work of "our greatest dramatists", but a beginning at least.

Within a month of the new company's arrival Holloway was hailing "The Rebirth of the Drama", citing "every-growing audiences" including, of course, "the thinking and discriminating section of the playgoing public" for whom the prospect of "a succession . . . of the most exclusive plays Northampton desires" seemed to be in sight at last (*NI* 24.4.1926). C. T. Doe, the general manager, worked quickly to make the Elephant Company (as it was known) part of the community, visiting local factories and encouraging members of the audience to suggest plays for production.

For the *Northampton Independent* the General Strike in May 1926 was merely an irritating diversion from its repertory campaign. Early in the month Holloway regaled his readers with accounts of the repertory movement in Bristol and Bath. In Northampton "the Elephant Company . . . are laying foundations – but upon them it is up to Northampton's theatre-going public to build a dramatic edifice worthy of the town and its large majority of intelligent citizens" (*NI* 1.5.1926). Later in the month letters of support were published (*NI* 22.5.26) from C. O'Brien Donaghey and P. B. Baskcomb, producer of the first episode in the 1925 pageant and the brother of two professional actors. A more cautious note was sounded by A. M. Walmsley (Senior English Master at the Northampton Town and County School) who made the valid comment that in Northampton the establishment of a repertory theatre "would not be so easy as in centres like Birmingham and Bristol, with their larger populations and University nucleus, or like Bath with its attractions as a residential centre" (*NI* 5.6.1926). All correspondents set great store by the creation of a Playgoers' Association to provide a nucleus of support and encouragement.

Meanwhile the Elephant Company went from strength to strength. Tom

Robertson's *David Garrick* and an adaptation of Charles Dickens's *A Tale of Two Cities* were staged by popular request. The ranks of the repertory lobbyists were swelled, an important recruit being Francis Graves, editor of the *Northampton Echo*. O'Brien Donaghey addressed the Rotary Club and discovered that amongst his audience was W. Pepper Cross O.B.E. chairman of the *Northampton Independent* directors and a member of the Northampton Theatre Syndicate, who encouraged him to formulate terms for the use of the Royal Theatre by a Northampton repertory company.

Much hinged upon a meeting chaired by Councillor J. G. Cowling, Mayor of Northampton, in his parlour in the Guildhall on the afternoon of 19 June 1926. O'Brien Donaghey recalled that the meeting "was extremely sticky and, at one moment, everything seemed hopelessly lost", to the particular consternation of Holloway, who had already written a glowing report for his journal of the same date. In the end all went well. Two committees were set up as the agenda had proposed:

> Two Committees be appointed; the first one of business men to discuss and draft a scheme for a Company to be floated in the town and county with the object of renting the Opera House and engaging a Repertory Company; the second to draft the constitution of a Playgoers' Club.[9]

The first committee comprised Councillor Harvey Reeves (chairman), Mr. Baskcomb (deputy chairman), Mr. Donaghey and Mr. Holloway (joint hon. secretaries), Councillor H. W. Dover, Mr. Reginald Brown, Mr. W. J. Bassett-Lowke, Mr. H. Musk Beattie, Rev. J. B. Dollar (Vicar of St. James's and chaplain to the mayor, who had played Thomas à Becket and produced that episode in the pageant) and a Rotary Club representative. The second committee comprised Mr. Compton James, Miss Wallace (of the High School for Girls, who had produced the second episode in the pageant), Mrs. Frank Panther, Rev. J. E. Evans, Rev. J. B. Dollar, Rev. J. Trevor Lewis R. D. and another pageant participant Rev. J. F. Winter.

Although civic endorsement was important the proposed repertory theatre had to be a commercial venture and accordingly the "Northampton Repertory Players Limited" needed to raise capital of £2,000 in £1 shares. Unless this could be achieved the whole venture would collapse.

As summer gave way to autumn the Elephant Company played on – twice nightly at 6.40 pm and 8.45 pm. At the end of July they had celebrated their two hundredth performance with Stanley Houghton's *The Younger Generation*. The repertoire hardly amounted to those "most exclusive plays" aspired to by Holloway. Harold Brighouse's *Hobson's Choice* was staged in September, Wilde's plays were popular and Alfred Sutro's *The Walls of Jericho* was on the bill for the four hundredth performance in November. The local branch of the Workers'

The Elephant Company's two hundredth performance at the Royal Theatre
7 August 1926. (Royal Theatre Collection)

Educational Association (vice-presidents included Margaret Bondfield M.P., A. M. Walmsley and his headmaster W. C. C. Cooke and Colonel John Brown of the Northampton Theatre Syndicate) responded to the spirit of the time with an evening class on Modern British Drama under the tutelage of Miss D. M. Clarke.

The momentum had not slackened and in early December the *Northampton Independent* proclaimed "all should be in readiness for the Northampton Repertory Players Ltd., as the new company is titled, to ring up their first curtain with the New Year". The objectives of the repertory company were clearly enunciated:

> The intention of the new company will be that originally propounded in these columns, i.e., to present the cream of dramatic entertainment with a company of first class artists directed by a leading producer. Furthermore the audiences will be closely linked alike to the theatre, the artists, and the plays through the medium of a Playgoers' Association, as members of which they may co-operate in the selection of forthcoming productions and may thus virtually choose their own entertainment.
>
> Who knows but that from these modest foundations may arise a dramatic edifice in Northampton rivalling those of Bristol, Bath and possibly even Birmingham. (*NI* 4.12.1926)

Northampton could scarcely claim to be in the advance guard of the repertory movement, the origins of which can be traced back to J. T. Grein's Independent Theatre (1891), the Stage Society (1899), Miss Annie Horniman's patronage of the Abbey Theatre, Dublin (1904) and the historic Vedrenne-Barker management at the Royal Court Theatre (1904–7). It was Miss Horniman's establishment of a repertory company at the Gaiety Theatre, Manchester in 1908, following her disenchantment with the Abbey, that constituted the first English repertory theatre. The Glasgow Repertory Company followed in 1909, Liverpool in 1911 and Birmingham in 1913. Subsequent significant developments included J. B. Fagan's Oxford Repertory Company (1923) and Hull in the same year; Terence Gray's Cambridge Festival Theatre (1926) and the Sheffield Repertory Company in 1928 (after nine years as an amateur society). By 1934 Cecil Chisholm counted "thirty-seven repertory companies . . . precisely the same number of companies are reported on tour".[10]

As George Rowell and Anthony Jackson have pointed out, in Britain the term "repertory" has not been used in the strict sense of building up a repertoire of plays each of which would be performed "no more than a week at a time but [be] brought back at frequent intervals according to public demand". Instead:

> Broadly repertory theatres in Britain have seen themselves as determinedly

non-commercial in approach, based in and serving a specific community or region and providing a wide range of plays, new and classic, challenging and popular.[11]

The means of achieving this common objective varied from place to place. In Manchester Miss Horniman's modest personal fortune from the family tea business provided a financial base, but although she received "more encouragement from Manchester than in all that time spent in starting Dublin [the Abbey]" she was insistent that "in England it will be purely a dramatic artistic venture on honestly commercial lines".[12] In Birmingham repertory grew out of the amateur Pilgrim Players and Barry Jackson's private means (derived from Maypole Dairies) enabled him to build his own theatre (opened in 1913) and support it with sizable subventions. In contrast the Liverpool Playhouse had no single patron, but issued 20,000 £1 shares which were spread amongst 900 shareholders whose diversity was reflected in a large board of directors consisting of "men of very differing outlook and interests".[13]

It was to the Liverpool model that Northampton corresponded most closely, though since, unlike Liverpool, it was renting rather than buying a theatre the capital required was comparatively modest. The first meeting of shareholders took place on 13 December 1926, when 1,630 (£1) shares were allotted to twenty-five shareholders, ranging from twelve with one hundred shares each to B. G. Holloway with a modest five (BM). All subscribed to the view that:

> While it will be run upon strictly business lines and no effort spared to ensure that shareholders shall receive as generous a return as possible, the primary object of the company is to provide good dramatic entertainment and this will always be paramount in its policy. (*NI* 18.12.1926)

The chairman of the board was the elderly Sir James Crockett, a prominent shoe-manufacturer and philanthropist. An enthusiastic theatre-goer from his youthful visits to the galleries of London theatres, Sir James's imprimatur gave the venture standing within the community. Although his personal patronage in no way equalled Miss Horniman's or Jackson's it was nevertheless said that "without Sir James in 1926 there would have been no company formed and that in 1929 without him the company would have come to an end" (PR 23.2.1931). W. H. Horton, chairman of the box-manufacturing firm Horton and Arlidge and a leading freemason, was deputy chairman on the understanding that much of the routine business would fall to him. Other foundation directors were: Mrs. Helen Panther (active in British Legion and Conservative circles) whose husband Frank was managing director of the huge shoe-manufacturing company J. T. Sears and Co. which in 1925 had over 3,000 employees; Francis Graves, editor of the *Northampton Echo* and a rotarian; H. Musk Beattie, also a rotarian and a solicitor, in which capacity he acted as secretary to the board (at an annual fee of £50 BM 25.1.1927); and W. J. Bassett-Lowke. Bassett-Lowke was the most interesting member of the board.[14] He had founded the internationally renowned model engineering company; he was a Fabian and a personal friend of George Bernard Shaw; he was the patron of Charles Rennie Mackintosh, who designed furniture and decor for 78 Derngate, and later of Peter Behrens for New Ways (1925-6), allegedly the most modern house in Europe. Bassett-Lowke's wife Jane was the daughter of Sir James Crockett's partner Frank Jones. Although the board represented a range of political and professional interests it was clearly reflective of the closely-interlocking "patriciate", the ruling-class which presided over Northampton between the wars. The true begetter of the repertory W. H. Holloway was not included on the board, but in all probability he considered that his work was completed and the venture could be carried forward by others.

The forum for theatre enthusiasts was the Playgoers' Association. P. B. Baskcomb, senior master of the Town and County Lower School, was elected chairman. He had played a significant role in advancing the repertory cause and had links with the acting profession through his two brothers (A. W. and Lawrence). Miss Irene Harding was hon. secretary. Although the purpose of the Playgoers was to support the theatre and provide a programme of lectures and talks, members were offered the inducement of "24 one shilling vouchers . . . exchangeable for tickets of admission . . . for £1" – a good return for their membership fee of 1s. (*NI* 18.12.1926).

There remained the critical appointments of general manager, producer and of course the acting company. N. Carter Slaughter's offer of his services as producer and manager was declined (BM 13.12.1926) but the legacy of the Elephant Company stood Northampton in good stead. C. Graham Cameron was appointed as general manager at £10 per week. South African born and widely travelled as soldier, actor and businessman, Graham Cameron brought a broader perspective to bear on Northampton's "Adventure in Repertory".

Notes

1. W. Macqueen-Pope *The Footlights Flickered. The Story of the Theatre of the 1920s*, 1959, p. 76.
2. See Lou Warwick *The Mackenzies Called Compton Incorporated in the History of Northampton Theatre Royal and Opera House 1884-1927*, 1977.
3. See Lou Warwick *Death of a Theatre A History of the New Theatre Northampton*, 1960.
4. Royal Theatre archives.
5. See Bache Matthews *A History of the Birmingham Repertory Company*, 1924; Thomas C. Kemp *Birmingham Repertory Theatre The Playhouse and the Man*, 1944; and J. C. Trewin *The Birmingham Repertory Theatre 1913-63*, 1963.
6. Anthony Parker *Pageants Their Presentation and Production*, 1954, p. 6.; see also Louis N. Parker *Several of My Lives*, 1928, Chapter IV.
7. Northampton Pageant programme in N.C.R.O..
8. Letter to T. Osborne Robinson dated 23.3.1973 in N.C.R.O..

9. Aubrey Dyas *Adventure in Repertory. Northampton Repertory Theatre 1927-48*, 1948, p. 18. Future references in text as *Adventure*.

10. Cecil Chisholm *Repertory: An Outline of the Modern Theatre Movement*, 1934, p. 14.

11. George Rowell and Anthony Jackson *The Repertory Movement. A History of Regional Theatre in Britain*, 1984, p. 2.

12. Rex Pogson *Miss Horniman and the Gaiety Theatre, Manchester*, 1952, p. 23.

13. Grace Wyndham Goldie *The Liverpool Repertory Theatre 1911-1934*, 1935, p. 57.

14. See Roland Fuller *The Bassett-Lowke Story*, 1984.

Abbreviations   BM – board minutes; PR – programme; AR – annual report.

CHAPTER TWO

In Business 1927–8

THE appointment of the Northampton Repertory Players' first producer (in modern parlance artistic director) was bound to be crucial, charged as he would be with responsibility for the company, the choice and production of the plays, as well as the financial well-being of the enterprise. Rather than offer the post for open competition the directors adopted a more informal procedure, as a result of which the secretary of the Bristol Players recommended Max Jerome, who had "carved the initial fortunes of the Bristol Repertory Company" (*NI* 18.12.1926). Graham Cameron met Jerome in London and the outcome was his appointment as producer at a weekly salary of £10 (BM 13.12.1926). The board's involvement, therefore, was at a remove.

Jerome's credentials seemed to be excellent: acting experience with Florence Glossop-Harris and Frank Benson; repertory in Liverpool and Stockton-on-Tees, as well as Bristol. Indeed in Liverpool in 1917 Jerome had taken over the general management on the resignation of W. Bridges Adams as producer and he was "proud of the fact that during his regime the Liverpool Playhouse was, for the first time, not only successful from an artistic point of view, but also a financial success" (*NI* 8.1.1927). Jerome's approach at Liverpool had been "a cautious policy in regard to plays and a strict economy in management. Salaries were kept low, the company small, and the expenses of production were reduced".[1] Jerome's financial prudence, which no doubt commended him to the Northampton directors, meant that the formative period of repertory was characterised by caution, to the disappointment of some of the more progressive supporters of the theatre.

By the time Jerome arrived in Northampton the company had been engaged by Cameron. Cameron had blended old faces with new, retaining Bluebell Glaid, C. T. Doe, J. Drew Carran, C. Harcourt-Brooke and of course himself from the Elephant Company and introducing Margot Lister, Arthur Hambling, Mildred Trevor, Maurice Neville, Enid Gwynne and Clifton James. Harcourt-Brooke was stage manager and Mildred Trevor assistant stage manager. Total expenditure on artistes (including producer and manager) was not to exceed £80 per week (BM 13.12.1926).

The members of that original company had found their way to Northampton by very varied routes. C. T. Doe had run away from home to join a circus in his native Australia (*NI* 26.2.1927); Clifton James, also an Australian, had fought as a "Tommy" at Delville Ridge (*NI* 19.2.1927); Irish born J. Drew Carran had achieved the unenviable double of seeing service both at Ypres (where he was gassed) and at Gallipoli (*NI* 1.1.1927); Arthur Hambling, born and educated (with Owen Nares) in Reading, had served in France and Italy. Although it was inevitable at this time that many actors would have been combatants in the First World War it is still intriguing to ask what it was that attracted such men, from non-theatrical backgrounds, to the stage. Was the lure of the theatre an extension of that escapism which had drawn audiences to *Chu Chin Chow*; a make-believe world after the hardship they had endured? There must have been more to it than that. Undoubtedly these soldiers turned actors had a capacity for hard work, a camaraderie and a phlegmatism which sustained them through the incessant grind of twice nightly weekly repertory. Amongst the actresses Mildred Trevor had done war work with the Red Cross and in a munitions factory and as a trainee actress had "played very often at lunatic asylums" (*NI* 22.1.1927). In contrast Bluebell Glaid (a stage name, of course, for Dorothy Barnes) had entered the theatre in a more dilettante way, her sister being at the Royal Academy of Dramatic Art (R.A.D.A.). Whatever their backgrounds and experiences this was the company revealed to an expectant audience as the curtain rose on the Northampton Repertory Players' first production, A. W. Pinero's *His House in Order*, at 6.30 pm on Monday 10 January 1927. The box office was presided over by Mrs. May Button, "the ever-cheerful and courteous manageress" for whom it was to be "the first of some 63,000 nights" in that capacity (*Adventure* p. 25). Ticket prices were below the bottom rate charged for the touring companies, being 2s. 4d. for the dress circle.[2]

As the audience assembled, the orchestra, under the direction of W. H. Collier, played a selection of pieces including German's *Merrie England*. Amongst those present were the Mayor and Mayoress of Northampton (Councillor and Mrs. James Peach), several borough officials (including the Librarian and the Tramways' Manager), members of the theatre board, with W. H. Holloway and Colonel John Brown. Although civic endorsement was important for the repertory, not a penny of the town council's £261,242 budget, which included £4,842, for the museum and libraries, was advanced to the cause (*NI* 12.3.1927). A message of goodwill was received from Barry Jackson, whose Birmingham Repertory Company's visits to the Royal Theatre had encouraged local enthusiasts. An informative programme (price 2d.) assured patrons that their comfort and convenience were the first considerations of the management and enjoined them to report "Any Incivility or Inattention on the part of an attache of the establishment". Clearly general manager C. Graham Cameron intended to keep his house in good order.

The choice of A. W. Pinero's *His House in Order* as the company's first play was unexceptionable and unexciting. Apart from being set "on the outskirts of a town in

17

the Midlands" it had no particular appropriateness to the occasion, but it was considered to be "one of Sir Arthur Pinero's best works" (*NDC* 11.1.1927) having enjoyed a run of thirteen months in its original London production twenty years earlier. The play stood up to revival reasonably well and after their understandable initial nervousness the company acquitted themselves creditably, despite the fact that "more than two thirds" of them "were called upon to impersonate characters twenty and thirty years older than themselves" (*Adventure* p. 25).

Amongst the audience there was "something of an intent concern that this was their baby, and they were going to see that it grew in the right direction" (*NDC* 11.1.1927) and at the conclusion of the performance they roundly applauded the "midwives" Cameron and Jerome when they appeared (in Jerome's case reluctantly) on stage. With gross income amounting to £342 and expenditure to £222, the company was off to a good start financially (BM 17.1.1927).

Jerome's first season, up to the short vacation at the end of July, totalled twenty-eight plays. Pinero reappeared with *Sweet Lavender* in March and A. A. Milne was also represented by two plays, *The Truth About Blayds* and *Belinda*. Jerome himself gave a forceful performance as Hilary Fairfield in Clemence Dane's *A Bill of Divorcement* and J. Drew Carran was convincing as the mysterious Stranger in *The Passing of the Third Floor Back*, an apt choice for Holy Week, by Jerome K. Jerome, who died in Northampton General Hospital on 14 June 1927. New plays and classic revivals, those twin talismani of the repertory movement, were in little evidence being represented by *Experiment*, a weakly constructed comedy, and R. B. Sheridan's *The School for Scandal* respectively.

The School for Scandal was noteworthy for three fine performances: C. T. Doe alternating temper and tenderness as Sir Peter Teazle, being particularly effective in the celebrated screen scene; Bluebell Glaid at her best as Lady Teazle; and J. Drew Carran making a dashing Charles Surface. But all the cast performed well and for once Jerome succeeded in welding his company into an ensemble. The acting was helped by splendid sets, the work of commercial artist Charles Maynard, whose Tara Studio was at 35 Sheep Street. Born in Liverpool, the son of an actor, Maynard had first tried his hand at scene-painting at the age of nine when he became friends with Albert Harker, son of Herbert Beerbohm Tree's celebrated scenic artist Joseph Harker. At fourteen Maynard ran away from home in the face of parental opposition to his calling and subsequently, after war service, he painted scenery "in some queer places – on board ship and in a cave in Northern India" (PR 14.11.1927). His contribution to *The School for Scandal* included Charles Surface's ancestral portraits. Charles Maynard can be regarded as the originator of the Northampton repertory's distinguished tradition in scenic design. No doubt his sets accounted in part for the success of *The School for Scandal* which was second only to *Raffles* (in which James Hayter joined the company) in popularity during the first season (PR 26.9.1927).

Aubrey Dyas (*Adventure* p. 30) states that "some 170,000 people" attended the first twenty-eight plays which, twice nightly, would have amounted to 336 performances. If Dyas's figures are accurate the average attendance was over 500 in a theatre with a capacity of only 532 seats plus the gallery.[3] The number of performances given by individual actors was published in the programme (29.8.1927) revealing that C. T. Doe, J. Drew Carran and Enid Gwynne had appeared in twenty-five plays each; Clifton James in twenty-four; and Bluebell Glaid and Margot Lister in twenty-two each. The company had certainly earned the garden party which Mr. and Mrs. Frank Panther gave in their honour.

The new season opened on 1 August 1927 again with Pinero (*The Second Mrs. Tanqueray*), but although Max Jerome had been retained as producer the board had decided "that the time had come to make a change" (BM 7.9.1927). Bassett-Lowke consulted St. John Ervine, the ascerbic critic and playwright, who recommended Rupert Harvey whom he described as a "competent producer and manager"[4]. Harvey came, on a temporary basis at £20 a week (BM 4.10.1927), from Bristol, where he had set up the Little Theatre. Harvey listed the accomplishments of his "ideal producer . . . not only . . . actor, stage-manager, prompter, property man and stage carpenter – he would be scientist and psychologist as well" (*NI* 29.10.1927). The quality of the plays chosen and the productions improved immediately. Shaw, Barrie and Shakespeare now found their place in the repertoire.

In Shaw's *Arms and the Man* "C. T. Doe was perfectly suited to the part of Bluntschli" and Bluebell Glaid was equally well cast as Raina against "original and aesthetic scenic effects" by Charles Maynard (*NDC* 22.11.1927). Within the limits of the equipment available Harvey achieved striking lighting effects, particularly in G. K. Chesterton's *Magic*, in which as an actor he (The Stranger) set the standard for his company: "He can wring the last ounce of meaning from a witty line and heighten a situation with a glance or gesture" (*NDC* 6.12.1927).

The choice of Christmas entertainment for a repertory company was a testing business. Conventional pantomime – "a back-slang, and possibly vulgar pantomime" (*NI* 10.12.1927) – scarcely accorded with notions of high artistic endeavour and yet some recognition of the season was called for. Despite its unseasonable title *A Midsummer Night's Dream* fitted the bill ideally, the company's first Shakespeare and yet a reassuringly accessible and entertaining piece.

Astutely judging public interest Harvey ran the production for two weeks, dropping twice nightly in favour of evening performances at 7.45 pm and matinees (except Fridays) at 2.30 pm and increasing ticket prices to 4s. 3d. for the front row of the dress circle.[5] Charles Maynard was charged with designing not only the sets, but also the costumes, shoes, wigs and even the ass's head. He rejected "the traditional white costume with gold key patterns [for] costumes of most delightful colours". Appropriately Maynard played the tailor Starveling. As

Puck James Hayter was made into "an old Peter Pan with some of Caliban's agility. His costume will give the appearance that he has just been cut from an old oak tree." (*NI* 7.12.1927). An augmented orchestra, directed by R. Richardson-Jones, played Grieg, Mendelssohn and Rupert Harvey's *Philomel*, specially composed for the occasion. Despite cast changes necessitated by illness Harvey (as Lysander) led his players (C. T. Doe as Bottom, Ailsa Grahame as Oberon, Bluebell Glaid as Hermia) to success in the most ambitious production undertaken by the company to date. It returned a modest loss of £47 (revenue £786, expenditure £833. BM 7.1.1928).

Harvey stayed on for the aptly chosen first anniversary production of Arnold Bennett's *Milestones* and in the birthday souvenir programme Graham Cameron gave a "Retrospection" on "Master N.R.P.'s first year". He observed that had the siren voices of "drab-minded ladies and gentlemen" prevailed Master N.R.P. would have been a "birth-strangled babe". Looking ahead he stated that although "it never has been, and never will be the object of the directors to endeavour to educate the theatre-going public of Northampton" it was "part of the duty of a Repertory Movement to see that playgoers of that town have an opportunity of witnessing and showing their attitude towards modern dramatic thought". He characterised Master N.R.P. as "a robust and sturdy little fellow. His prospects are rosy and his pluck unending". In fact Master N.R.P.'s guardianship during his first year had been uncertain, but as he entered his second his upbringing came into the hands of a man supremely well-suited to nurture his strengths and develop his potential – Herbert Prentice, to whom Rupert Harvey (on behalf of the board) had offered the post of producer (at a weekly salary of £15) in October 1927 (BM 25.10.1927).

Notes

1. Grace Wyndham Goldie *The Liverpool Playhouse 1911–1934*, p. 118.

2. The Repertory Company operated the "Early Doors" system, which effectively imposed a premium on advance booking. Thus stalls were 2s. 4d. Early Doors, 2s. Ordinary Doors; pit stalls 1s. 6d. and 1s. 2d., dress circle 2s. 4d. and 2s., upper circle 1s. 6d. and 1s. 2d., pit 1s. and 8d., gallery 6d. and 4d..

3. Minor adjustments were made to seating during the early seasons, but the division of the auditorium was basically 142 orchestra stalls, 94 pit stalls, 87 pit, 87 dress circle, 122 upper circle, plus the gallery.

4. St. John Ervine *The Organised Theatre A Plea in Civics*, 1924, p. 172.

5. Early doors prices: first row dress circle 4s. 3d. second and third rows 3s. 6d., stalls (incl. pit stalls) 3s. 6d., pit 1s. 10d., gallery 8d.. The usual differential was applied to Ordinary Doors.

CHAPTER THREE

Herbert Prentice 1928–32

HERBERT M. PRENTICE was born in Marple, Cheshire in June 1890, a brilliant mathematician he received his education in Manchester, by then the cradle of the repertory movement, at the School of Commerce and the university. He took a scholarship training scheme with the Great Central Railway Company in Sheffield where he lived, with his wife Marion, at the Hostel of Settlement. Over dinner there one night the Prentices were discussing drama with friends and resolved to do a play at the Settlement. John Galsworthy's *The Silver Box* was duly staged for six nights from 24–9 November 1919. Prentice was described as:

> A man of impeccable artistic taste with great ideas and enthusiasm with which he was able to inspire his friends, he soon gathered round him a band of amateurs of varying degrees of capability but fired with his own unbounded love of the theatre and the urgent desire to express themselves in this medium.[1]

Although the Sheffield venture remained amateur its fortunes flourished to the extent that Prentice was appointed as salaried (£400 p.a.) director in April 1921. His productions included Greek tragedies, Frank Taylor's *The Carthaginians*, the first English performance of Toller's *The Machine Wreckers*, St. John Ervine's *The Ship* and a revival of *Twelfth Night* "in which he introduced a system of psychological lighting" (PR 7.11.1927). Prentice was also a talented set and costume designer, several examples of his work being shown at the International Theatre Exhibition of 1923.

In 1926 when Terence Gray founded the Cambridge Festival Theatre, Prentice became its resident producer, alongside his Sheffield associate Harold Ridge as general manager and electrician and Norman Marshall, recently graduated from Oxford University, as stage manager. Just turned thirty Gray, educated at Eton and Magdalene College, Cambridge had no professional theatre experience, but he had distinctive ideas and a large enough fortune to enable him to reconstruct the dilapidated early-nineteenth-century Theatre Royal into a sophisticated playhouse with an innovative open stage backed by a permanent curved cyclorama, an up to date German lighting system (costing £2,000) and an auditorium of elegant simplicity. Prentice's role in this venture has been insufficiently recognised; Gray was unequivocal:

> In the first place it is quite probable that the Festival Theatre would never have come into existence if Mr. Prentice's work in Sheffield had not given Mr. Ridge and myself confidence that there was a producer in England whose work warranted the inception of such an enterprise . . . he alone . . . would appear to be qualified to carry an advanced repertory enterprise on his shoulders. (PR 26.3.1928)

The dual principles upon which Gray founded his theatre were that the producer "was no longer the servant of the playwright but his master" and the rejection "of any form of realism".[2] The repertoire was significantly different from the conventional Horniman or even Jackson fare. Opening with *The Oresteia* of Aeschylus, Prentice progressed to Strindberg, Chekhov, Capek, Pirandello, Shakespeare and Sophocles. Rehearsals were generous (four weeks) and the year was divided into three eight week seasons to coincide with the university term. The ambience of the theatre was highly cultivated – a fine restaurant, with the best wine list outside London; even the programmes were unusual, white print on black paper to make them legible in the dark.

As Graham Woodruff has written "the Festival theatre had an upper middle class theatre audience".[3] He quotes the *Cambridge Chronicle* to the effect that 55 per cent of the audience came from the university (35 per cent undergraduates, 20 per cent senior members), 30 per cent from the city and 15 per cent from outside Cambridge. Amongst this 15 per cent were several interested parties from Northampton. Predictably in the vanguard was W. J. Bassett-Lowke, accompanied by P. B. Baskcomb and H. Musk Beattie, whose reactions the *Northampton Independent* was characteristically ready to publish. Of the double bill of Fiona Macleod's *The Immortal Hour* and Lady Gregory's *The Workhouse Ward* Bassett-Lowke wrote:

> The wonderful surroundings and decorations of the theatre and the marvellous stage setting, which it would be impossible to see anywhere else in England, made the production a most impressive and lasting memory. (*NI* 12.3.1927)

In May 1927 B. G. Holloway (W.H.'s son) and Max Jerome repaired to Cambridge to see Elmer Rice's expressionist drama *The Adding Machine*, in which as Holloway reported "the mirror is held up to the innermost thoughts of man and to the registrations of his subconscious mind" (*NI* 7.5.1927). In answer to his own question "Should a similar production be offered in Northampton?" Holloway admitted that amongst his companions the opinion was divided. Max Jerome left no doubt about his views in a letter published the following week. Reasonably enough he pointed out the difference between Northampton and

Cambridge, then he unleashed his venom on the play: "a play that deals with the contortions, in this world and the next, of a sensual and depraved mind . . . [it] is calculated to plant seeds of a dank and unwholesome line of thought." As to staging *The Adding Machine* in Northampton "No, a thousand times no!" (*NI* 14.5.1927).

This public exchange of views clearly indicated a gulf between Jerome and at least one of his directors. When Jerome took his leave a few months later Prentice's appointment as his successor signalled the intention to move towards greater experiment. Why Prentice should have been lured away from the heady refinement of Cambridge to the uncertain prospect of Northampton remains a mystery, though Gray's doctrinaire proprietorship was perhaps becoming irksome. The technical and financial resources of Northampton were manifestly inferior to Cambridge; the workload much more burdensome. Prentice must have realised that his experience in Sheffield would stand him in better stead in his new appointment than would his indisputably impressive achievements in Cambridge.

For most of his time in Northampton Prentice combined the duties of general manager with those of producer. During the latter stages of Prentice's regime Peppino Santangelo was successively assistant manager, business manager and manager in which capacities he relieved Prentice of some of his administrative duties. As Santangelo indicated, in an article "How a Play is Produced. A Peep Behind the Scenes at the Opera House" (*NI* 10.10.1931), Prentice's artistic workload was onerous enough. Having selected and read (several times) the play, the producer "must be able to visualise the setting, the lighting effects, and the action of the players". As at Cambridge Prentice "drafted out to scale every little detail of furniture and property . . . in its proper place with explanations for the different stage departments".

Lighting was an important feature of Prentice's productions and an essential complement to his set designs. As early as 1925 Harold Ridge had dedicated his book *Stage-Lighting for 'Little' Theatres* "To Herbert Prentice, Director of the Sheffield Repertory Company". In September 1931 Ridge's firm of consulting engineers, Ridge and Aldred, submitted a detailed report on the Royal Theatre's electrical installations to Prentice, advising "we are not prepared to attempt any piecemeal patching up, as in our opinion things have gone too far and the risks are too great" (N.C.R.O.). The board negotiated with the Northampton Theatre Syndicate to share the cost of £350 (BM 28.4.1931 and 13.5.1931). Prentice's meticulous deployment of lighting, both technically and "in the scheme of colour used by the producer while setting the scene" (*NI* 10.10.1931) was apparent in his stage work.

Casting, within the constraints of a permanent company, was "itself . . . an art", avoiding type-casting, stretching the talent at his disposal. At the first rehearsal on Tuesday the company would "read the entire play from the script.

Places, movements, positions and groupings are plotted out, but there is no attempt at characterisation. The second rehearsal is devoted to characterisation with places. It is so important that the actors know their stage positions, as it helps them to remember their lines so much more easily." Already "the first act is committed to memory". At the third rehearsal (Thursday) attention is concentrated on "pause, intonation of voices, and the general development of the characters". Lines were gone through again and again until the producer was satisfied. In Cambridge Prentice spent six hours' rehearsal on the brainstorm scene in *The Adding Machine* although on stage it lasted only sixty seconds – a luxury unaffordable in Northampton. On the fourth day Prentice observed from the stalls, pausing at the end of each act to comment and correct. By then no books were permitted, but the prompter was kept busy. By Saturday the cast was expected to be word perfect for "the perfect rehearsal", though in practice their day of rest on Sunday was probably used to perfect their lines. On Monday with the opening two performances looming up, costumes, wigs and make-up were donned and music and lighting put into place. No wonder that Prentice referred to the "infinite amount of work" involved in rehearsal "as almost every movement of the eyelid has to be rehearsed and memorised" by each actor "who is under terrific nervous strain for hours at a stretch".

The selection of suitable plays, at the rate of one a week, was a task requiring consummate skill. Each play had to be short enough – or capable of being cut – to play twice nightly. Performing rights and royalties had to be satisfactory. The size of the cast (and the range of parts) had to be within the compass of the permanent company. If it was too large additional players – usually amateurs – would have to be engaged and although a smaller cast gave some actors a welcome week off it was uneconomic to be paying too many actors whose services were not used. Requirements (and cost) of scenery, costumes and lighting had to be considered. But the overriding imperative was the taste of Northampton's theatre-goers, which was not very sophisticated or elevated:

> Northampton audiences are perhaps more constant in their taste and it is almost certain they will respond to any plays by authors like Somerset Maugham, Coward and Lonsdale. Crook plays that are cleverly constructed, together with certain plays of Shaw, are also popular, while some of the late Victorian and Edwardian dramatists like Sutro and Sir Arthur Pinero have always proved successful. Sir James Barrie is also popular, but most of his plays are unfortunately too long for twice nightly performances.
>
> The plays that are certainly disliked in Northampton are the ones that deal with slum life in obscure surroundings, and dialect plays. Impressionistic plays have never yet been tried at the Northampton Repertory Theatre, except when "R.U.R." was produced . . . an excellent result. (*NI* 2.1.1932)

The league table of success in Prentice's first eighteen months reveals that between January and July 1928 the three most successful plays were: *Tilly of Bloomsbury* by Ian Hay, *Hindle Wakes* by Stanley Houghton and another Ian Hay piece *The Sport of Kings*. In the second half of 1928 *Grumpy* by Horace Hodges and T. Wigley Percival led H. A. Jones's *The Lie* and Ian Hay's *The Happy Ending*. During the winter–spring of 1929 (when the future of the company was in jeopardy) Prentice's own *Alice in Wonderland* headed Jean Webster's *Daddy-Long-Legs* and Walter Hackett's *Ambrose Applejohn's Adventures*.

An analysis of the two hundred plus plays produced during Prentice's term of office indicates just how restrictive the taste of Northampton was. Somerset Maugham led with ten plays. Noel Coward and Frederick Lonsdale followed with seven and six respectively, each achieving a reprise (*Hay Fever* and *On Approval*). Ian Hay, so prominent in the league tables, furnished five plays solo and three collaborative pieces, two of them with P. G. Wodehouse. Shaw was the only "serious" dramatist to make a showing, with four plays. H. A. Jones (three), Stanley Houghton (three), John Galsworthy (two), J. M. Barrie (two) and Oscar Wilde (two), were in evidence, but Pinero had declined to a single production. A. A. Milne provided four plays, John Masefield and John Drinkwater two each, St. John Ervine and Benn Levy three each.

Plays produced twice – a clear indication of popularity – were – in addition to *Hay Fever* and *On Approval* – : Masefield's *The Witch*, Sutton Vane's *Outward Bound*, Benn Levy's *This Woman Business*, H. A. Jones's *The Lie* and *Ambrose Applejohn's Adventures*. In contrast classic revivals were represented only by *She Stoops to Conquer*, *The School for Scandal* (already done by Jerome) and *Le Malade Imaginaire*; there was no full length Shakespeare. *The White Lady*, *The House of Crooks* and *Three Blind Mice* were the only new plays. Prentice countered an article by St. John Ervine (reproduced from the *Observer*) complaining about the difficulty encountered by dramatists in getting new plays performed by referring to the "pages of utter trash masquerading under the name of 'a play'" through which he was consistently obliged to read. He recalled that even at the Festival Theatre, Cambridge, which was favourably disposed to original work "Quite a number of manuscripts were submitted but surprisingly few were even worthy of consideration" (PR 17.9.1928).

Their shared difficulty in finding new plays was about all that Cambridge and Northampton had in common. From the twenty-six productions (several of them made up of one-act plays) which Prentice staged at the Festival Theatre he considered only one play *Absorbing Perdita*, retitled *Perdita Comes to Town*, by actor T. G. Saville, to be suitable for Northampton. His experience in Sheffield stood him in better stead and he repeated such former successes as Shaw's *Fanny's First Play*, *Candida*, *Misalliance*; Barrie's *Mary Rose*; Galsworthy's *The Silver Box*; Granville-Barker's *The Romantic Young Lady*; St. John Ervine's *The Ship*; Synge's *The Playboy of the Western World* and C. B. Fernald's adaptation of

Chiarelli's *The Mask and the Face*. Detailed comparison of the repertory theatres during this period would be a fascinating line of enquiry, but by way of example the Birmingham Repertory Company (admittedly with a smaller turnover of plays) produced only one work by Somerset Maugham during the period in which Northampton produced ten.

If Prentice's scope for play selection was severely restricted he could at least ensure the highest standard of performance. He was strikingly successful in attracting actors and actresses of outstanding ability. Inevitably there was a large change consequent upon his arrival, with only C. T. Doe remaining long. Cambridge was naturally a fruitful recruiting ground with Vivienne Bennett, Bertram Heyhoe, Godfrey Kenton, T. G. Saville, Guy Naylor, Curigwen Lewis and Marion Prentice all coming from the Festival Theatre.

From the late nineteenth century onwards the composition of the acting profession had altered markedly. No longer were recruits drawn predominantly from acting families, but rather from the professional classes whose offspring enjoyed a good education affording them a choice of career. This pattern is clearly evident from the programme pen portraits of the corps of actors and actresses who enlisted for the rigours of weekly repertory in an unfashionable company in a Midlands county town.

Godfrey Kenton (Louth Grammar School and St Paul's Theological College Lincoln) and Noel Howlett (King's School Canterbury, Leeds University and Mirfield Theological College) were both intended for the church. Terence Duff (St Paul's School) and Max Adrian (Portoro Royal School) both came from military families. Noel Morris was another product of St Paul's, whose war record included Ypres (where he was gassed) and Arras (where he was shot down in an aeroplane). Guy Naylor, the son of a Cambridge don, was educated at Radley and St John's College, Cambridge; Philip Yorke at Shrewsbury School and Corpus Christi College Cambridge. Scotsborn Donald Gordon attended Highgate School and James Hayter (born in India) the Dollar Academy in Scotland. T. G. Saville was "educated privately".

Attendance at one of the London drama schools was an increasingly common form of training: Kenton studied at R.A.D.A. as did Gordon and Hayter. Apprenticeships were served with the Charles Macdona Players (J. Laird Hossack and Donald Gordon), with Lena Ashwell (Kenton) Ben Greet (Duff), Robert Atkins (Gordon), Rupert Harvey at Bristol (Hayter) and of course Terence Gray's Festival Theatre as already listed. Not one of the above-mentioned actors came from a theatrical family.

A similar pattern is discernible amongst the actresses in the company. In May 1929 (PR 7.5.1927) Marion Prentice was described as "the only member of the N.R.P.'s past or present cast whose father [Robert J. Smith for twenty-seven years producer to the Stockport Garrick Society] has been connected with the stage". A later recruit Sheila Millar came from a theatre family, but received a conventional middle-class education at the Convent of the Sacred Heart in Bath. Joan Douglas "a typical English girl" to whom "tennis, golf and swimming are second nature" (PR 26.10.1930) was representative of the background of most of the female members of the company. Her interest in acting began at school (in her case Westcliff, Weston-Super-Mare) as it had for Vivienne Bennett (Convent of the Ladies of Mary, Forest Hill), Elma Carswell (Bournemouth High School), Molly Francis (King Alfred School, Hampstead), Olive Milbourne (Ravensfield College, Hendon), Diana Carroll (Hall School, Weybridge) and Lois Obee (Aberdeen High School). Curigwen Lewis's amibitions were fired by eisteddfods as well as her schooling in Llandrindod Wells. Single-sex education benefited girls more than boys in their dramatic aspirations. Apart from the traditional training in dance and ballet the whole range of dramatic roles became available to them.

Despite Noel Coward's injunction to Mrs. Worthington ("Don't put your daughter on the stage, Mrs. Worthington")[4] the prejudices of well-to-do parents against the stage as a career for their daughters were weakening. True that after studying at Aberdeen University Lois Obee "much against the inclination of her parents . . . decided to adopt the stage as a career" (PR 17.10.1932) and did so only after training at R.A.D.A.. The growing reputation of the principal drama schools eased many an aspiring actress's ambitions. Vivienne Bennett attended R.A.D.A. as did Curigwen Lewis and Olive Milbourne. Elma Carswell studied at the Central School and the Froebel Institute; Molly Francis with Dame May Whitty at the Etlinger School of Arts; Athol Fulford with Lady Benson; and Joan Douglas at the Guildhall School. Vera Draffin, having failed to enter R.A.D.A., attended a school of cookery (as did Joan Douglas for a time), but even that proved to be useful: "I've taken maids' parts so many times that I feel that my lessons in domesticity in Buckingham Palace Road have not been quite in vain."

These actresses were by no means novices. Vivienne Bennett had played Puck for Bridges Adams at Stratford in 1921 whilst still at school. Curigwen Lewis's appearance in an eisteddfod at the age of seven had been acclaimed. During their time at the Festival Theatre Cambridge both actresses had given accomplished performances, in particular Vivienne Bennett's Juliet and Salomé and Curigwen Lewis's ("the little Celtic Lady of Cambridge") Cleopatra in Shaw's *Caesar and Cleopatra*. Elma Carswell had worked with Lillah McCarthy; Molly Francis at the Old Vic and Athol Fulford, born in China and educated in Australia, was another example of the "large proportion of actors and actresses who have originated from countries so many thousands of miles away [who] have met together in a work-a-day provincial town to co-operate in the growth of the Repertory Movement in Northampton".

Just why these young and talented professionals should have been drawn to Northampton in particular is something of a puzzle. The obligation not only to a weekly change of play, but also to twice nightly performances made Northampton an especially tough assignment compared with other more

The Importance of Being Earnest by Oscar Wilde 1931. Noel Howlett as John Worthing, Vivienne Bennett as Gwendoline, Curigwen Lewis as Cecily and Max Adrian as Algernon. (*Adventure in Repertory*)

prestigious repertory theatres. The top salary of £7 a week (BM 20.5.1930) was scarcely an inducement. Undoubtedly Herbert Prentice's reputation as a producer was a strong incentive and clearly he brought out the best in his company. Prentice's determination to avoid type-casting combined with the exigencies of weekly repertory to give actors a wide range of parts, both in terms of length and character type. Nevertheless actors inevitably found their forte in roles to which they were particularly well suited.

During two spells in Northampton (he left to work at the Old Vic in 1928-9) Godfrey Kenton, gifted with a magnificent voice, combined versatility with an urbane style which suited him to the mercurial Saben in Coward's *The Queen Was in the Parlour*. Juvenile parts included Simon Bliss (*Hay Fever*) and in a more intensively sincere vein Wilde's Gerald Arbuthnot (*A Woman of No Importance*). He played Hubert in the scene from *King John* which constituted Prentice's only Shakespearean offering and as the General, in Prentice's most ambitious choice, *R.U.R.*, was "a show unto himself" (*NDC* 17.7.28). As the Stepson in Masefield's *The Witch* he gave "a performance of artistry in which is presented, with power and conviction, the struggle between his joy in his love of the beautiful witch and his duty to his father and his priestly calling" (*NDC* 4.3.30).

Of the other actors Bertram Heyhoe performed the Father in *The Witch* with appealing dignity and was admired as Tarleton in Shaw's *Misalliance*. In that play Noel Howlett was a fastidious Lord Summerhays and he included amongst his other successes Charles II (J. B. Fagan's *And So To Bed*), John Worthing (*The Importance of Being Earnest*) and Sir Peter Teazle (*The School for Scandal*). Max Adrian was the Charles Surface in Sheridan's play (the Christmas production for 1930) and in the following spring he rose to the challenge of several important roles: Wilde's Algernon Moncrieff, Eugene Marchbanks in *Candida* and Christy Mahon in Synge's *The Playboy of the Western World*. During his years in Northampton James Hayter developed his distinctive talents for eccentric comedy in such roles as Bunny in *Raffles*, Lob in *Dear Brutus*, Pepys in *And So To Bed*, the Drunken Priest in *The Witch*, Archdeacon Daubeney in Wilde's *A Woman of No Importance* (to which he returned nearly forty years later in the 1967 London revival), Sir Oliver Surface in *The School for Scandal* and Burgess in *Candida*.

Godfrey Kenton, Noel Howlett, Bertram Heyhoe, Max Adrian and James Hayter all progressed to distinguished careers in the theatre.

The most impressive range of parts to fall to any performer were those played by Vivienne Bennett during her years with the company (1928-31). She demonstrated her professionalism in July 1928 when Joan Ingram, who was playing the title-role in L. N. Parker's *Magda*, was incapacitated by a fall from a horse. The company did not extend to understudies, but "At the shortest notice and without rehearsal, Vivienne Bennett gallantly stepped into the breach and gave a remarkably fine performance" (*Adventure* p. 43). The following week she deputised for Joan Ingram in C. K. Munro's boarding-house comedy *At Mrs. Beams* and the week after that gave a poignant study as Helena in *R.U.R.*

The diversity of repertory casting was apparent in *The Romantic Young Lady* in which Vivienne Bennett appeared as the eighty year old Dona Barbarita; nearly two years later she shed decades and changed her sex to appear as Prince Arthur to Kenton's Hubert in the scene from *King John*. By then she and Kenton were husband and wife. The off-stage lives of repertory players, who became part of the community, exercised considerable fascination on audiences. Thus of Queen Krazia in Coward's *The Queen Was in the Parlour*, "their marriage in real life . . . cannot fail to add piquancy to the occasion" (*NDC* 3.9.29). The couple ran the gamut of relationships from brother (Simon Bliss) and sister (Sorel Bliss) in *Hay Fever* and to husband (Simon) and wife in Barrie's *Mary Rose* in which Vivienne Bennett scored a personal success in the title-role. Vivienne Bennett subsequently played the child Margaret in Barrie's *Dear Brutus*, Gwendolen in Wilde's *The Importance of Being Earnest* and Pegeen in *The Playboy of the Western World*.

Other actresses seized their opportunities: Elma Carswell as O'Neill's Anna Christie; Marion Prentice as Masefield's Witch and J. B. Fagan's Mistress Pepys;

Alice in Wonderland Curigwen Lewis as Alice 1928. (*Adventure in Repertory*)

Joan Ingram in Sybil Thorndike's role as Elinor Shale in H. A. Jones's *The Lie*; Olive Milbourne as Lady Bracknell and Candida; and Sheila Millar as Maugham's Victoria in *Home and Beauty* and Raina in *Arms and the Man*.

Two special talents were nurtured in the Prentice years, those of two very contrasting actresses: Curigwen Lewis (later Mrs. Andrew Cruikshank) and Lois Obee (in later life Sonia Dresdel).

As the Romantic Young Lady of G. Martinez-Sierra's comedy (translated by Granville-Barker) Curigwen Lewis took "the extremely difficult title role . . . as though she had been acting the part for years" (*NDC* 14.8.1928), but it was as Lewis Carroll's Alice, in Prentice's own adaptation, already seen in Sheffield, that Curigwen Lewis won the hearts of Northampton audiences:

> What shall we say of Miss Curigwen Lewis as Alice? Perhaps she could not be paid a bigger compliment than to be told that the Alice of our book acquaintance was not nearly as ingenue, as sweet, and as brightly curious as she. (*NDC* 24.12.1928)

There followed Poppy Faire in *Ambrose Applejohn's Adventures*, Perdita in *Perdita Comes to Town*, Wilde's Cecily Cardew and Hester Worsley, the puritanical

30

young American in *A Woman of No Importance*.

Lois Obee was an actress of very different mettle. She made her mark immediately as Mrs. Pottle in *Baa-Baa, Black Sheep* and quickly progressed to stronger roles: Deborah Cane "an outstanding performance" (*NDC* 19.1.1932) in *Interference*, followed by "another brilliant performance" (*NDC* 26.1.1932) as the Eurasian Daisy in Maugham's *East of Suez*. She gave "vivid emotional performances as Paula in *The Second Mrs. Tanqueray* and Elinor Shale in *The Lie*" (*Adventure* p. 69).

From time to time Prentice found it necessary to augment his company from the amateur ranks, making the following appeal in the theatre programme (19.11.1928):

> I should be glad if any of our patrons who are willing to assist with the Christmas production of "Alice in Wonderland" by acting as supers, would give their names in . . .

Over the years many local enthusiasts trod the boards of the Royal Theatre: P. B. Baskcomb; Ernest Reynolds (later the author of important books on theatre history); artist Henry Bird (whose long association with the theatre culminated in his magnificent act-curtain); J. F. Brown, son of Colonel John Brown, who adopted the stage name of John Barton; Lady Henley of Watford Court; and longest serving of all, Rose Walding, who at this time dashed from her duties at the town's library to take her place on the stage.

Week after week Prentice succeeded in welding his company into an effective ensemble. The judgement on Shaw's *Fanny's First Play* stands as an example:

> From every member of the cast we get an admirable performance, and there is also a team work about the whole production which contributes a great deal to the general success and excellence of the presentation. (*NDC* 27.5.30)

Scenic design had long been one of Prentice's accomplishments and a major feature of both his Sheffield and Cambridge productions. Following a dispute over his contract Charles Maynard was dismissed (BM 10.1.1928). He subsequently threatened court action (BM 8.5.1928). W. J. Bassett-Lowke was a client of the Bonaventure Press in Fish Street where he had noticed the talent of a young commercial artist upon whom he prevailed to help the theatre out of its emergency. Thus began the remarkable partnership between Tom Osborne Robinson and the Royal Theatre, which was to endure for nearly half a century.[5] His starting salary was £4 10s. a week (BM 24.1.1928).

The eldest of Charles and Kate Robinson's three sons Tom was born at Gypsy Cottage in Kingsley Road, Northampton on 26 March 1904. He showed precocious enthusiasm for the children's operettas produced by his mother, but the family's strict nonconformist ethos was certainly not calculated to foster a theatrical career. Neither was his education at the Town and County School. In 1921 Tom's father (by then a garage proprietor) took his son to see Diaghilev's Russian Ballet in *The Sleeping Princess* at London's Alhambra Theatre – with decor and costumes by Bakst. This experience removed any lingering doubts about his future and Osborne Robinson later recorded "I knew then that nothing would stop me from designing scenery and costumes".

When he left school in the following year Osborne Robinson took a job with the Bonaventure Press (5s. a week) and for the next six years spent his evenings studying at the Northampton School of Art (then in Abington Street), where his talent was recognised by the principal, Lewis Duckett. His early work showed his flair for originality of design and use of colour and in 1926 he so impressed the college authorities that he was awarded a travelling scholarship of £10 for two weeks in Paris. For Tom Osborne Robinson the call from the Royal Theatre in January 1928 was the summons to his destiny. Initially he combined his theatre work with his job at the Bonaventure, but nevertheless within four months he had personally painted some twenty-five sets.

The actual set designs, all circumscribed by the narrow proscenium arch of under twenty-one feet wide, were still Herbert Prentice's. In the summer of 1928 Prentice visited Germany "to inspect various new devices for securing magnificent effects with the simplest possible means", being particularly impressed with the use of plain black velvet curtains and the superiority of the Schwabe-Hasait lighting system, which in England had "an undeserved bad name" despite its use at the Festival Theatre, Cambridge (PR 8.10.1928).

In fact Prentice's predilection for the expressionist style of setting had already been evident in two Northampton productions: C. B. Fernald's version of Chiarelli's *The Mask and the Face* (30.4.1928) and Karel Capek's *R.U.R.* (16.7.1928). Even in the more naturalistic "A Room in the House of Count Grazia" in the former play the walls were in strong primary colours, the doors scarlet and the sky Italian blue. "The Drawing Room in Mrs. Domain's House" in *R.U.R.* was "in a semi-expressionistic manner".

> The basis or groundwork of the scene was black with bright yellow lines. Scenery and furniture were carried out in straight lines and angles to interpret the spirit of the play. The colour of the scenery in this scene was lupin-blue and silver.[6]

The prevailing lighting was "greenish blue" with "essential points picked out in shafts of white light" and red "superimposed on the whole scene . . . each time Radius entered" (PR 16.7.1928).

These sets attracted national interest being reproduced in *Drama*, the journal of

Setting for Karel Capek's *R.U.R.* by Herbert Prentice and Osborne Robinson 1928. (*Adventure in Repertory*)

the British Drama League, as was the set for Coward's *The Queen Was in the Parlour*. In each case the credits were for scenery "designed by Herbert M. Prentice and executed in the studio and workshop of the Northampton Repertory Players".

However few plays in the Northampton repertoire lent themselves to Prentice's personal and preferred style of design and increasingly Osborne Robinson's contribution was acknowledged. For *The Green Goddess*:

> The hand of Mr. T. Osborne Robinson, the Company's scenic artist, is welcome. Who else but Mr. Robinson would have designed such striking mountain scenery as we see in the first act? (*NDC* 6.8.1929)

Often it was Osborne Robinson's colour sense that enlivened the set designs:

> There is but one scene in "Misalliance" and Mr. Prentice and Mr. Osborne Robinson have together given us a truly delightful setting of a spacious modern loggia, and, of course, with those telling touches of vivid colour that so characterise the Repertory productions. (*NDC* 7.10.1930)

33

Again for *The Witch*:

> Primarily, though, "The Witch" is a triumph for Mr. Herbert Prentice and
> Mr. Osborne Robinson. The groupings and the lighting, the brilliant
> clear-cut colourings and the effectiveness of the settings – particularly the
> last beautiful cathedral scene – make the story that is unfolded to us the
> most enthralling ever. (*NDC* 4.11.1930)

Prentice was adroit in harmonising stage groupings with his set designs to create
an overall pattern. Lewis Duckett "noted well – and delighted in – the tendency to
form symmetrical groups of actors". He approved "designs showing 'Black and
White' interiors, simple masonry, and simple panelling", but saw "no special
virtue in cold reds, and 'modern' art, unless severely held in check" (PR
7.1.1929).

Costume was of course intrinsic to the visual effect. In contemporary plays the
actors provided their own, but period pieces such as *The Importance of Being
Earnest* offered scope: "The 'etching' effect of the second scene is unusual and
effective" (*NDC* 7.4.31). The other senses were not neglected, music having been
carefully chosen and receiving, in the case of *And So To Bed*, special rehearsals for
the songs.

The demands placed upon Prentice as producer are too self-evident to require
reiteration. In addition he was answerable to the board for the financial and
administrative affairs of the theatre. The board was relatively stable. W. H.
Horton became chairman on the resignation of Sir James Crockett in 1930 and
was himself succeeded by Mrs. Helen Panther in 1932. P. B. Baskcomb, long a
supporter of the theatre, joined in 1928 as the Playgoers' Association's nominee.
Whatever their achievements on stage the Northampton Repertory Players Ltd.
were confronted by recurrent difficulties.

By March 1928 average weekly costs had risen by £90 to over £320 (BM
6.3.1928) and Prentice was required to economise. Despite the success of *Alice in
Wonderland* over Christmas 1928 attendances plunged in the new year, partly due
to external factors (wintry weather, illness, bad trade) beyond the theatre's
control. Attendances for John Masefield's *Good Friday* in Holy Week reached the
lowest ebb. Audiences rallied for Lonsdale's *On Approval* and the *Daily Telegraph*
(28.3.1929) appealed to "the more public spirited citizens of Northampton" to
safeguard the theatre's future. Ironically the Playgoers' Association felt alienated
by the board's failure to communicate its reported decision to close the theatre.
The Playgoers' indignation; Sir James Crockett's guarantee of a bank overdraft
"up to £500" (BM 7.2.1929); and a further issue of shares (BM AGM 27.5.1929)
ensured that the closure was only temporary and after a summer season in Bath
the company returned to the Royal. The theatre experienced another bad patch
in the autumn of 1931, this time largely because of "theatre-goers resenting the

theatrical fare offered to them" (*Adventure* p. 67). By that stage however there was no serious doubt about the continuation of repertory, the lease with the Northampton Theatre Syndicate having been renewed for a further five years in January 1931. The practice of subletting the Royal to touring companies during a summer repertory vacation alleviated some of the pressure. In the summer of 1930 the Prentices, the Kentons "and several other personalities associated with the Northampton Repertory movement" accompanied the Bassett-Lowkes on a de-luxe Mediterranean cruise aboard the *Arandora Star* (*NI* 23.7.30).

The sense of being part of a national repertory movement was strong during the Prentice years. Barry Jackson extended his activities to the Malvern Festival Theatre in 1929 and his maxim that a National Theatre was "the proper apex of the repertory movement" was often invoked. The prospect of a National Theatre was in the forefront of many minds, but in the meantime Elizabeth Scott's new Shakespeare Memorial Theatre rose on the banks of the Avon at Stratford, being officially opened by the Prince of Wales in April 1932 with a performance of *Henry IV*, in which Gyles Isham (of Lamport Hall) played Prince Hal. The forum for much of this activity was the British Drama League, founded in 1919 by Geoffrey Whitworth. Although much concerned with amateur drama the League was also a firm supporter of repertory and generally held its annual conference in a town which had a flourishing repertory theatre.

That the British Drama League should hold its 1929 conference in Northampton, so soon after the inception of the repertory company and in the wake of its threatened closure, was largely thanks to W. J. Bassett-Lowke. The League's intention was that "one of the results of the visit would be that townspeople would rally to the support of that splendid institution".[7] Under Bassett-Lowke's encouragement the local community turned out in force to support the occasion. The packed weekend (25–7 October 1929) began with the Mayor's reception at the Guildhall, thence to the Royal Theatre where Mrs. Panther welcomed the delegates prior to an Address by Lord Lytton and – at last – "a notably fine performance of *The Queen Was in The Parlour* by the Repertory Players". On Saturday Prentice guided the delegates around the theatre before they repaired to the Carnegie Public Library for the formal proceedings. After dinner at the Angel Hotel, presided over by Lord Henley, the members returned to the library for a talk by Professor Gilbert Murray on "Dramatic Training" and two performances by Women's Institute teams, one from Harlestone, the other a mixed group organised by Lady Henley. On Sunday morning Rev. Trevor Lewis preached a special sermon at the parish church of All Saints and the conference concluded with a luncheon for over one hundred hosted by Lord and Lady Henley at Watford Court.

The conference was notable for the contributions of two men: Gilbert Murray, the classical scholar and translator, and Robert Young, then Labour M.P. for Islington. Although Murray's involvement with the British Drama League was long-standing his presence in Northampton was due to his kinship with the Henleys. Murray's wife Mary was Lady – Dorothy – Henley's sister, both of them daughters of the ninth Earl of Carlisle. The sisters had been theatre enthusiasts since their childhood at Castle Howard where they performed in family entertainments. In *Major Barbara* Shaw based Adolphus Cusins on Murray, Barbara on Lady Mary and Lady Britomart on the formidable Rosalind, Countess of Carlisle – to identify Barbara's sister Sarah with Lady Dorothy and her suitor Charles Lomax with the future Lord Henley can only be speculative (and unflattering). Lady Henley was a leading figure in amateur (particularly Women's Institute) drama in the county and from 1926 to 1955 regularly produced plays in the library theatre at Watford Court. Her correspondence with Murray reveals that he was an unenthusiastic participant in the Drama League conference. He wrote "But I have only to make an appearance and with a little stimulant can easily face two companies of Women's Institutes".[8]

It fell to Robert Young to move the resolution:

> That this Conference of the British Drama League, believing that the Government is in sympathy with the idea and establishment of national Theatre and would favourably consider a practical and agreed scheme to this end, requests the Council to take early and energetic measures to achieve this great object.[9]

Clearly there was a feeling that the new Labour government was sympathetic to the National Theatre scheme. Young referred to Prime Minister Ramsay MacDonald's encouraging reply to a question on the matter in the House of Commons in July 1929 and Geoffrey Whitworth, secretary of the League, read out a letter from J. R. Clynes, Home Secretary, endorsing "the contribution [of the theatre] to improved National character and understanding".

The resolution was passed by sixty-two votes to ten, but passing resolutions was easy enough, actually creating and running any theatre was, as the Northampton pioneers knew, a very different matter. In an article specially written for *Drama* (October 1929) to mark the League's Northampton conference Francis Graves referred to the town's advantages ("an actual theatre, and not a converted chapel or warehouse") and its disadvantages: "the necessity of playing twice nightly" and "the smallness of the public who love the theatre and the peculiar sensitiveness of Northampton people to any suspicion that they are being educated".

Although in January 1929 Prentice experimented by running one once nightly production per month twice nightly was ineluctable. As a system it offered a wider choice of performances to audiences, many of them accustomed to the flexibility of cinema attendance. The price exacted on plays (forty pages cut from Maugham's *Caesar's Wife*) and players was a high one to pay. As Graves reported to the Playgoers in April 1929 "another thousand regular attendants at the theatre each week" (*NDC* 9.4.1929) would solve the problem and give repertory the core of support it needed. Various incentives were deployed: season tickets, lucky numbers in the programmes and free tickets for a second visit: the management was assiduous in its help with transport – parking arrangements, late buses and trains. Even the support of the Playgoers' Association was removed in February 1930 when they ceased activities.

Producer, designer and general manager Prentice resolutely pressed on, but following the poorly supported autumn 1931 season he suffered a breakdown. T. G. Saville stepped in to produce several plays and Prentice resumed his duties early in 1932. Nevertheless Barry Jackson's invitation to take over the Birmingham Repertory Theatre in June that year must have been irresistible. W. J. Bassett-Lowke, undoubtedly Prentice's firmest supporter on the theatre board, described him as "very reserved" preferring to be known by his stage works of which "the impressionistic play is the type at which he excels", regrettably a type of play which "would not appeal to a Northampton audience" (PR 6.6.1932).

During his three and a half years in Northampton Prentice had made little headway in extending the tastes of local audiences, which persistently restricted his choice of plays. Though he accommodated their preferences and tolerated twice nightly performances, he was uncompromising in his standards of production and acting and so he ensured a respectable reputation for the theatre both locally and nationally and, above all, its survival.

Notes

1. T. Alec Seed *The Sheffield Repertory Theatre A History*, 1959, pp. 1–2.

2. Norman Marshall *The Other Theatre*, 1948, pp. 53 and 59. See also Richard Cave *Theatre in Focus Terence Gray and the Cambridge Festival Theatre*, 1980.

3. Graham Woodruff " 'Down with the Boot-faced': Public Relations at the Festival Theatre, Cambridge" in *Theatre Research International* v. 1., no. 2., February 1976, p. 117.

4. Sheridan Morley *A Talent to Amuse*, 1974, pp. 210–11, quoted the lyrics, composed in 1933.

5. For biographical information on Tom Osborne Robinson see *Patron Extraordinaire A Tribute to Osborne Robinson OBE*, 1976; and Colin Robinson *Thomas Osborne Robinson OBE Beginnings*, 1977.

6. *Drama* v. vii, no. 10, October MCMXXVIII, p. 13.

7. *Drama* v. viii, no. 10, October MCMXXIX, p. 48.

8. Letters in Lady Henley's papers in N.C.R.O.

9. Geoffrey Whitworth *The Making of a National Theatre*, 1951, p. 171.

CHAPTER FOUR

Robert Young 1932-5

AFTER interviewing several candidates the board appointed Robert Young as Prentice's successor from August 1932. He and Northampton were of course known to each other through his participation in the 1929 British Drama League conference, as Young recalled:

> Three years ago I paid my first visit to Northampton to move the resolution at the British Drama League Conference in favour of a National Theatre. Previously I had seen Mr. Ramsay MacDonald in the House of Commons and gained his encouraging support. (*NI* 8.10.1932)

In 1931 MacDonald's and Young's political fortunes received a set-back and Young lost his Islington seat, but his political credentials would have commended him to at least one member of the Northampton repertory board: W. J. Bassett-Lowke, who had been elected as a Labour councillor for the borough in 1931. Not that Young needed any special pleading, his qualifications for the job of producer being beyond dispute.

Born in Manchester in 1891, he was educated at Manchester Grammar School and then travelled widely to South America, South Africa and New Zealand, where he enlisted in the expeditionary force as one of only ten white men in a Maori regiment. He was badly shell-shocked at Gallipoli and subsequently wounded at Messines Ridge. After the war he studied with Lady Benson before joining her husband's company and he later worked (as an actor) at Stratford, with J. E. Vedrenne, Arthur Bourchier and Lena Ashwell.

On his election to parliament Young was dubbed "the Actors' M.P." and took a prominent role in the move to create an actors' union – Equity. The failure of a musical show *Open Your Eyes* in September 1929 incensed members of the profession against the activities of what they regarded as bogus managements. On 8 October a large open meeting was held at London's New Theatre (lent by Bronson Albery) for the purpose of fusing the two existing professional organisations for actors – The Actors' Association and the Stage Guild. According to Joseph Macleod:

> it was perhaps Young who made the most impact, when he rose to move:

The Northampton Repertory Players in 1932.
Front row L-R: Sheila Millar, Lala Lloyd, Lois Obee (Sonia Dresdel), Robert
Young, Joan Kemp-Welch, Jane Tann, Oswald Dale Roberts, Doreen Morton.
Back Row L-R: Eric Phillips, Stringer Davis, Osborne Robinson, Noel Howlett,
Peppino Santagelo, Herbert Bradford, Donald Gordon, Peter Rosser, Fred Pratt.
(Royal Theatre Collection)

> That this meeting urges the Actors and Actresses of this country to form
> and unite in one effective organisation and abandon every consideration
> which might prejudice this result.
>   It was carried enthusiastically.[1]

Young's commitment and enthusiasm were beyond question, his tact and
diplomacy were not. He offended the Actors' Guild by appealing to it to disband.
In 1951 Felix Aylmer recalled that "when everything had gone nicely according
to plan, the New Theatre meeting was wrecked by the irruption of Young (on the
platform) with his appeal for the disbanding of the Guild".[2] On 1 December
Young absented himself from another meeting at which Ben Webster's motion
that a British Actors' Equity Association be formed was carried without dissent.
Young became member no. 2 and proudly maintained his membership until his
death, aged ninety-three, at the actors' home Denville Hall in 1985.[3]

Although Young's parliamentary career was widely referred to in Northampton,
his role in the formation of Equity was not. As producer he was inevitably directly
concerned – on the management side – with the conditions of service of his
company. However he viewed this function his tenure was marked by tensions
and disputes with both the board and performers, but these seem to have arisen as
much from his temperament (as evidenced at the New Theatre meeting) as from

the clash of divided loyalties.

Young approached his duties as producer methodically and energetically. He was reported as working "80 hours a week, but would not exchange his job for a royal crown". He was in the theatre by 10 o'clock each morning and after dealing with correspondence for half an hour, he rehearsed until 2 p.m., usually stationing himself in the front of the dress circle. He aimed to keep three weeks ahead of his company and devoted his afternoons and evenings to studying plays, discussing wigs and costumes and interviewing artistes. Although he regarded Sunday as a day of rest for the actors he regularly worked for six to eight hours. He claimed that:

> The system under which we work is largely responsible for the excellent spirit of co-operation and good will which exists in the theatre. The company consistently give me loyal support and they are very keen on their work. (PR 30.1.1933)

On his appointment Young retained the services of four key members of the company: Donald Gordon, Noel Howlett, Lois Obee and Sheila Millar. New recruits included Joan Kemp-Welch and Oswald Dale Roberts. Educated at Roedean Joan Kemp-Welch had trained as a dancer and a teacher before gaining experience in repertory, the West End and films. Oswald Dale Roberts, a clergyman's son, attended Shrewsbury School and Exeter College, Oxford graduating in 1912. A versatile sportsman he played hockey, soccer and cricket for his college, accomplishments which no doubt commended him to Frank Benson, with whom he worked for three years. Whilst with Benson Roberts met his future wife Violet Cecil, who, like Joan Kemp-Welch, had trained as a dancer with Espinoza. Gassed at Passchendaele Dale Roberts resumed his theatre career as a stage director for Henry Baynton.

Young's ability as a producer was apparent in the quality of work achieved by his company in, for instance, Maugham's *The Painted Veil*:

> At the last there is a tremendously important feature of the play, the acting of Miss Lois Obee in a heavy role. Miss Obee's work can be compared with anything seen at the Repertory Theatre. The acting throughout is, indeed, outstandingly good this week. Mr. Donald Gordon in the part of the implacable husband. Mr. Noel Howlett as the rogue Charles Townsend. Miss Joan Kemp-Welch, as the Mother Superior. Mr. Stringer Davis as the wise man of the piece Waddington – all these and a long cast of others are brilliant in a brilliant play . . . The unusual settings, too, . . . create an atmosphere quite their own . . . They represent some of Osborne Robinson's best work. (*NDC* 20.9.1932)

Twelfth Night by William Shakespeare 1933. "A City in Illyria" by Osborne Robinson. (*Adventure in Repertory*)

Early in 1933 in L. N. Parker's *The Cardinal* Oswald Dale Roberts rose "to tremendous heights of dramatic power . . . It is indeed a triumph for Mr. Oswald Dale Roberts, but one must also mention Mr. Stringer Davis, Miss Lois Obee, and Miss Sheila Millar. But all the players rise to the occasion superbly." (*NDC* 31.1.1933) The production and performances were commended by the national press and delegates at the Conference of the Repertory Theatres' Association which met in the town.

Unlike his predecessor Young tackled Shakespeare. First, in February 1933, *Twelfth Night*, which returned a profit of £69 (box office income £312 BM 7.3.1933):

> With Noel Howlett's dignified Orsino, Sheila Millar's attractive Olivia, Lois Obee's engaging Viola, Donald Gordon's appealing Feste, Oswald Dale Roberts's jovial Sir Toby and Robert Young's richly comic portrayal of Sir Andrew . . . (*Adventure* p. 76)

The Merchant of Venice followed in April, running for two weeks (profit of £36 in week one, loss of £99 in week two BM 11 and 19.5.1933), with Roberts giving a powerful performance as Shylock well matched by Lois Obee's charming Portia.

Cecil Chisholm considered Northampton to be one of the few (alongside only Birmingham, Bristol and Liverpool) repertory theatres capable of staging the bard successfully. He wrote of Young:

> Few repertory producers have experience of doing poetic drama on the grand scale. Robert Young of Northampton, is an exception, since he has spent much of his stage life on Shakespeare work.[4]

When Chisholm visited Northampton in May 1933 to see Arnold Bennett's *Sacred and Profane Love* he enthused over Lois Obee's performance as Carlotta Peel:

> I recollect a performance of Arnold Bennett's *Sacred and Profane Love*, produced by Robert Young at the Northampton Repertory. In this piece of *bravura*, a typically romantic, yet hard-headed Bennett heroine has to save a pianist of genius from dope. In so doing she is called upon to run up almost the entire dramatic scale from complete innocence to sophisticated cosmopolitan cynicism; from the lightest comedy to the darkest of tragic suggestions, and she must keep one hand on a continuous romantic undertone, while the other is exerting all manner of realistic trills and cadenzas. A young actress, Miss Lois Obee, passed quite easily from the uncertainties of the provincial girl in love with a great artist to the self-assurance and poise of the professional woman. She was alternately as youthfully high falutin' and as mordantly cynical as Bennett himself could have desired. Better still, she caught the romantic undertones with beautiful fidelity.[5]

At the end of the season Lois Obee provided "a piece of *bravura*" of her own making. After the final performance of H. H. Davies's *The Mollusc* on 15 July 1933 she "stood with a bouquet clasped in either arm and the suspicion of tears in her eyes" for what she described as "the hardest farewell it has ever been my lot to bid". Having thanked the audience for its kindness she proceeded in progressively more sombre terms:

> I must take this opportunity of thanking the directors. I am sure they have done their best for me, also the manager, Mr. Peppino Santangelo, who has always been so courteous and helpful to me, as he is to everybody. We all think on this side of the curtain that it is a great pity that the same courtesy and consideration is not extended in every department of the theatre.
>
> My only reason for leaving you so suddenly and so abruptly is that I found it utterly impossible to go on working here any longer under the present method of production and as in my opinion next season will be even worse, I feel I must leave while I still have my health and sanity – what little of the latter I do possess. (*C&E* 17.7.1933)

Young had already left on holiday, but it was clear that he was Miss Obee's target. In a press interview she claimed that "we are all treated like amateurs", subjected to long waits and discouraging remarks during rehearsals. H. Musk Beattie, as secretary to the board explained that Miss Obee had originally applied for and been given a contract (£6 a week) for the next season. Her decision to resign dated only from 12 July. Whatever their reasons Joan Kemp-Welch, Stringer Davis (already embarked on his fifteen years' courtship of Margaret Rutherford whom he married in 1945), Ronald Hickman, stage-manager H. M. Bradford and manager Peppino Santangelo (whose "association" with Lois Obee was alluded to by Young BM 1.8.1933) also left the company, but Sheila Millar, Donald Gordon, Peter Rosser and Oswald Dale Roberts wrote a letter disassociating themselves from Lois Obee's remarks:

> We deplore the fact that she thought fit to include us in the unfortunate passage of her speech, and we deprecate the introduction of any personalities, or suggestion of personalities in her speech from the stage. (*C&E* 17.7.1933)

Matters did not rest there. Young issued a writ for slander through his solicitor H. Musk Beattie and Miss Obee was obliged to pen a retraction:

> On that occasion I spoke under considerable stress and I now realise that what I said might be taken as an aspersion on the professional reputation and competence of Mr. Robert Young. I desire to withdraw without qualification anything which might be so construed and I should like to take this opportunity of acknowledging the very considerable extent to which Mr. Young's skill and experience have contributed to the success of the Repertory Players' productions. (*NI* 7.10.1933)

Even this unqualified letter of retraction was not the full extent of Lois Obee's humiliation; she was obliged to change her name – to Sonia Dresdel – before she could get her promising stage career underway again. Meanwhile Young consolidated his position. The departure of the stage manager H. M. Bradford may very well have been contrived in order to enable Young's wife Doris Littell to take over the position. In practice the conjunction of husband and wife in two such crucial roles as producer and stage manager served only to heighten tensions within the company.

Ironically the next incident concerned Sheila Millar, who had rallied to Young's support at the time of Lois Obee's outburst. An attractive actress her career had progressed from a charming Lydia Languish in *The Rivals* through a lovable Elizabeth Barrett in *The Barretts of Wimpole Street* and an engaging Mother Grubble in *Jack and the Beanstalk* to Nora in *A Doll's House*: "[Miss Millar] rose to the occasion [with her] best piece of acting for some time" (*C&E* 30.1.1934).

At a special meeting on 25 January 1934 the board received a letter from Young saying that "he had suspended Miss Millar for insubordination".[6] He cited the stage "log-book" which indicated "a number of missed entries by Miss Millar in the past three weeks". Evidently there had been previous complaints, including "gossip with persons outside the theatre" (BM 17.10.1933), but the board was

> . . . of the opinion that the Producer had acted unwisely in suspending Miss Millar without consultation with the Board, or the Chairman, and that the proper course was to have reported her delinquencies to the Board. It was further felt that the state of affairs revealed as between Miss Millar and the Stage Manager appeared to have contributed to the difficulties.[6]

The board decided "to invite certain of the more responsible members of the Company to meet the Board in order that the Board might form an opinion as to the causes of the friction which appeared to exist between the Stage Manager and Miss Millar". A further special meeting of the board followed on the 26 January to which Young submitted a letter stating that "he could not admit the right of any artist to offer judgement on the sufficiency and behaviour of the Stage Manager". The board felt that "it could not admit any question as to their right to hold such an investigation" and therefore had no alternative but to accept the Youngs' resignations.

At the next – regular – board meeting on 30 January the Youngs withdrew their resignations on the understanding that they intended to leave at the end of the season "for reasons unconnected with the theatre". The board acceded, but reiterated its view "of the unwisdom of the disciplinary action against Miss Millar" and stated that any recurrence of such behaviour would result in the dismissal of both parties. At the 6 February meeting Peter Rosser, another of Young's erstwhile supporters, made "certain complaints against the Producer", but the board considered these to be of a personal nature not requiring its intervention.

In May 1934 the Youngs retracted their impending departure and the board agreed that their contracts should be renewed for a further season. When that season got underway in the autumn of 1934 two young recruits Nigel Patrick and Ruth Gower left within weeks. Young reported to the board on 28 August that "he had been obliged to terminate the engagements of Miss Ruth Gower and Mr. Nigel Patrick". The official public version was that "They were not completely happy here . . . they have taken advantage of better offers" (*NI* 7.9.1934), but not surprisingly speculation ran rife and the board protested to the *Chronicle and Echo* about its handling of the story.

Young's period in office was characterised by recurring incidents of this kind, which undeniably seem at odds with his political views and his support of Equity. Clearly everyone working in twice nightly weekly repertory was subject to considerable stress, which the personalities of Young and his wife evidently exacerbated, but Prentice, too, had noted "the atmosphere of discontent and insubordination . . . among the company" (BM 19.1.1932). Nevertheless these tensions do not seem to have had an adverse effect on the quality of the company's work, indeed they were in part the consequence of Young's exactingly high standards.

Like Prentice Young was keenly aware of the importance of play selection within the constraints under which he was obliged to operate:

> There are about forty-eight plays to be chosen every year, and, of course, there are not enough really suitable good plays to fill each week. For instance, we cannot produce every London success here. Some contain too many characters, others have a theme which may not appeal to local audiences. From London successes one turns to the classics, and here again many problems arise . . . The work of selecting plays is full of pitfalls. Not only must the plays be as good as possible: they must be varied in their sequence, otherwise our audiences weary of similar themes. Further, we have to bear in mind the limitations of our material in flats, and also the physical limitations of staff . . . We have to avoid two big productions following one another, for we do not have enough flats, etc., to make six different full-stage scenes. (Those flats in use for one play cannot be used for the following week.) So the plays have to be balanced one against another in plot, simplicity of setting, and size and nature of parts. (*Adventure* p. 95)

In any case the repertoire was changing as Cecil Chisholm observed: "But what about the giants of yesterday – Shaw, Galsworthy, Masefield, Granville-Barker and Hankin? I am afraid they are rapidly becoming *vieux jeux* . . . These bulwarks are now definitely gone."[7] In Northampton Shaw was the exception, possibly aided by the advocacy of his Fabian friend W. J. Bassett-Lowke and a sense of political fellow-feeling on the part of Young. *Arms and the Man, You Never Can Tell, Pygmalion, The Devil's Disciple* and *Major Barbara* were all revived.

Surprisingly H. H. Davies was represented by three plays all within two months in the summer of 1933. In contrast with Prentice Young produced only three Maugham plays, one Lonsdale and not a single Coward. Of contemporary dramatists J. B. Priestley supplied two pieces and Eden Phillpotts three, but "Mr. van Druten became the most favoured playwright" (*Adventure* p. 88) with five works. New plays were no more in evidence (only Edward L. Stanway's *The Power and the Glory*) and after his initial success with Shakespeare (*Twelfth Night* and *The Merchant of Venice*) Young produced only *Othello*. Other classical revivals were confined to Molière (*Le Malade Imaginaire*) and the ever-dependable Sheridan (*The Rivals*). Ibsen was represented by *A Doll's House*, Ferenc Molnar by *The Play's the Thing* and Elmer Rice by *See Naples and Die* and

Counsellor-at-Law. Young extended the run to a second week on five occasions: L. N. Parker's *The Cardinal* (which received a further one week revival), *The Merchant of Venice*, Eden Phillpotts's *The Farmer's Wife*, *Caesar's Friend* by Campbell Dixon and Dermot Morrah, and Charles Hawtrey's resilient farcical comedy *The Private Secretary* first seen in London in 1884.

Cecil Chisholm judged Rudolf Besier's *The Barretts of Wimpole Street* as "the most popular play in the repertory theatre today" and Northampton was no exception, its appeal enhanced by Oswald Dale Roberts's performance in Cedric Hardwicke's role as Edward Moulton-Barrett. One London visitor was "forced to admit that there was little to choose between Cedric Hardwicke in the West End and Oswald Dale Roberts in Northampton" (*C&E* 17.11.33).

In Eden Phillpotts's *Yellow Sands* Roberts assumed Hardwicke's mantle even more literally:

ENTERPRISE
Through the efforts of Mr. P. B. Baskcomb, B.A., we have managed to secure the original hat and coat that was worn by Sir Cedric Hardwicke in "Yellow Sands". It [sic] will be worn by Mr. Oswald Dale Roberts.
(*PR* 12.2.1934)

Drawing many of its plays from West End successes, which by their nature included strong roles for stars, the repertory company needed the services of such a powerful actor as Oswald Dale Roberts who, though he could not command star status on the metropolitan stage, easily assumed a comparable pre-eminence in the humbler orbit of Northampton. Dale Roberts, a forceful actor, albeit in a somewhat outmoded style, possessed a fine stage presence and powerful elocution. He was the sheet-anchor of the company during Young's regime; between December 1933–June 1934 he appeared in twenty-five out of twenty-eight plays. His popularity on stage was enhanced by his athletic prowess in the theatre's cricket and hockey teams and by the involvement of his wife and two young children in the local community.

Two contrasting recruits, Freda Jackson and Errol Flynn, were to proceed to prominence in their chosen spheres. Freda Jackson[8] arrived in Northampton in August 1933 at the age of twenty-five after working as a teacher for two years. Like Lois Obee, she had received a university education – in her native Nottingham. Miss Jackson's status for her first five months in Northampton was that of pupil, which meant that she received no salary. She had originally applied to Herbert Prentice, by then at the Birmingham Repertory Theatre, but, since the pupil system did not operate there, he advised her to try Northampton. The pupil arrangement was confined to actresses, young actors being in such short supply that they could command a salary from the outset. The dedication of the pupil actress extended not only to supporting herself without salary, but also to providing an adequate personal wardrobe for modern plays, a much more onerous requirement than for her male colleagues.

Of the twenty-one productions staged during Freda Jackson's apprenticeship (August–December 1933) she appeared in thirteen. Her roles were generally minor (Cook in *You Never Can Tell*, The Lady with the Baedeker in *See Naples and Die*, A Parlour Maid in *Art and Mrs. Bottle*, but the exigencies of weekly repertory projected her into Priestley's *Dangerous Corner* as Miss Mockridge, described by the author as "your own idea of what a smart middle-aged woman novelist should be". Miss Jackson's was judged to be "a fine performance" (*C&E* 19.9.1933).

The pupil system was long-standing. During the late nineteenth century certain theatres, notably Sarah Thorne's at Margate, became reputed as training grounds for young actors. Pupils at Lady Benson's school received opportunities in her husband's companies, but some managers were less scrupulous, using unpaid labour to underpin their enterprises. Not surprisingly, given his involvement in Equity, Young took his responsibilities for pupils seriously. Miss Jackson described him as a brilliant teacher, instilling in her precepts (such as keeping head and body movement to a minimum) which stood her in good stead for the rest of her career.

At its meeting on 4 December 1933 the board received "a letter . . . from Miss Freda Jackson asking to be placed on the salary list, and it was decided to pay her £3 a week salary commencing after Christmas". Miss Jackson's appearances now became more frequent, twenty-four out of the twenty-eight plays covered in that period. The board now insisted that artistes "'stand by' in Northampton, even if not cast" (BM 19.7.1932). Minor roles (Chinese mute in *Bulldog Drummond*, A Parlour Maid in *The Fake* and A Page Girl in *Good Morning, Bill*) still recurred, but by the summer vacation she had jumped a generation to play Mrs. Higgins in *Pygmalion* and scored two personal successes: Desdemona in *Othello* and Katharine Howard in Clifford Bax's *The Rose Without a Thorn*.

Miss Jackson was commended for "her sweetly gracious Desdemona – a really sensitive interpretation" (*C&E* 6.3.1934). In the Bax play "as Katharine Howard – whose beauty like a rose without a thorn, seemed to hold out to Henry a promise of returning youth – Freda Jackson gave the play unity and force. A lovely performance . . . She possesses that rare quality, that fluidic thing, call it magnetism or what you will, that seemed to waft itself like a vapour across the footlights" (*Adventure* p. 86). In the "modern miracle play" *Caesar's Friend* Freda Jackson achieved a powerful effect as Zillah, a Blind Woman (the only non-biblical character) with Oswald Dale Roberts in top form as Pilate.

In contrast she was supremely regal as the Queen in Edward L. Stanway's new play *The Power and the Glory* showing her flair for comedy. In a reprise of L. N. Parker's *The Cardinal* she traversed generations in "the important part of the Cardinal's [played by Oswald Dale Roberts] mother . . . [whom she] invested

The Power and the Glory by Edward L. Stanway 1934. Noel Howlett as H.M. King Ferdinand XIV. Freda Jackson as H.M. Queen Sophia, Nicholas Phipps as H.R.H. The Crown Prince Alex and Oswald Dale Roberts as Schnitzler. (Programme 29.10.1934)

with exquisite tragedy" (*C&E* 5.3.1935). She played another formidable dowager, Lady Britomart in Shaw's *Major Barbara*.

Whatever the rigours, hardships even, endured by a young actress in weekly repertory, Freda Jackson's early career and subsequent success provide abundant evidence of its excellence as a training ground.

With Errol Flynn the element of proof is often elusive. Like so many other recruits to repertory in Northampton Flynn found his way from afar, in his case Australia. He wrote a characteristically colourful account (*NI* 17.3.1934) of his journey via New Guinea including incidents (Showers of Poisoned Arrows; One Lone White Man) which suggest that his dramatic imagination was already well developed. In his autobiography he recalled driving to "Northampton, a dowdy, dreary place where they manufactured boots" and being interviewed, in his dingy office, by Robert Young "a grey haired, fine-looking man".[9] Flynn claimed that Young, a keen cricketer who captained the theatre eleven, was more concerned about his prowess on the field than the stage, but in December 1933 the cricket season was a rather remote prospect and in any case Young was fully alert to the prospect of engaging an actor of such fine physique for juvenile roles.

Flynn's own account of his months in Northampton is manifestly inaccurate. Certainly he did not play Othello, as he claimed, neither did Freda Jackson like "onions and beer", and the assault upon him by "a woman of great wealth"

Freda Jackson (Programme 7.5.1934)   Errol Flynn (Programme 7.5.1934)

during a visit "to her beautiful country house" is equally suspect. His energetic love life, despite the surveillance of his landlady, and his recurrent motoring offences – there were five of the latter by March 1934 (*C&E* 7.3.1934) – have passed into legend. More reliable are the other actors' recollections of Flynn. Freda Jackson remembered him as "a Greek god . . . like a burst of sunshine in our dark grey world". The appearance of this "god" in a company which already had its fair share of personality clashes was bound to increase tensions. Zillah Grey, a contemporary, recalled that Doris Littell, Young's wife, was a "disciplinarian" as stage manager, as Sheila Millar's experience had demonstrated. Doris Littell "drove him [Flynn] so hard that he would talk loudly in the wings or tread heavily upstairs and slam doors just to annoy her. Finally, when the end of the season came . . . he intercepted her on the stairs. He slapped her so hard that she fell all the way down . . . He could easily have killed her." Clearly Flynn experienced some of the antagonism which had afflicted Lois Obee, Sheila Millar and Nigel Patrick.

Young's own role as mentor to this raw recruit is more creditable and corroborates Freda Jackson's experience:

I soon realised he knew nothing of the technique of acting so I arranged for him to attend private lessons in stage technique two afternoons a week. I trained him in walking the stage, in easy, graceful movements and in voice technique. He rapidly improved. He played small parts in four months' work with surprisingly good results.[10]

In fact Flynn was by no means confined to small parts and as soon after his arrival in Northampton as mid-January 1934 he "made a splendid villain" (*C&E* 15.1.1934) as the sinister blackmailer Krogstad in *A Doll's House*. In the following month Flynn gave what Aubrey Dyas considered to be a "satisfying and sincere performance . . . easily his best piece of acting" as Joe Varwell, the communist nephew of the wealthy octogenarian Jennifer Varwell, in Eden Phillpotts's *Yellow Sands*. Other substantial parts included Geoffrey Sands in *The Fake* and Dr. Davy Adair in *Paddy the Next Best Thing*.

The workload undertaken by such inexperienced performers as Freda Jackson and Errol Flynn was formidable. For Christmas 1933 the repertory company staged its first pantomime *Jack and the Beanstalk* which played matinees to full houses "enraptured by the colourful scenery painted by Mr. Tom Osborne Robinson . . . the giant's turreted castle . . . the giant's monster kitchen . . . the monster copper, the six-foot bottle of Phizic . . . and his gorgeous costumes" (*C&E* 28.12.1933). In addition in the first week the same company was appearing twice nightly in *The Thirteenth Chair* and in the second in Pinero's *Sweet Lavender*. The mornings were necessarily taken up with rehearsals. One day early in 1934 several members of the company also gave a broadcast of Stanley Houghton's one-acter *The Dear Departed*. Thus, as Aubrey Dyas summarises:

> Actually, the work accomplished on Wednesday, 3 January 1934, was in the morning a rehearsal of *Bulldog Drummond*, followed by a rehearsal of the broadcast, in the afternoon a performance of *Jack and the Beanstalk*, and in the evening two performances of *Sweet Lavender* and the broadcast of *The Dear Departed*. Surely this achievement constitutes a record for any repertory theatre in the world. (*Adventure* p. 82).

Young did ensure that his company received some additional emoluments for this marathon workload. Artistes were paid "at the rate of one-eighth of full weekly salary for each performance" of the pantomime (BM 19.12.1933). The B.B.C.'s fee of £16 15s. for the broadcast of *The Dear Departed* was divided as follows: five artistes at £2 2s., one at £1 15s., Young and Richard Summers (business manager) £2 2s. each and Fred Pratt (the stage carpenter) £1 (BM 2.1.1934).

The board minute book (for the period December 1933 to May 1936) provides invaluable information about the financial dealings of a repertory company at this period. Cecil Chisholm reckoned "that a company of repertory actors cannot be got for less than £80 per week. For it is impossible to cast a series of modern plays with a permanent cast of less than eleven people. A really able actress capable of a wide range of roles cannot be found for less than £10 per week."[11]

Capable actors and actresses did in fact work in Northampton for significantly less than £10 per week. When the board agreed the salaries for the forthcoming season at its meeting on 19 June 1934 Oswald Dale Roberts was re-engaged at £7 per week, Peter Rosser at £6 and Donald Gordon at £5 10s. Dorothy Galbraith led the actresses at £6, with Zillah Grey on £3 10s. and Freda Jackson on £3. Another five artistes were to be engaged at aggregate salaries of £23 per week, making a weekly total of £54, well below Chisholm's norm.

As producer Young received £12 per week. This figure is placed in context by reference to the salaries paid to officials of Northampton Borough Council: Town Clerk £1,400, Chief Constable and Medical Officer of Health £1,000 each, the Secretary of Education £650 and the Borough Librarian £600 (*NI* 19.8.1933). The producer's salary was therefore much the same as that of the town's principal education officer and librarian. Local government reorganisation makes direct comparison now difficult, but it is clear that Young was relatively much better rewarded than his modern counterparts.

Even so the life-style of those leading citizens who constituted the board was of an altogether more privileged kind. Mrs. Panther travelled widely – to Australia in 1934, on the Queen Mary's maiden voyage in 1936 and to Brazil in 1937. She continued to extend hospitality to the company at her home Boughton Hall. John Brown, chairman of the repertory's landlords the Northampton Theatre Syndicate was knighted in the New Year Honours list of 1934 and later that year he joined the repertory board in place of Francis Graves. In the same year the Northampton Theatre Syndicate bought the freehold of the scenic studio and dressing rooms at the Royal Theatre, which it had hitherto held only on lease. During Mrs. Panther's frequent absences abroad Brown acted as chairman. Clearly there were advantages in his membership of both boards, but during Young's years the theatre's finances were remarkably untroubled.

Attendances were generally good. The number of regular weekly seat holders increased to 1,000 (PR 2.7.1934) and up to 1,300 (PR 27.8.1934). The debate about twice nightly continued, but Northampton became less out of step: "London, by the way, is following our example . . . The Duke of York's is to become twice nightly . . . Twice nightly has some advantages . . . men can go straight from work to the theatre . . . or have plenty of time to go home and have a meal before attending the second performance" (PR 13.10.1932). It was the life-style of variety and cinema applied to the theatre. Even St. John Ervine weighed in with an *Observer* article (7.3.1933) on the virtues of twice nightly:

The theory that players would be overworked is largely tosh . . . the player in a modern comedy earns his money easily [Ervine had London long runs in mind] . . . The fact is that the average theatre is uneconomically used . . . for only two and a half hours a night.

In practice the discussion moved on to the possibilities of two week long runs, which Young introduced with the five plays already listed. At its meeting on 30 July 1934 the board devised a rule of thumb approach:

If the total Box Office Returns for the first three nights of that week amount to approximately £100, but not otherwise the Board shall have power at that meeting, if they think it desirable from every (including the financial) point of view, to authorise the continuance of the play for a second week.

For the purposes of this meeting two directors shall constitute a quorum.

By modern standards this was short-term planning indeed, but the theatre generally decided its programme only a few weeks ahead and this system did accord with the repertory principal of running popular plays for longer. As Young informed audiences this would enable the company "to enjoy a few days respite from constant rehearsals" and the theatre to maximise its box office revenue (PR 13.8.1934).

Box office returns for each play were presented to the board. This income, together with that from programmes and other sources (refreshments) was balanced against expenditure to give a profit or loss for each play. Unfortunately the items included in expenditure were not directly related to the specific costs of any given production, but included such general bills as might fall in that week. Nevertheless the box office income is a useful indicator of popularity ranging in two consecutive weeks from £209 1s. 2d. for Miles Malleson's *Conflict* (14.5.1934) to £372 16s. for Gertrude Page's *Paddy the Next Best Thing* (21.5.1934). Two major items of expenditure were directly related to income: entertainment tax and authors' royalties, the former being £44 7s. 11d. and £78 3s. 1d. and the latter £12 10s. 1d. and £31 12s. 7d. for those two weeks. For the week of *Pygmalion* (29.1.1934) Shaw with £12 13s. 2d. came off much worse than H.M.'s Treasury with £56 6s. 11d..

Aubrey Dyas entitled his chapters on Young's tenure "Smoother Sailing" and "Successful Years". His play selection was rather more adventurous than Prentice's, production standards were at least comparable, audiences were more numerous and consequently financial crises were avoided. Indeed the surviving accounts for the company for the year ended 31st March 1934[12] reveal a satisfactory financial state with box office income totalling £14,799 8s. 2½d. for the 1933-4 season producing a modest profit of £145 11s. 3d. to be added to the balance of £1,094 4s. 8½d. brought forward from 1932-3 – a total surplus of £1,239 15s. 11½d.

Aubrey Dyas, who maintained contact with Young after he left Northampton, tactfully omitted any reference to Young's altercations with his company and board. By nature Young tended to be tactless, autocratic and peremptory, but his professional skills were not in doubt. The presence and personality of Young's wife, Doris Littell, in the crucial role of stage manager raises the old doubt about the wisdom of employing married couples in the same theatre.

Unhappily Young's departure was marred by further controversy. In the spring of 1935 he indicated his definitive intention to resign in order to return to politics, though in fact he was unsuccessful in the subsequent general election. The board set in motion the process for appointing his successor, who was to commence his duties on 27 May, prior to Young's departure on 8 June. Although his contract was subject to only four weeks' notice on either side, Young claimed that it was "the invariable custom in the Profession that a Producer must end his work at the end of the season". Ironically he declined to take part in a public farewell, for which Lois Obee's might have provided him with a model, and the board felt it necessary to publish a three page insert (PR 17.6.1934): "To our Patrons. Mr. Young's Criticisms. A Reply."

Despite regret that Young's achievements should be soured in this way the board's A.G.M. on 12 June 1935 "was a very happy one, the shareholders being gratified at the profit made during the past year".[13] Nearly £300 was allocated to reseating the theatre during the summer break. For all its off-stage dramas Young's stewardship had been a fruitful one and he handed over a thriving enterprise to his successor.

Notes

1. Joseph Macleod *The Actor's Right to Act*, 1981 p. 179.
2. Ibid p. 195.
3. Obituary in the *Stage* 4.4.1985. Young made his last acting appearance with Peter Sellars in *I'm All Right Jack*. He was the author of *Cricket on the Green*
4. Cecil Chisholm *Repertory An Outline of the Modern Movement*, 1934 p. 130. The book cover incorporates Osborne Robinson's design for "A Street in Illyria" for the Northampton production of *Twelfth Night*.
5. Ibid pp. 141–2.
6. The Minute Book of the Board of the Northampton Repertory Players 4.12.1933 to 7.7.1936 in the Royal Theatre archive.
7. Chisholm op. cit. pp. 122–124.
8. I am indebted to the late Freda Jackson for several conversations recalling her first engagement at the Royal Theatre.
9. Errol Flynn *My Wicked Wicked Ways*, 1960 repr. 1969, pp. 157-63.
10. Charles Higham *Errol Flynn The Untold Story*, 1980 pp. 64-7. Higham also recorded Zillah Gray's recollections.
11. Chisholm op. cit. p. 217.
12. In N.C.R.O.
13. Copy in N.C.R.O.

CHAPTER FIVE

Peake and Trough 1935–7

THE saga of Robert Young's resignation (or rather resignations – threatened, withdrawn and finally recriminatory) gave the board ample opportunity to determine its procedure for appointing his successor. At its meeting on 25 March 1935 the board noted the "large number of applications . . . received" and on 1 April it drew up a preliminary short-list of six: Bladon Peake, Shayle Gardner, Worrall Thompson, Maurice Brian, Christopher Fry and Oswald Dale Roberts. Each was interviewed by the chairman and one or more of the directors and a final short list, consisting of Peake, Thompson and Dale Roberts, was invited for interview on 24 April. The exclusion of Christopher Fry from this list is noteworthy, not only because, with hindsight, his future distinction as a dramatist is known to us, but also because as director of the Tunbridge Wells Repertory Players (1932–5) he was a well-qualified candidate. Oswald Dale Roberts, already the company's leading actor and stand-in producer would have been a safe and popular choice, but "After long and careful consideration it was decided to appoint Mr. Bladon Peake on a monthly engagement at a salary of £12 10s. per week" (BM 24.4.1935). By way of consolation Dale Roberts's weekly salary was increased by 10s..

Compared with his predecessors, who were virtually appointed by invitation, Bladon Peake had been selected as a result of a lengthy, formal procedure. The man preferred to the numerous other applicants was a rather unorthodox choice since his experience had been gained mainly in the amateur theatre. Born in Cheshire, the son of a nonconformist minister and a bareback rider in a circus, Peake had moved to East Anglia, first as a farm student and then on the Great Eastern Railway. He met Nugent Monck and became involved in the Norwich Players, an amateur society which in 1921 had reconstructed a former church as the Maddermarket Theatre on the Elizabethan principles of William Poel for whom Monck had staged several productions before the First World War.[1] Following his experience in Norwich Peake became co-founder of the Birmingham Municipal Players – subsequently the Crescent Theatre – where he was stage director from 1931 to 1934. Whilst in Birmingham Peake "met and became firm friends of Mr. Oswald Dale Roberts and Mr. Herbert Prentice" (*NI* 6.9.35). His other credits encompassed directing several pageants (including Stratford-upon-Avon), writing and producing plays for the B.B.C. Midland

Region and a spell at the Abbey Theatre, Dublin.[2] Latterly he had been involved with W. B. Yeats and Ashley Dukes in the re-formation of the Poets' Theatre, London (*C&E* 29.11.1937).

It had been the board's intention that by taking up his appointment on 27 May, well before the summer closure, Peake would be "in a position to advise the Board as to the re-engagement of artistes already employed and the replacement of those whom he did not wish to engage" (PR insert 17.6.1935). In practice the re-engagement of most of the existing company was approved at the board meeting on 18 June: Oswald Dale Roberts (£7)[3], Donald Gordon (£5 10s.), Patrick Crean (£5), Philip Dale (£4), M. Leverett as stage manager £4 10s.), Betty Larke-Smith (£6), Freda Jackson (£4 10s.), Katherine Page (£4), P. Dadswell as assistant stage manager (£3). Peake was given discretion "to engage other artistes provided that the weekly outlay did not exceed £70". One important newcomer was Olga Murgatroyd, a former pupil of Frank Benson's with repertory experience in Birmingham and Manchester.

This was the team at Peake's disposal for the autumn season of 1935 and several notable performances were given, not least by Oswald Dale Roberts: Polydamas in *Marriage à la Mode*, Sir Hector Benbow M.F.H. in *Thark*, Henry Horatio Hobson in *Hobson's Choice*, Dr. Kirby in *Eden End*, Baptista in *The Taming of the Shrew* and Edward Moulton-Barrett in a reprise of *The Barretts of Wimpole Street*. But the last named was Dale Roberts's farewell performance. In fact the choice of the pre-Christmas play had been changed (from *Family Affairs*) in order to give audiences an opportunity to see their favourite actor in his most acclaimed role. The theatre programmes (9.12.1935 and 16.12.1935) reverberated with expressions of mutual appreciation, but the truth was less companionable the board having resolved at its meeting on 22 October "that Mr. Oswald Dale Roberts be informed that his engagement would not be continued after the last week in January [1936]". Donald Gordon's engagement was also terminated and at the following meeting on 29 October Freda Jackson's notice was "received and accepted". Dale Roberts made a characteristically gracious and loyal farewell speech: "For 30 months I have tried to live as a decent citizen of this kindly town. It will be a big wrench to depart." He paid tributes to many members of the theatre staff by name, including Peake "for his sympathy and understanding of a man, alas, so much older than other members of the company", and advised Northampton to hang on to Osborne Robinson "this brilliant local genius" (*C&E* 23.12.35).

As Lady Bracknell might have remarked to lose three leading actors exceeded the bounds of both misfortune and carelessness. There appears to have been a mutual incompatibility between Peake and actors of this style and calibre. Lesser lights such as Patrick Crean and Philip Dale remained and were joined by competent performers including George Mudie and Paul Harford, both from careers in touring, but Mudie's remark that he "gave up touring for Repertory as it is less trouble on Sunday" (PR 8.6.1936) seems symptomatic. The spark which had ignited the talents drawn to Northampton by Prentice and Young was missing and the fact that the board felt obliged to "emphasize a special point, no amateurs are employed in Repertory Theatre productions" (PR 31.8.1936) enforces, rather than suppresses, doubts about the calibre of acting. The next month the board discussed "the inadequacy of certain of the male members of the company" (BM 15.9.1936).

A visiting critic observed:

> the company . . . did not seem anything like as good as when I saw them a few months ago . . . Oswald Dale Roberts has left (for Hull, I heard), and Freda Jackson, the most promising youngster in my recent experience, has gone up to town. (*Birmingham Weekly Post* 21.2.1936)

However the same critic went on to list some of the plays due for production over the following weeks: Galsworthy's *The Roof*, Shakespeare's *Macbeth*, Elmer Rice's *The Adding Machine* and Gordon Daviot's *Richard of Bordeaux*, concluding wryly: "Then people say you can't see good plays in the small provincial towns."

Undoubtedly it was in the selection of plays that Peake was at his most imaginative. Within weeks of taking up his appointment he introduced Northampton audiences to Chekhov (a favourite of Nugent Monck's) in a double bill with Quintero's *The Women Have Their Way*. Peake's earnestness about play selection is indicated in the board's minutes for 8 August 1935:

> A discussion took place as to the methods of selection of plays and it was resolved that a Play Selection Sub-committee should be appointed, whose duty would be to settle and present periodically to the Board for final decision a preliminary list of suitable plays. It was further resolved that this sub-committee should consist of the Chairman, the Producer and the Manager.

The selection of plays was taking on a new significance in relation to entertainment duty. At the board meeting on 3 September 1935:

> The Director-Secretary read a communication received from the Commissioners of Customs and Excise in reference to the application for exemption from Entertainment Duty. This asked for a copy of the last balance sheet, the Memorandum and Articles of Association of the Company, a list of representative plays produced, and a list of plays in respect of which exemption was sought.
>
> In relation to this last requirement it was decided to furnish a list of plays, and the following were selected to compose the list . . .

The list submitted conforms to the plays actually staged between 9 September and 25 November except that *Too Young To Marry* was dropped in favour of *The Wasps' Nest*, a new play by Adelaide Eden Phillpotts and Jan Stewart. That the twelve titles should include works by such reputed dramatists as John Dryden, Ben Travers, Harold Brighouse, Pinero, J. B. Priestley and Shakespeare suggests that the selection was made with the endorsement of the commissioners in mind.

The stumbling block to tax remission proved to be the company's constitution rather than its repertoire. On 1 October 1935 the board heard that "the company as at present constituted did not qualify for exemption from Entertainment Duty", but that further consideration would be given if the company amended its constitution. After further negotiations with the commissioners and consultation with legal counsel (at a cost of £20 0s. 6d) the decision was taken to wind up the original company and register as a new non-profit-distributing company of the same name. As the *Explanatory Memorandum* of 28 December 1935 outlined the two conditions for exemption from entertainment duty were:

(a)   that the plays performed shall be of an educational nature.

(b)   that any profits made by the theatre are not paid to the Shareholders but are devoted to the purposes of repertory [in lieu of which shareholders were to receive interest on their investment fixed at 5 per cent p.a.].

By accepting these conditions the new company stood to save an average of £2,250 per annum. This remission of tax could be regarded an an early form of subsidy, carrying, like its later manifestations, certain conditions. In all probability Peake welcomed the requirement "that the plays performed shall be of an educational nature" perceiving it as an instrument through which he could stage the type of plays which he, in any case, preferred. In practice the danger was that the choice of less popular plays would result in a box office shortfall in excess of the benefits of tax remission.

The annual report (dated 21 May 1937) of the board for the first financial year (to 15 February 1937) under the new system confirmed these fears:

Unfortunately, the saving in Entertainments Duty has been largely offset by the diminution in the Box Office receipts, which, in the view of the Board is due partly to the factor last mentioned [increased competition in the local field of entertainments], but is also to some extent attributable to the fact that, after ten years of Repertory, the novelty of the venture has lessened.

In fact the remission had amounted to £1,110 5s. 4d. (considerably less than estimated and itself affected by the decline in box office). Nevertheless "The actual nett profit in the year's working is £306 5s. 4d., which . . . may be regarded as fairly satisfactory."

Although not explicitly identified by the board the choice of plays was clearly a significant factor. Not that Peake was relieved of all the constraints which had hedged in his predecessors. He wrote of "three conditions . . . The first – is it [the play] available for Repertory production? The second – is it sufficiently short or can it be cut so that it can be produced twice nightly? And the third – is the cast too long for us to produce it, even if we have a certain number of additional players?" (PR 1.6.1936).

Clearly Shaw's *Back to Methuselah*, which was proposed by some patrons, failed on the second and third counts. Nevertheless it is surprising that, in marked contrast to Young, Peake did not stage a single play by Shaw. Conversely Coward, banished entirely by Young, was re-instated by Peake, sharing top honours – of three plays each – with Dryden and Priestley. At last Northampton saw Elmer Rice's *The Adding Machine*, but it played to only half-full houses, as did Jacques Deval's *Mademoiselle* when the *Daily Mirror* (22.3.1937) columnist visited Northampton.

To try to wean Northampton audiences onto plays "of an educational nature" without the inducement of seeing their established favourites in the cast was a risky undertaking. St. John Ervine provoked controversy when, after a visit in Autumn 1937, he wrote of the poor behaviour of Northampton audiences. Nevertheless the management persevered with inducements, introducing a voucher scheme "Are You a Voucherite?" (PR 23.8.1937). A system of colour-coding for posters displayed a level of sophistication probably above the heads of most patrons:

> For Tragedies, Drama and Thrillers, the lettering will be printed in bright Red. For plays covering the range of domestic drama, the title will be printed in Black, and Light Comedies and Farces in Green.
> As you walk along the street just a glance at the posters will tell you what type of play you will be seeing at the Repertory Theatre. (PR 16.8.1937)

When George Fearon wrote an article on Northampton for *Theatre World* (November 1937) he described the board as consisting of "Two solicitors, a toy-train maker, a school-master and an architect", who, "through their efforts . . . have seen to it that their work-people are able to enjoy the best that the theatre can offer". Fearon referred to the "munificence of local people" – "munificence" rather than "municipal". The mid-1930s were in fact years of considerable civic pride and progress. The Technical College had opened in St. George's Avenue in 1932 where it was joined by the Art School in 1937.[4] W. J. Bassett-Lowke had pioneered the construction of the public swimming baths which were completed in October 1936. In the following year the United Counties bus station added to the convenience of theatre-goers.

That under Bladon Peake the Northampton Repertory Players tried to elevate themselves to a position of national attention is not entirely separable from the

The directors of the Northampton Repertory Players: Solicitor H. Musk Beattie, Schoolmaster P. B. Baskcomb, Shoemaker Mrs. Helen Panther, Toy Train Maker W. J. Bassett-Lowke and Soldier-Architect Sir John Brown. (*NI* 19.11.1937)

aforementioned manifestations of civic achievement. The two principal planks of Peake's promotion of the theatre were Shakespeare and Dryden. His production of *The Taming of the Shrew* in November 1935 inaugurated a short-lived experiment of playing only one performance on Mondays:

> To the Aldermen, Councillors and members of the Corporation, we extend a hearty welcome and hope the party will thoroughly enjoy our presentation . . . (PR 25.11.1935)

As Cecil Chisholm had observed, when praising Robert Young's Shakespearean productions, few repertory directors were equal to the challenge of the bard. Olga Murgatroyd gave a forthright performance as Katherine partnered by Alastair MacIntyre as Petruchio. Osborne Robinson's sets were admired.

When Peake returned to Shakespeare for the second – and last – time in March 1936 the more exacting demands of *Macbeth* (of which he had staged an innovative, but unsuccessful, production at the Abbey Theatre, Dublin) revealed that he was "not without ambition", but his approach to casting was contrary. Instead of allocating Lady Macbeth to Olga Murgatroyd, whose strong stage presence and experience as Katherine seemed to make her a natural choice for the part, he wasted her talents on Fleance – "reckless extravagance" (*C&E* 17.3.36). Lady Macbeth was played by Betty Larke-Smith, originally a musical comedy actress, whose only previous Shakespearean role had been the Widow in *The Taming of the Shrew*. Betty Larke-Smith gave a clear if rather slow and monotonous performance, labouring under the "natural disadvantage of a charming personality" (*C&E* 17.3.1936). The Thane was played by Alastair MacIntyre who, having been born and educated (Fettes) in Edinburgh, at least came from the right side of the border, but far from scaling the dramatic heights his Macbeth emerged as "the almost pathetic victim of inordinate ambition" (*ET* 17.3.1936). The middle ranks were less "o'er parted" – Patrick Crean as Malcolm and Philip Dale combining A Wounded Sergeant, Young Siward and the Porter.

The most powerful effect of the production came not from the actors, but from the one member of the Northampton company who was genuinely knocking at the door of national recognition: Osborne Robinson, who provided a "profusion of brilliant effects" as set and costume designer. The basis of the set was "two pillars (symbolising Macbeth and his wife) which dominate every scene, and through whose cleverly concealed transparency the spirits of the murderous couple are often made visible in a most arresting fashion" (*NI* 20.3.36). Two other similar devices were employed: "The gradual unfolding of the trees into the three witches . . . and again . . . the shadows of the dread spectres seem to rise out of the cauldron whilst gasps from the younger members of the audience help to show how convincing this scene is" (*C&E* 17.3.1936). Like *The Taming of the Shrew*, *Macbeth* attracted large attendances (2,000) from schools and returned a profit of £34 (BM 24.3.1936).

Such captive audiences could not be relied upon for Elmer Rice's *The Adding Machine* which posed "intricate difficulties to a producer and theatre unequipped with special stage, lighting and sound apparata" (*NI* 3.4.36). Nevertheless Peake and Osborne Robinson (over-)compensated for this with such ingenuity that the audience's capacity to identify with the plight of the tragicomic figure of Mr. Zero (Patrick Crean) was forfeited:

> . . . this aspect is completely lost in a series of unnecessarily complicated effects and unsuitable scenery, of great mechanical ingenuity but relatively little importance. (*C&E* 31.3.1936)

In the famous brainstorm scene (upon which Prentice had lavished such attention in Cambridge) audiences and Patrick Crean himself were left "gasping and blinking by the sudden flashes of light and nightmare noises" (*Adventure* p. 103). The loss of £53 was reduced to £30 by the new tax concession (BM 7.4.1936).

Marriage à la Mode by John Dryden 1935. (*Adventure in Repertory*)

Shakespeare and expressionist plays were important emblems of a repertory company's credentials, but they were not distinctive and inevitably invited comparison with other companies. Northampton with its close proximity to Stratford, where the new Memorial Theatre had opened in 1932, was particularly conscious of its humbler status. If Northampton was to develop as a theatre of more than local significance it needed to establish its expertise in the work of a particular dramatist, preferably one with local associations. John Dryden, poet laureate and author of twenty-seven plays, had been born in the county at Aldwinkle in 1631, though it had to be admitted that his subsequent association with his birthplace was slight.

In his introduction to an edition of Dryden's (selected) plays the scholar George Saintsbury confessed that "I am not fond of the theatre", but admitted "I should like to see one of these plays acted". In fact between the wars the opportunities of seeing one of Dryden's plays on stage were relatively numerous. *Marriage à la Mode* (1672) had been revived by Nigel Playfair at the Lyric Theatre, Hammersmith in 1920 and again in 1930; in 1928 it had been staged at both the Birmingham Repertory Theatre and at the Festival Theatre, Cambridge. Thus merely to perform *Marriage à la Mode* was not particularly remarkable. Peake's acumen lay in elevating what was still basically a twice nightly one week production into a Dryden festival – "To Rival Malvern?" (*NI* 30.8.1935). This he

61

achieved by exploiting the local connection, reinforcing the occasion with exhibitions of Dryden books and memorabilia in the theatre and at the town's library and national publicity.

Within weeks of taking up his appointment Peake had obtained approval for the production of *Marriage à la Mode* (BM 18.6.1935) for the week of 12 August. It was postponed until 16 September "owing to numerous requests received from playgoers all over the country" (PR 12.8.1935). The London newspapers were reported as being "very enthusiastic on our being so ambitious"; to encourage them the board (17.9.1935) approved the expenditure of 15s. for advertising in the *New Statesman*.

The additional time was valuable to the theatre's design team, the board having resolved "that the costumes to be used in Dryden's play should be made in the theatre. The estimated approximate cost being £15" (30.7.1935). The costumes were the work of Nancy and Ellen Pratt to the designs of Osborne Robinson, who also designed the settings (executed by the theatre's carpenter Fred Pratt) and the wigs (made by Leslie Pickering). The whole visual effect was co-ordinated in black and white, as Peake's production of Molière's *The School for Wives* at the Abbey Theatre had been. Robinson even proposed black and white make-up, but this was resisted by the actors on the grounds that facial expression would be limited and that the risk of confusing characters, already dressed in the same colour scheme, would be increased in a play which had an excess of plot complications. Visually the production made a powerful impact:

> Rarely has a more exquisite or original picture in sheer black and white been painted on a stage canvas than that offered by the combination of scene and costumes . . . (*NI* 20.9.1935)

Period music by G. B. Lully and Henry Purcell helped to create mood and pace, the latter being – in the tradition of Monck's work at the Maddermarket – brisk. The company still included Freda Jackson whose Melantha, an affected lady, was "most effectively done and never overdone" (*NI* 20.9.1935). Oswald Dale Roberts (Polydamas), Donald Gordon (Palamede), Katherine Page (Doralice) and Miss Jackson were all commended for their "beautiful performances" by the *New Statesman* which considered that "The Northampton Repertory Theatre has done a fine and courageous thing" (*Adventure* p. 112).

As well as the critics of the national press the production attracted such distinguished visitors as Sir Archibald Flower, chairman of the Shakespeare Memorial Theatre and his artistic director Ben Iden Payne. Parity with the celebrated Stratford theatre seemed to be attainable for at least one week in the year. *Marriage à la Mode* was a *succès d'estime* with which Northampton proclaimed that it not only had a house dramatist, but that it could stand up to national scrutiny in the execution of his work. Furthermore, whereas Nigel

Playfair had lost money on his 1930 revival of *Marriage à la Mode*, the Northampton box office receipts were a healthy £288 8s. 7d., leaving a profit of £55 17s. 6d. on the week.

Whilst *Marriage à la Mode* was an obvious choice for the first Dryden festival finding another stage-worthy vehicle from the rest of the dramatic canon was by no means easy. Peake selected the tragicomedy *The Spanish Fryar* (1681) with its serious usurpation plot and its equally complicated subplot about the monstrously corrupt Friar Dominic. Compression was inevitable for twice nightly presentation and though this clarified the action the piece remained "the sheerest museum play". Again Osborne Robinson's designs attracted the greatest attention:

> His [Peake's] use of a permanent setting makes for speed and the set itself is so skilfully devised that there is no impression of restriction. Court, street and house in Saragossa are achieved simply and quickly. Mr. Osborne Robinson has designed setting and costumes and has shown refinement and good taste in his use of colour. The bravery of the costumes is kept within limits of elegance by a delicate white and gold motif, which also appears in the curtains. (*Birmingham Post and Journal* 23.9.1936)

Sir Martin Marr-All by John Dryden 1937. (Royal Theatre Collection)

Sir Martin Marr-All by John Dryden 1937. Setting by Osborne Robinson. (*Adventure in Repertory*)

Although now without the talents of Dale Roberts, Donald Gordon and Freda Jackson, the cast, including Patrick Crean (Torrismond), Betty Larke-Smith (Teresa), Olga Murgatroyd (Elvira) and George Mudie – somewhat diffident about the low comedy of the title-role – acquitted themselves well, combining "so thoroughly as a team that the acting honours were almost equally divided" (*NI* 25.9.1936) in Peake's swiftly moving production.

During a visit to the Royal Theatre in the week preceding the 1937 Dryden festival Dame Sybil Thorndike "very graciously addressed members of the Company on the 'Team Spirit' that must prevail in Repertory" (PR 20.9.1937). Visitors to the revival of *Sir Martin Marr-all*, Dryden's 1667 comedy written in collaboration with the Duke of Newcastle, included Sir Archibald Flower and Iden Payne, Bache Matthews from Birmingham and "Tyrone Guthrie, fresh from his triumphs in directing the first Buxton Festival" (PR 27.9.1937). Unfortunately local support for what Samuel Pepys had described as "the most entire piece of mirth, a complete farce from one end to the other, that certainly was ever writ", was scanty – "it was rather depressing last night (the opening of the third annual week) to see so thin a house" (*Birmingham Mail* 21.9.37). Nevertheless it would have been some compensation that the critics of the national press (*The Times, Sunday Times* and *Daily Telegraph*) made their way to Northampton where Osborne Robinson's designs again excited attention:

64

A permanent setting on a miniature scale suggests space, and, for variety, an exterior becomes an interior by an uncompromising turn of the handle in full view of the audience. This ingenious device is admirably suited to artificial comedy. The costumes by Osborne Robinson are boldly designed, and preserve all the fashion of the period in a brilliant mixture of colours. They would do a credit to any West End production: in a provincial theatre, their originality and opulence are astonishing. (*Birmingham Post and Journal* 22.7.1937)

All the more astonishing with a total budget of £50.

In the *Spectator* novelist Graham Greene was equally impressed: "a charming set made up of dolls' houses and diminutive steps and streets, round which Sir Martin wanders like Gulliver in Lilliput . . Push a house round by a handle and another scene is ready in its interior just large enough from the second floor to the ground to hold two or three characters" (*Adventure* p. 114).

The limitations of weekly repertory were more apparent in the acting: in the title role Anthony Pelly "will be better when he has had more time" and George Mudie "though rather mature for Warner . . . rattled along with unfailing fluency, even when the words he utters sound more like his own than Dryden's". Donald Gordon, now back in the company, provided ballast as the lustful Lord Dartmouth and the "leading women are portrayed with confident assurance by Misses Molly Cullen, Helen Irving, Iris Sutherland and Gwladys Black Roberts" (*Birmingham Mail* 21.9.1937).

Undoubtedly the three Dryden festivals succeeded in attracting national attention to Northampton. However despite its size Dryden's dramatic canon had limited scope for modern production, even in Northampton where local pride fought an unequal battle with an inbred resistance to such novelties. The calibre of the acting in the second and third plays (which even after remission from tax recorded losses of £61 and £116 respectively) was barely equal to the challenge and only Osborne Robinson's designs salvaged distinction from the treadmill of weekly repertory.

Indeed Osborne Robinson was the major beneficiary of the Dryden productions, which brought him to national attention at an opportune moment in his career. Tyrone Guthrie's invitation to him to design for the Old Vic in 1937 was almost certainly a direct consequence of having seen his work in *The Spanish Fryar*. At the Old Vic Robinson was responsible for the designs for Laurence Olivier's *Hamlet* (subsequently seen at Elsinore) and *Richard III* with Emlyn Williams. Lilian Baylis offered Robinson the permanent job as scene designer and painter at her theatre, but he declined. He did, however, go to Stratford in 1938 to design costumes and scenery for *Macbeth*, with Gyles Isham in the title-role. If Robinson was ever to break away from Northampton this was the time, but instead he immersed himself deeper in the community adding Art College evening classes in stage design to his duties at the theatre. Remuneration cannot have been a major consideration, but at least the board recognised his talent with such extra payments as that of £3 3s. "in respect of special services rendered in connection with the pantomime" (14.1.1936) – that pantomime was *Sinbad the Sailor* for which copies of the costume designs survive.

One activity for which Osborne Robinson's services were not required was broadcasts for the B.B.C. Midland Region. Peake, with his previous experience in radio, developed this work, which had been initiated by Young.[5] *Caesar's Friend*, a popular piece on stage in Northampton, was broadcast on 25 August 1935 and repeated (with cast changes) on Good Friday 1936: "The Players come from the Northampton Repertory Company, which is always good for something outstanding" (quoted in PR 13.4.1936). On 23 August the company broadcast *The Squirrel's Cage*, a play specially adapted for the radio by Tyrone Guthrie, from Geoffrey [sic] Wynn's novel" (PR 10.8.1936). St. John Ervine's *The Ship* followed in April 1937.

For most of Bladon Peake's period as producer the business affairs of the theatre were under the control of Richard Summers until he left to become manager of the New Theatre in July 1937. He was replaced by F. W. Cotter Craig from the Theatre Royal, Birmingham. The Northampton Repertory Players' lease from the Northampton Theatre Syndicate had come up for renewal in May 1935, when the board sought to extend it for seven years, with a breaking clause at four years "and if possible the inclusion of an option to purchase at £15,000" (BM 28.5.1935). At the meeting on 4 June Sir John Brown (in his capacity as landlord) intimated that the breaking clause would have to be mutual, to which the repertory board would not agree, but he "gave his personal assurance that the Syndicate would not sell the property without first offering it to the Repertory Company".

By the time Peake tendered his resignation in November 1937 the lease was again a subject for discussion between the board and the syndicate. There had been rumours of possible closure during that summer and on 8 December Musk Beattie wrote to Sir John Brown requesting the suspension of the "clause in the lease under which we are under obligation to pay six months' rent in advance". With the repertory company's bank account overdrawn by £600, nearer £800 if outstanding accounts were paid, the situation was serious indeed. In his reply of 20 December Sir John agreed to a reduction in "Retention money from 6 months to 3 months" (N.C.R.O.).

Thus the financial state of the Northampton Repertory Players at Peake's departure was precarious despite, or perhaps because of, the remission in entertainment duty. He had responded to the condition that the repertoire should include more plays of an educational nature, but he had failed to carry audiences with him. His productions of those plays were often undercast and relied for their effect upon the burgeoning talent of his scenic designer Osborne Robinson.

Anticipating Peake's departure Musk Beattie wrote to Sir John Brown (8.12.1937):

> We are hopeful that changes that are taking place in the personnel behind the curtain will in course of time result in an improvement in box office results. (N.C.R.O.)

The board invited Oswald Dale Roberts "to accept engagement as Producer at a salary of £10 per week, this to be reviewed in three months time" (BM 7.12.1937), but Dale Roberts could not extricate himself from his current contract.

Notes

1. The conversion cost £3,300; the theatre's capacity was 220.
2. See Hugh Hunt *The Abbey, Ireland's National Theatre 1904-1978*, 1979, pp. 148-9.
3. Dale Roberts's increase of 10s. per week seemed to have been overlooked.
4. See David Walmsley compiler *An Ever-Rolling Stream. The On-Going Story of the Development of Higher Education in Northampton and Northamptonshire*, 1989.
5. Additional payments for radio work had been stipulated in Peake's contract.

CHAPTER SIX

Storm Clouds and Conflict 1937–45

THE man charged with the task of stabilising the fortunes of repertory in Northampton was William Sherwood. Born in Dublin Sherwood had adopted a stage career after war service and a spell in the Indian Army. "An actor, a scenic designer of considerable talent, and the author of six plays", Sherwood was certainly not lacking in experience, Northampton being "the nineteenth repertory company with which I have been associated" (*NI* 29.12.1937).

Shortly after Sherwood's arrival a Repertory Circle (similar to the erstwhile Playgoers' Association) was established to galvanise public support. One hundred people attended a meeting on 23 January at which Dr. Eric Shaw was unanimously elected chairman. Sherwood addressed the gathering on his vision for the theatre, proclaiming that "the forthcoming programme of plays . . . were designed to please the majority" (*NI* 28.1.1938).

This deference to the public taste was nothing short of mandatory. Two letters from the repertory manager and licensee F. W. Cotter Craig to Sir John Brown reveal the extent of the crisis. On 16 March 1938 Craig sent "the returns for the last few plays, some make interesting reading and some, alas, not so satisfactory". The returns for *Mary Rose* (12.2.1938 loss £9 17s. 2d.); *The Silent House* (19.2.1938 profit £11 18s. 11d.); *The Celebrity* (26.2.1938 loss £35 6s. 9d.) and *Nell Gwyn* (5.3.1938 loss £31 12s. 4d.) may have been merely "interesting", but "The experiment of Squaring the Circle [7.3.1938] seemed nearly to round off the Repertory Theatre!!!" – the deficit on this Russian comedy was £138 12s. 6s..

Craig believed that "we will do better with *Jew Süss*, and the next few weeks, as our plays are more suitable for Northampton audiences". Ashley Dukes's *Jew Süss* failed to live up to expectations (loss £94 12s. 4d.) and the next two plays also turned in losses (*Queer Cargo* 26.3.1938 £82; *Caesar's Wife* 2.4.1938 £34 9s.). In his accompanying letter (6.4.1938) to Sir John Brown Craig wrote:

> I am sorry there does not seem to be any improvement in business but I hope that whatever new arrangements are made, they will have a beneficial effect on the one thing that matters at the moment i.e. the Box Office.[1]

An "Informal Committee" (including B. G. Holloway, W. H. Fox and Talbot Butler) met on 12 April 1938 to produce a survival plan, a major element of which was the re-engagement of such artistes as Dale Roberts and Donald Gordon (BM 12.4.1938). Sherwood's solution was to rely on revivals of established repertory favourites (*Candida, Mary Rose, Yellow Sands* and *Charley's Aunt*), partly because of their proven record at the box office and partly because, after eleven years and five hundred productions, the supply of plays new to Northampton was drying up. One exception was J. B. Priestley, who was represented by three works (*People at Sea, I Have Been Here Before* and *Time and the Conways*) during 1938.

In *People at Sea*, a play of ideas set on the S.S. Zillah bound for Central America Sarah Churchill appeared as Miriam Pick, maid to Diana Lismore (Dorothy Fenwick) "a well-known English actress". Although her part in that play was modest Sarah Churchill certainly qualified as "a well-known English actress", albeit principally because of her famous father and her much publicised marriage to Vic Oliver rather than her acumen on the boards. Her abilities were put to test in the next production *Romeo and Juliet*.

Described as "the most ambitious programme presented by the Northampton Repertory Company since its inception 11 years ago" (*C&E* 25.5.1938) the production was spared two performances on the opening night, but thereafter Chorus's "two hours' traffic of our stage" had to be observed almost literally for the customary twice nightly schedule (6.30 pm and 8.50 pm).

In the summer of 1937 Osborne Robinson had attended a production of the play at the Foscari Palace in Venice which he recalled with enthusiasm: "The vast stage, built on a scale of a film set, provided for almost continuous action", but although his sets for the confined Royal Theatre stage were "as realistic as possible", they required frequent changes for the eighteen scenes (in five acts) into which the play was divided. The "outstandingly effective . . . frontcloth" was inevitably "used continuously" (*C&E* 24.5.1938). Robinson also provided original costume designs (executed by Mrs. F. Pratt assisted by Mrs. Musk Beattie and Mrs. Ives) for the company of forty, twenty-two of them amateur supers.

Of the performances Sarah Churchill was "an appealing childlike Juliet"; Arthur Lawrence a forcefully manly Romeo; Rosemary Johnson's Nurse, Richard Fisher's Mercutio and Neil Tuson's Tybalt were all satisfactory, but as Friar Laurence George Mudie showed his customary inability to use the lines set down for him. John Fothergill, whose father the eccentric innkeeper ran The Three Swans Hotel in Market Harborough, appeared as Balthazar.[2]

In September 1938 Osborne Robinson had another fine opportunity to display his talents in *The Circle of Chalk*, James Laver's version of the six hundred year old Chinese drama. The cast included the young David Tomlinson (as Chang Ling) and the return of Oswald Dale Roberts (at a weekly salary of £8 BM 8.6.1938) in no less than three parts.

By the end of September 1938 Neville Chamberlain had signed the Munich agreement with Hitler, thereby claiming the prospect of "peace for our time". Sherwood's choice of *The Insect Play* by Joseph and Karel Capek (17.10.1938)

The Insect Play by Josef and Karel Capek 1938. (*Adventure in Repertory*)

showed that he did not consider the theatre to be divorced from events in the world outside. Completed in 1923 the play had been successfully staged by Nigel Playfair at the Lyric Theatre, Hammersmith in the same year. Reducing the conflict of the First World War (in which Karel had fought for the survival of his native Czechoslovakia) to the level of the battle between the Black Ants and the Yellow Ants for the vital territory lying between two blades of grass the Capeks created a damning indictment of human aggression.

The Royal Theatre programme (10.10.1938) previewing *The Insect Play* quoted the Bishops of London, Southwark and Willesden and proclaimed:

> In presenting the play to Northampton audiences, we feel certain that we are not only fulfilling the aims of Repertory, but we are endeavouring as far as we can to inculcate a spirit of Peace and Goodwill among men.
>
> "THE INSECT PLAY" is full of thought. It is not only amusement and entertainment, but it gives those who see it something very deep to ponder over, and encourages them to try to propagate a deeper and more human feeling toward Men and Nations.

Amongst those who witnessed the Northampton production the *Northampton Independent* (21.10.1938) reviewer wrote:

> . . . what a pity it is that drama such as this cannot be directly harnessed to

the cause of Peace and the solution of humanity's over-bearing problems.

I would like to stage this play before an audience consisting of the whole of the world's leaders and, co-incidentally, in every theatre of every nation.

In Northampton Osborne Robinson excelled himself with striking costumes and settings. Oswald Dale Roberts as the Tramp and Arthur R. Webb as the Lepidopterist were ably and amply supported by the resident company, augmented by the Phyllis James School of Dancing and the Boy Scouts.

Although the objective of peace commanded almost universal support the threat of war had clearly not been removed. As early as May 1938 Sir John Brown, theatre proprietor, architect and soldier, had resigned from the repertory board "Owing to the pressure of his important duties at the War Office and consequent frequent absence from Northampton" (*NI* 6.5.1938). He was succeeded by Dr. Eric Shaw, chairman of the Repertory Circle.

In August 1938 Brown had received a letter (N.C.R.O.) from a firm of London solicitors (Philcox, Sons and Edwards) enquiring on behalf of a client "if there is any possibility of renting the same [the Opera House] next season" (19.8.1938). No longer shouldering a divided duty Brown's reply revealed a distancing from the interests of the repertory company:

The Opera House has been run for the past 10 years as a Repertory Theatre by the local people. They have, I believe, another 3 years Lease of the Theatre, but owing to the deaths of many of those interested there is a distinct possibility of their being willing to give up their Lease. (23.8.1938)

Although nothing came of these negotiations subsequent correspondence between the repertory board and the syndicate indicates that the tenants were in such dire financial straits that they were obliged to confront the possibility that their lease might be terminated.

In February and March 1939 the repertory board negotiated a reduction of its annual rental from £1,500 to £1,000, conceding that in exchange the syndicate would be released from liability for repairs to the building and would have "the right to sell the property should an advantageous offer be received during the currency of the present lease" (Musk Beattie to Talbot Butler Northampton manager of the National Provincial Bank 18.3.1939 in N.C.R.O.). Initially both parties overlooked insurance, but this became a matter of contention.

The syndicate argued – ingeniously – that "insurance is only an elementary precaution against the liability for repairs rendered necessary by fire" and should therefore be borne by the repertory board which had accepted responsibility for repairs (Becke, Green and Stops to Musk Beattie 12.4.1939 in N.C.R.O.). Mrs. Panther stood her ground and in the end the insurance premium (£65 14s. 2d. on a value of £29,100) was shared by landlord and tenant. Adequate insurance is only prudent at all times, but in the spring of 1939 it had an added imperative.[3]

Whilst the board negotiated with the syndicate to secure the future of repertory, Sherwood marshalled his forces on stage. The summer season concluded with Laurence Housman's celebration of the life and reign of the Queen-Empress *Victoria Regina*, at the conclusion of which Franklin Davies warned the audience that without stronger support the company might not sustain an autumn season. The Northampton Repertory Players journeyed to Buxton where they presented a season of six plays between 3 July and 12 August. Meanwhile Robert Young brought his County Players (including Freda Jackson) from Tonbridge to occupy the Royal Theatre.

In retrospect the portents of 1939 seem all too clear, but attitudes towards Germany were by no means uniformly hostile. The theatre programme (9.1.1939) extolled Goering's action (influenced by his wife, a former actress) in removing entertainment tax "its abolition has been the salvation of the theatre in Germany" where "the theatre is now flourishing". There was even an actors' old age pension fund, financed by a levy – equal to a farthing – on every ticket. The Northampton Anglo-German Club (Sekretarin: Miss K. Billingham) advertised its meetings in the programme (23.1.1939) with the reassurance "Dieser Klub ist nicht politisch". More dubious were the activities of "the Anglo-German friendship society known as The Link" one of whose thirty branches was in Northamptonshire. Its president was the fiercely patriotic and "anti-Bolshevik" Captain George Drummond of Pitsford Hall, whose daughter Edwina occasionally graced the repertory stage as an amateur. The chairman of the local branch was W. J. Bassett-Lowke, whose admiration for the engineering, commercial and civic achievements of Germany was well-known, but he "asked to be relieved of his duties in consequence of the pressure of his public work" (*NI* 11.8.1939). The Home Secretary, Sir Samuel Hoare, had alleged that The Link was an instrument of German propaganda, but the Northampton branch denied any such activities.

Even during the summer of 1939 continental travel occupied several Northamptonians. Osborne Robinson's destination was Corsica, whence he returned through Marseilles and Paris observing lamps coated with dark blue paint and blinds drawn down. A more hazardous journey was that undertaken by W. H. Fox, a future chairman of the repertory board, to rescue his daughter from Paris on the very eve of hostilities.

In Terence Rattigan's *Harlequinade* Dame Maud Gosport recalls:

> It was 1914 I played Juliet, dear. I remember the date well, because the declaration of war damaged our business so terribly.

Sherwood's plans for the opening production of the autumn season had already been changed from Priestley's *Johnson Over Jordan*, for which the author withdrew permission, to Shaw's *The Millionairess*, which was scheduled to open

72

on Monday 4 September. The declaration of war on the previous day resulted in the closure of all theatres. Amongst the most vehement protests was G. B. Shaw's:

> Bernard Shaw Up in Arms.
> "What agent of Chancellor Hitler is it who has suggested that we should cower in darkness and terror for the duration? The closing of theatres and picture houses is a master stroke of unimaginative stupidity. During the last war 80,000 soldiers on leave were amused every night and theatre rents rose to a fabulous figure. Are there to be no theatres for them to keep thousands of children out of mischief and traffic dangers?" (*NI* 8.9.1939)

Shaw was of course overlooking the nature of the new conflict with its threat of bombing raids to which large assemblies of theatre-goers would be particularly vulnerable. Happily in Northampton the closure was brief indeed. Permission to re-open was given on Saturday 9 September and by selecting Gerald Savory's comedy *George and Margaret*, which the company had already performed in Buxton, live theatre was resumed on the following Monday. Adolf Hitler achieved one reform which had eluded Northampton for twelve years – black-out restrictions meant that henceforward performances would be once nightly only.

The programme (11.9.1939), whilst giving clear instructions about evacuating the theatre (within five minutes) and the locations of the nearest air-raid shelters, echoed Shaw's sentiments about the value of theatre in wartime:

> The national work the stage did in the last war came generally to be admitted . . . Plays are needed as antidotes to war. Plays, if they can raise laughter, are rich in blessing; they can even inspire citizens, men and women alike, with a new strength, courage and energy, which may last until the war is over and won.

On the same page there was a call for increased support: "We want to strive for a regular weekly patronage of 5,000 people."

During the opening months of the conflict the Northampton Repertory Players took up the challenge of keeping the curtain up. Members of H.M. Forces were admitted at the special rate of 1s. on Mondays and Tuesdays. All members of the audience were required to bring gas masks and exhorted not to leave them behind. Members of the A.R.P. were reassured that if their duties necessitated them leaving before the conclusion of the play a ticket for another performance would be available free of charge. In time sugar was no longer provided for interval drinks and motorists were asked not to switch on their headlights until they had left Guildhall Road. These minor irritants apart the theatre actually enjoyed its release from the twice nightly treadmill and was able to mount plays which had hitherto been impossible.

Geneva, Shaw's satire on European politics written when he was eighty-two, was given its repertory première on 25 September (once nightly at 7 pm with Thursday and Saturday matinees). Osborne Robinson provided "one of the best [settings] he has done" and "the company were magnificent" (*C&E* 26.9.1939). Sherwood, whose personal style was relaxed but competent, had now gathered a company of solid talent around him. Arthur R. Webb (combining A Bishop with his duties as stage manager) and Franklin Davies (Commisar Posky) were to remain as stalwarts through the war years. Colin Douglas (A Jew), with his powerful physique and distinctive voice, had joined the company having tried farming in New Zealand prior to training at R.A.D.A. (*NI* 14.4.1939). Rosemary Johnson (who married Sherwood) led the three women in the cast as Begonia Brown "Camberwell personified". John Whiting, the son of a local lawyer and later a distinguished dramatist, appeared as The Betrothed. Their efforts were rewarded by good audiences, producing a profit of £89 plus £24 tax exemption (BM 3.10.1939).

Romeo and Juliet made an early return on 2 October at the initiative of Godfrey Kenton and Vivienne Bennett, who gave their services to their old theatre as a gesture of encouragement in difficult times. They supplemented the stock company (Rosemary Johnson as the Nurse, Arthur Lawrence as Mercutio, Franklin Davies as Escalus, Colin Douglas as Tybalt) with Lawrence Baskcomb as Friar Laurence and Michael Eden, Lady Henley's son, who had been a prominent member of the Oxford University Dramatic Society from 1933-6 (PR 2.10.1939), as Paris. This sense of her profession's responsibilities during the war was characteristic of Vivienne Bennett, who, together with Bernard Miles and Harold Scott, founded the Market Theatre to take "a programme of short plays, mime, song and dance" to schools and village halls across the land.[4]

The loyalty which Northampton inspired in former members of the company was reflected by the return of Donald Gordon to play Bill Boanerges, a role he had created with the author's tutelage in the original Malvern production of *The Apple Cart* in 1929. One actor who was sadly destined never to return was Oswald Dale Roberts. Devastated by the death of his beloved wife in April 1939, Roberts had subsequently suffered "from intermittent nervous breakdowns"; in October his body was found at the foot of the Avon Gorge, a fall of 250 feet. The Bristol jury returned an open verdict (*NI* 27.10.1939).

Shaw was in evidence again in 1940 with *The Doctor's Dilemma* in February and *St. Joan* in March. *St. Joan* is an ambitious choice at any time and it was no exaggeration to say "it will tax us to the hilt" (*PR* 19.2.1940). However the cast "regarded by most of us as a better balanced company than there has been there in its [the Repertory's] 14 years of history" (*C&E* 26.3.1940) acquitted themselves superbly from Rosemary Johnson's Joan "blending naivety and intensity" to Lawrence Baskcomb's crafty Archbishop, Colin Douglas's manly Dunois and Franklin Davies's polished Warwick. Total profit amounted to £84.

St Joan by George Bernard Shaw 1940 with Rosemary Johnson as Joan of Arc. (*Adventure in Repertory*)

It had been hoped that *St. Joan* might justify a second week, but this was not the case, instead as spring gave way to summer attendances declined. With the conduct of the war in such a critical state (the evacuation of Dunkirk in late May/early June) it was not surprising that the population was otherwise preoccupied. At the end of each performance of Helen Jerome's adaptation of *Jane Eyre* during the week of 8 July Franklyn Davies appealed for support for the theatre. Predictably the *Northampton Independent* rallied to the cause:

Must Repertory Theatre Go Too?
Soon they MUST close unless Northampton rallies its patronage and interest at once. (5.7.1940)

Happily *Jane Eyre* was (and has continued to be) popular with local audiences, "3,914 persons paying for admission" (PR 22.7.1940). The combination of threat and exhortation sustained attendance for the next two plays (*Sheppey* 1,965 and *Sixteen* 3,152). Thus although William Sherwood resigned in August 1940 to take up a more lucrative position in York, he had the satisfaction that Northampton was one of only three (together with York and Harrogate) "out of the sixteen original members of the Repertory Theatres' Association" still functioning (*Adventure* p. 135).

The scale of this achievement was formidable. The basic ingredients of the theatre: plays and actors, as well as audiences, were in short supply. With West End theatres re-opening more hesitantly than those in the provinces commercial managements were taking out their own tours instead of releasing plays for repertory production. The acting profession was suffering from the apparently contradictory ills of unemployment and shortages. An Equity report stated that "of the 5,000 members of the Association there were 4,000 unemployed [plus a further 4,000 backstage and front-of-house staff]" (PR 3.6.1940) and "Gradually the ranks of the younger actors are being denuded of artistes as the calling up for service of the different groups comes along. Arthur Lawrence and Colin Douglas registered last Saturday week" (PR 3.6.1940).

Even those actors in work were precariously placed as the programme (8.7.1940) revealed:

> It may not be generally known, but had it not been for the sacrifice of the artistes and staff in consenting to a scheme of salary payments on the basis of box office receipts, the Repertory Theatre would have had to close its doors long ago.

The sliding scale was based on weekly box office income ranging from £150 to £250 (in steps of £25) producing in the case of Sherwood a minimum of £5 and a maximum of £13. Other artistes were on pro rata rates, with a guaranteed weekly minimum of £3 (BM 26.9.1939). Contracts (such as Marjorie Sommerville's - 9.6.1941) stipulated rigorous conditions, several of them (e.g. complaints) stemming from the disputes in the 1930s. In 1943 Arthur Leslie resigned as producer because the board would not relax its "rule against joint engagements" by employing his wife (BM 16.3.1943).

Partial salvation lay in the extensive use of amateurs. In January 1940 Sherwood noted that in his productions to date "there have appeared 65 professional artistes, 70 amateurs, 5 dogs, 1 parrot, 1 monkey, 1 hen" (PR 15.1.1940). As early as October 1939 "our friends from the amateur ranks" were welcomed for their help in the production of *Romeo and Juliet* in which they mustered eighteen, including Norman Gibbs as Sampson and Maurice Dunmore as Balthazar. Between autumn 1939 and spring 1940, when he left to join the Royal Artillery Service Corps, Dunmore appeared in a dozen roles, several of which were quite substantial. Substantial enough to require him to absent himself from his office at the county council to cross Guildhall Road at a prearranged time to attend rehearsals - "his most outstanding performance was as Brother Martin in *Saint Joan*" (PR 15.4.1940).[5] Other regular amateurs included Florence Fancourt, an accomplished actress who could match any of the professionals in her acting talents and who from June 1941 received £2 2s. a week "as expenses when she plays" (BM 24.6.1941); Rose Walding whose experience went back to the early days of repertory; and George Bradshaw the colourful landlord of the

Black Boy public house until his death in January 1940. Even W. J. Bassett-Lowke trod the boards, as the Second Customer in *Sheppey*, imperfectly disguised as B. J. W. Ekwol. Professionally Bassett-Lowke's company was making an important contribution to the war, culminating in preparations for the Normandy landing in 1944. "Combined Operations headquarters were said to have had the most up-to-date fleet of models of landing strips and equipment in the world" (*D.N.B.*).

Needless to say there were no understudies, though the strain of the work (and in early 1940 an epidemic of German measles) often resulted in illness amongst the company. In February 1940 Rosemary Johnson, Margaret Greene and Arthur R. Webb were all on the invalid list. Rosemary Johnson's role as Moya Lexington in Rattigan's *After the Dance* was taken over at the last moment by Miss Alison Horstmann who "for one so young in experience acquitted herself well" (PR 5.2.1940).

Inevitably the department which suffered the most acute deprivation was Osborne Robinson's. A conscientious objector[6] Robinson responded to the situation with a firm commitment to uphold the standards of theatre work. Accustomed as he was to eking out his modest budget Robinson had to use even greater resourcefulness in recycling the material at his disposal. The production of *Murder on the Second Floor* was only made possible "by the good offices of His Worship the Mayor, Ald. H. A. Glenn" whose family building firm Messrs. Glenn and Sons "kindly loaned us timber, balustrades and doors for the structure of The Second Floor in the second act of this week's play" (PR 5.8.1940).

Costumes posed another problem. Even with its distinguished record for making its own costumes for period plays the theatre was obliged to resort to hiring them. In the case of *Pride and Prejudice* in October 1940 "On the Saturday previous to the production neither the costumes nor the wigs had arrived" (PR 7.10.1940). A member of the theatre staff J. S. Owen volunteered to drive to London early on Monday to collect them and though he returned with the costumes in time for the dress rehearsal, the wigs were trapped in transit. The cast used considerable ingenuity in dressing their own hair in period.

Shortly afterwards Osborne Robinson solicited donations to the wardrobe:

All gifts to the collection of costumes etc. are much treasured and they are well taken care of. We still do not possess specimens of the extreme "Oxford Bags" and "Plus Eights", nor of any day-dresses and millinery of the 1920s. (PR 21.10.1940)

An extreme example of the vicissitudes of war was the failure of the play texts of *Little Ladyship* to arrive on time for the first rehearsal on Tuesday morning although they had been dispatched on the previous Thursday:

Luckily, we already had the full scripts and parts of "INDOOR

FIREWORKS", which was to have followed "LITTLE LADYSHIP", and so Mr. Brookfield put this play into rehearsal at once on Wednesday morning. (PR 4.11.1940)

The normal practice was to issue scripts to actors on the Saturday prior to the commencement of rehearsals (BM 18.3.1941).

By then William Brookfield had succeeded William Sherwood, with whom he shared lengthy repertory experience as well as his christian name. After war (1914–18) service in the artillery Brookfield had toured in several plays before setting up his own repertory company which he had run for eleven years in such locations as Bradford, Manchester and Luton (*NI* 30.8.1940). His accustomed venues being designated as danger zones he had come to Northampton, accompanied by his wife actress Hilda Malcolm. Brookfield's contract was "at £10 a week, subject to the sliding scale" (BM 21.8.1940), but this norm, based on weekly receipts of £251-275, could fluctuate from £6 (£150-170) to £12 (over £300) (BM 13.11.1940).

The word coined to sum up Brookfield's tenure was "REPEATORY", but he was astute in his choice of plays and audiences responded accordingly. He was judged to have come through his first production – Dodie Smith's beguiling family drama *Dear Octopus* – in September 1940 "with flying colours". In the best tradition of repertory Rosemary Johnson aged for Marie Tempest's role of the (grand-)matriarchal Dora Randolf. Marjorie Sommerville was the lovable and long-suffering companion Fenny.

As the equally long-suffering second Mrs. de Winter in Daphne du Maurier's *Rebecca* "Marjorie Sommerville has rarely touched greater heights". The play ran for two weeks with Anthony Blake giving an "immaculate interpretation" as Maxim de Winter and the company's corps of mature actors (Franklin Davies, Donald Gordon, Arthur R. Webb and Lawrence Baskcomb) all comfortably accommodated with suitable character parts (*C&E* 26.11.1940). Osborne Robinson's sets recaptured a more gracious age.

By the beginning of 1941 the repertory company had consolidated its position. The accounts for the year ending 15 February 1941 showed a profit of £535, compared with a loss of £86 in the previous year. The roll of permanent seat holders had increased to 1,200 a week (PR 10.3.1941) as local supporters were joined by evacuees, visitors (local hotels were filled with Londoners in search of a quiet weekend) and of course the military, one of whom wrote:

> In these days, when so many theatres have been compelled to close down, it comes as a great pleasure to see well-filled and enthusiastic houses at Northampton . . . But Northampton SHOULD be 'repertory-minded', for few towns can boast such a splendid record of excellently presented plays. (PR 10.2.1941)

The management felt "confident that all our patrons . . . will remain loyal to us despite the slight increase [bringing the top price for the dress circle up to 3s. from 2s. 6d.] in the price of their seats, and we assure them that every endeavour will be made to keep up the very high standard of plays and productions which has always been our policy" (PR 17.2.1941).

Revivals dominated the repertoire, but there were exceptions. In March 1941 Robert Ardrey's drama, of the disillusioned journalist who becomes a lighthouse keeper on Lake Michigan, *Thunder Rock* was staged despite the fact that a West End revival had opened. Shaw retained his prominence with *Fanny's First Play* (12.3.1941) and *Major Barbara* which was described in the producer's note as "as fresh and topical today as when it was written". Peggy Diamond, who had joined the company in the previous September with experience in Watford, Peterborough and Leicester, was "an impressive Major Barbara" and "Franklin Davies [was] . . . grandly individualistic as Undershaft" (*C&E* 13.5.1941).

Although casts now tended to be compact, Brookfield did not flinch from the occasional large-scale production of which the Christmas 1941 show *Pickwick* was an ambitious example, incurring a loss of £141, offset by tax relief of £70 (BM 6.1.1942). The programme (now reduced to a single sheet with two folds) listed forty characters, which inevitably meant some doubling and the use of amateurs. In addition to directing the production Brookfield played Pickwick "in real traditional style" (*C&E* 27.12.1941). Clothing so many actors in period costume was no small task, but Osborne Robinson's resourcefulness was evident:

Costumes are here in plenty; to delight the eye, to help to sustain the old-world atmosphere and to contribute largely to the success of a warm and colourful production. (*NI* 2.1.1942)

And again for the revival of *The Doctor's Dilemma* in February 1942:

It is amazing how well the Repertory Theatre has surmounted the clothes rationing so as to allow Miss Diamond to appear in the most beautiful gowns that were so much a feature of Mrs. Dubedat.

After five valuable years of service as business manager, F. W. Cotter Craig was succeeded by J. E. Stephenson. Dr. Eric Shaw had resigned from the board, owing to his heavy responsibilities in wartime, to be succeeded by accountant W. H. Fox, who had audited the Northampton Repertory Players' books since the outset in 1927. In May 1942 Brookfield bade farewell to Northampton. His place was temporarily filled by George Roche, already a popular member of the company (Mr. Jingle in *Pickwick*, Cutler Walpole in *The Doctor's Dilemma*). In October 1942 a permanent appointment was made in Arthur Leslie, who was also a member of the company (Sir Patrick Cullen in *The Doctor's Dilemma*) with twenty-six years' experience in the profession including "ten years in repertory in the north of England" (*Adventure* p. 138).

The highlights of Leslie's short – seven months – tenure were Shaw's "Fantasia in the Russian Manner" *Heartbreak House* in November 1942 and Ibsen's *Hedda Gabler* in March 1943. Shaw again proved to be topical and Peggy Diamond scored a personal triumph as Hesione Hushabye, as she also did as Hedda:

> Peggy Diamond plays Hedda with brilliance and a high sense of tragedy. She leads us up to an emotional climax with poise and beauty – and moves throughout with the finish and quality of a great repertory actress. (*C&E* 30.3.1943)

The concept of "a great repertory actress" (at a basic £7 a week) might appear contradictory, but in fact the presence of performers of sufficient charisma and stature to scale the heights of the main roles in the repertoire, was perhaps the single most important ingredient for repertory success. Some (Peggy – Margaret – Diamond was one *Adventure* p. 171) went on to distinction in the West End; for

The School for Scandal by R. B. Sheridan 1943. David Hofman as Joseph Surface. Mary Whitfield as Lady Teazle and Lawrence Baskcomb as Sir Peter Teazle. (Royal Theatre Collection)

others (Oswald Dale Roberts) repertory was the extent of their orbit, but their achievements were no less significant for that.

In April 1943 the Northampton Repertory Players welcomed Alex Reeve as their fifth producer since the outbreak of war. Despite this rapid turnover continuity had prevailed, largely because of the constraints on performers, plays and audiences common to all holders of the office. Alex Reeve's pre-war experience had been as producer of the Welwyn Thalians, who had won the British Drama League Community Theatre Festival and thereby attracted the commendation of Tyrone Guthrie. His salary was £17 per week (BM 6.4.1943).

Initially Reeve contented himself with routine revivals (*Hobson's Choice, The Millionairess, The School for Scandal, Hindle Wakes* and *Gaslight*), but in September 1943 he produced the first new play to be seen at the theatre since board director H. Musk Beattie's *The Rest is Silence* in April 1940.

Burning Gold was by Dr. Falkland L. Cary and A. A. Thomson, both of whom lived in Harrogate. The theatre proclaimed the importance of new work:

No theatre should offer a menu consisting of revivals of well-known plays, least of all a repertory theatre. Any art which lives in the past alone lacks vigour and vitality. It is therefore essential for the future of the theatre that new plays should be produced and new playwrights encouraged. (PR 13.9.1943)

Burning Gold was described as being as topical as Terence Rattigan's *Flare Path*. Set at Woodbury Manor the ancestral home of Lady Caroline Woodbury (Peggy Diamond) and her family during 1939–40, the play explored the conflict between the older generation's struggle to uphold traditional values and the younger generation's modernity and realism. Thus it brought face to face "two worlds – the old world of the landed gentry, tradition and security and the new world of big business, social change and shifting values" (PR 20.9.1943). Northampton responded well to the play, no doubt encouraged by the casting of old favourites in leading roles.

Another strong drama was an adaptation of Zola's *Thérèse Raquin, Thou Shalt Not*, with Hilda Malcolm giving a compelling performance as Madame Raquin. 1943 was rounded off with *1066 and All That* judiciously updated with "little topical and local touches" (*C&E* 28.12.1943), which played to full houses and established a pattern of packed audiences for the ensuing year. Clifford Bax's *The Rose Without a Thorn*, with Yvonne Marquand in Freda Jackson's old role as Katharine Howard, was successfully recalled to service and other old favourites included Coward's *The Queen Was in the Parlour*, Barrie's *Dear Brutus* and Shaw's *Arms and the Man*. Shaw, Coward and Priestley shared the honours with three plays each.

The commitment to new writing was honoured with Falkland Cary's *Candied*

Peel in December 1944, though this was a less ambitious piece – "a pot-boiler pure and simple" *C&E* 5.12.1944 – than *Burning Gold*. Nevertheless Cary discoursed on the play and its Northampton production at considerable length in his manual *Practical Playwriting*. He had tested the title with eight repertory producers, six of whom, including Reeve, assured him of its suitability. Its aptness relied merely on the leading character's penchant for candied peel and the action of the comedy-thriller revolved around mysterious happenings at a weekend party at his home. Cary was delighted with Reeve's production "If ever Production and Playing had made a play this was the occasion". He was particularly pleased with Peter Tremlett's performance as the lead, James Ondersley, "precisely and exactly, down to the smallest detail, as I had visualised it". As Mrs. Cortonhart Dorothy Fenwick excelled his expectations "the part . . . was recreated as something altogether better, less obvious and more effective than I had written".[7]

Tremlett and Dorothy Fenwick were still in the company for another Cary première *Murder out of Tune* in October 1945, with which the author again professed himself highly delighted: "I think the Producer and the Company at Northampton excelled even their work in the two plays of mine which they had previously produced." Arthur R. Webb "typified everything I had visualised for my detective" and Mary Russell as Mrs. Trochell had created "something that was altogether better than my original character and made the part an outstanding and brilliant success".[8] Since Cary had expended only ten days writing *Murder out of Tune* this was less surprising than might be expected. Otherwise the last year of the war relied heavily on Coward and Priestley (three plays each) and Shaw and St. John Ervine (two each), who collectively accounted for nearly a quarter of the year's forty-three productions.

In the summer of 1945 the Royal Theatre hosted a production of *Romeo and Juliet* under the auspices of C.E.M.A. (Council for the Encouragement of Music and the Arts) which had been set up in January 1940 to promote the arts with the aid of government funding. George Rowell has described C.E.M.A. as "The Civilians' E.N.S.A.".[9] Back in October 1943 part of the repertory company led by Peggy Diamond had undertaken an E.N.S.A. tour of Hubert Griffiths's *Nina*. On 5 May 1944 a number of repertory theatre leaders met in a temperance hotel in Birmingham to found the Conference of Repertory Theatres (C.O.R.T.). Although these developments arose out of the conditions of war they were harbingers of the future for repertory theatres – a future in which subsidy and all its trappings were to assume a central role.

Ironically, after the uncertainties of 1939–40, regional repertory theatre had enjoyed a period of almost unexampled prosperity. Charles Landstone records that between May 1943 and May 1946 the Theatre Royal, Bristol made a cumulative profit of £16,000, though half of this came from bar takings.[10] Exemption from entertainment duty had to be sought for "every play, by whatever author . . . with the exception of Shakespeare, Sheridan and other classical authors e.g. Ibsen and most probably Shaw" (BM 1.2.1944). The sliding scale for salaries was abolished in May 1944 (BM 23.5.1944).

Those who had advocated a central role for the theatre at the outset of hostilities had been proved right. Compared with the First World War there was a greater readiness to support more serious and meaty fare, the theatre had not been a mere diversion. However even by V.E. Day in May 1945 Landstone detected a decline in standards of productions and audience attendances. A vast new public had been created for the theatre, but he calculated that only a residue of 20 per cent could be relied upon to form "the backbone of support for the Repertory Theatre movement in the years of peace".[11]

Notes.

1. Northampton Theatre Syndicate papers in N.C.R.O.. Entertainment tax was paid on all these productions, which implies that the theatre was no longer enjoying exemption.

2. See John Fothergill *Confessions of An Innkeeper*, 1938, p. 269.

3. At the same time the New Theatre was insured for £54,000.

4. Charles Landstone *Off-Stage A Personal Record of the First Twelve Years of State Sponsored Drama in Great Britain* 1953, p. 21.

5. I am indebted to Maurice and Alison Dunmore for their recollections of this period.

6. *Northampton Independent* 9.6.1939 recorded that "There are 1,423 militiamen in Northamptonshire and 23 conscientious objectors, 10 of whom registered from Northampton." BM 21.1.1941 reported that "Mr T. Osborne Robinson had registered for military service, and it was decided to support an application for deferment of his calling up."

7. Falkland L. Cary *Practical Playwriting* nd, p. 167.

8. Ibid p. 170.

9. Rowell and Jackson *The Repertory Movement*, p. 77.

10. Landstone op. cit. p. 126.

11. Ibid pp. 60-1.

CHAPTER SEVEN

Subsidiary and Subsidy 1946–1951

AFTER the years of wartime austerity and with the relaxation of rationing (clothing as well as food) still a remote prospect in post-war Britain John Gielgud's glittering revival of Oscar Wilde's *Lady Windermere's Fan* at London's Haymarket Theatre in August 1945 caught the mood of the times. A talented cast included Athene Seyler, Isabel Jeans, Dorothy Hyson, Geoffrey Toone and Denys Blakelock, but the acting "with one or two conspicuous exceptions" was judged "scarcely worthy of its ornate setting" (*The Times* 22.8.1945). Instead it was "the gorgeousness of the setting and the splendours of the costumes" by photographer turned designer Cecil Beaton which attracted attention.

Early in 1946 the Northampton repertory company followed the metropolitan example with its own production of *Lady Windermere's Fan*. The cast, with Dorothy Fenwick as Mrs. Erlynne, Reginald Thorne as Lord Darlington and June Ellis as Lady Windermere, was creditable, but again it was the sets and costumes – by Osborne Robinson – which made the greatest impact:

> The Northampton Repertory Company this week give Oscar Wilde's play the production it deserves, and the sets and dresses it deserves, no more could be said than that . . . The richness of the ball scene earned applause from last night's audience. (*C&E* 29.1.1946)

The production was such a success that it was retained for a second week thereby enabling more playgoers to marvel that "such a standard could be achieved in a small provincial theatre presenting a different play each week" (*NI* 8.2.1946), as well as producing a total profit of £383 (BM 12.2.1946).

The resources at Osborne Robinson's disposal were obviously much more limited than those enjoyed by Gielgud and Beaton, but the war years had already tested and proved the Northampton designer's capacity for inventiveness. Some indication of the budget for post-war weekly repertory is given in a pamphlet *The Staff and Expenses of a Typical Repertory Theatre in 1945*, published in February 1946.[1] Salaries were still at pre-war levels ranging from £10 each per week for the manager and producer down to £2 10s. for student actors. The scenic designer's salary was £8 and his weekly budget (for furniture and costume hire and the purchase of materials such as paint, canvas and screws) was barely £10. Osborne Robinson's wages were raised to £15 a week in May 1946 (BM 28.5.1946). Acting salaries ranged from £15 (Lionel Hamilton) to £3.

Lady Windermere's Fan by Oscar Wilde 1946. (Royal Theatre Collection)

Such straitened working conditions did not deter members of the profession from engaging in repertory work. The *Stage Guide* for 1946 stated that the total of "repertory theatre and travelling companies . . . has now mounted to 238 and is steadily growing".[2] Many of these companies, principally those without their own theatres, were commercial undertakings on the lines of the companies which had visited the Royal Theatre before 1927. Naturally enough the longer established and more prestigious repertory companies were at pains to distinguish themselves from these more dubious ventures. The Conference (later Council) of Repertory Theatres (C.O.R.T.) had been formed to advance their work collectively.

Northampton's sense of its superior status was voiced in October 1947 at the time of negotiations between Equity and the repertory sub-committee of the Theatre Managers' Association. These negotiations were directed at the plight of members of minor commercial companies who were earning £3 a week with no payment for rehearsals or weeks-out. As a member of C.O.R.T. Northampton observed the Equity minimum wage of £4 and proclaimed:

Northampton's repertory theatre is a non-profit-making undertaking and the conditions under which the artistes are engaged and under which they work have gained the theatre a reputation second to none in repertory circles. (*NI* 24.10.1947)

85

Osborne Robinson painting the set for *Dick Whittington*. (*C&E* 18.12.1947)

The treatment and remuneration of artistes were important not only as ends in themselves, but also as the means of ensuring high quality work on stage.

Northampton stuck to its commitment to new plays. In March 1946 *Crackling of Thorns* by C.E.M. Joad the philosopher and radio Brains Trust personality attracted widespread interest for its first professional production. The substantive scenes, for which locations included a youth hostel and a national school, advanced the author's ideas on the reduction of the nation's population. These were interspersed with duologues between Mr. Playwrite and The Critic (Mr. James Aggravate – alias for James Agate) discussing the craft of playwriting. Joad attended the first night, but although he had lent Alex Reeve, making one of his rare stage appearances as Mr. Playwrite, one of his suits he was less than enthusiastic about the identification of the character with himself:

Being the same size as Joad he [Reeve] was able to make himself up to resemble him, beard and all, and when he imitated Joad's squeaky voice the impersonation was very funny. Joad was a famous public figure . . . and the audience quickly recognised the character and fell about. When Joad came to see the show his lack of amusement was positively Queen Victorian. In the bar afterwards he told Reeve, "I'm sure I don't speak in that squeaky voice." He said this in such a squeaky voice that we thought he was being funny, and laughed. But he wasn't, and in his subsequent radio broadcasts it was noticeable that his voice had gone down quite a few semitones.[3]

Northampton audiences were grateful for this light relief in Joad's cerebral and undramatic play, which lost £33 (BM 12.3.1946).

The redoubtable Dr. Falkland L. Cary continued to provide new plays for Northampton. *Without Vision* was a sequel to *Burning Gold* following the fortunes of Philip Woodbury, the blind ex-pilot, now a dynamic and revolutionary M.P. advocating world disarmament. At least Cary was an adept enough playwright to temper his proselytising with some lively characterisation, in particular the voice of the old-guard church the Rev. Charles Olphert who, in Lionel Hamilton's polished performance, almost stole the play. Another recent recruit to the company Ronald Radd had "an enjoyable time as the irrepressible R.A.F. type, Jacko" (*C&E* 31.9.1946). A modest profit of £61 was made (BM 8.10.1946).

Lionel Hamilton, playing the Governor, redeemed another rather intense new play *The Man in the Market Place* (by Justin Power and Ronald Wilkinson) a reworking of the gospels (*John* 18–19 and *Luke* 22–23) for Holy Week 1947. Cary (in collaboration with Philip King) returned with a further première *Madame Tic-Tac* with its central character of a deaf–blind woman written expressly for

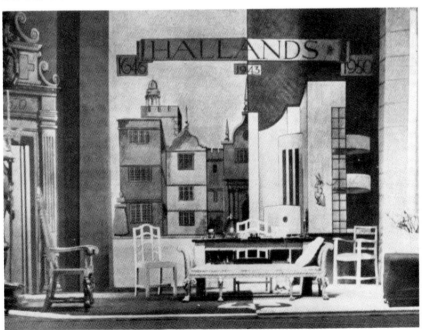

Without Vision by Falkland L. Cary 1946. (*Adventure in Repertory*)

Dorothy Fenwick. Dorothy Fenwick legendarily expressed regret that her customised character was not dumb, as well as blind and deaf, but Northampton audiences, beguiled by the play's description as a thriller and their loyalty to author and cast, gave it "a tremendous ovation" (*C&E* 26.8.1947). Audiences were similarly deferential to Val Gielgud's new play *Man's Company*, a tale of a commando raid on the French coast, in October 1947, the first night of which was attended by the author and Clemence Dane. Miss Dane, whose *A Bill of Divorcement* (1921) had been recurrently popular with repertory companies before the war, felt inspired to address the Northampton audience at the final curtain, "she rose massively [from her seat in one of the boxes] to acknowledge the acclaim of Northampton's public . . . A hush fell as she began: 'Dear people of Nottingham . . .'"[4]

However although new plays did not shrink from contemporary themes the lure of escapism, which had dominated the theatre *during* the First World War, tended to dominate it *after* the Second. Turgenev's *A Month in the Country* was another opportunity for splendid (mid-nineteenth-century Russian) period settings by Osborne Robinson as well as fine performances by Arthur R. Webb, Reginald Thorne, Arnold Peters and "a newcomer Lionel Hamilton" who gave "the husband a depth which he might easily lose" (*C&E* 9.4.1946). J.M. Barrie's costume drama *Quality Street* was "an invitation to forget the jangling post-war days for a quiet English street" (*C&E* 28.5.1946) and for Coward's *The Marquise* "Osborne Robinson has conjured up a rich set, with costumes near-Watteau; it is a triumph" (*C&E* 28.5.46). A return to Wilde with *An Ideal Husband* again sustained a second week with Colin Douglas back in the company (as Sir Robert Chiltern) and Lionel Hamilton "polished, urbane and persuasive" as Lord Goring (*C&E* 20.5.1947).

The Northampton Repertory Players were holding onto their reputation and audience. An indication of their standing was their inclusion in a seven week C.O.R.T. sponsored season at the Shakespeare Memorial Theatre, Stratford-upon-Avon in early 1948 when the company performed *The Lass of Richmond Hill*, W. F. Lipscomb's play about the Prince of Wales (Lionel Hamilton) and Maria Fitzherbert (June Ellis) seen in Northampton the previous autumn. The other repertory companies deemed to be worthy of inclusion in this Festival of English Repertory were York, Colchester, Sheffield, Oldham, Windsor and Oxford.[5]

Ironically the Northampton company's appearance at the Stratford festival was preceded by outspoken criticism at home concerning the inadequacies of its revival of Shaw's *Saint Joan* in January 1948. Observing that the space available to him was "as precious as a clothing coupon book" the *Chronicle and Echo* (19.1.1948) reviewer pulled no punches. He found the production (three and a half hours including the Epilogue) "under-rehearsed", the company "under strength" and Alex Reeve's production "too static in parts, badly grouped in

The Marquise by Noel Coward 1946. (Royal Theatre Collection)

others". June Ellis, a "gallant little trouper" was miscast as Joan, though she salvaged some good moments. Other casting was open to criticism: Franklin Davies had scored a personal success as the Earl of Warwick in the previous 1940 revival, but instead of capitalising on his experience in that role Reeve cast him as Robert de Baudricourt, assigning Warwick to Lionel Hamilton, who would have been well-suited to the Inquisitor for whom Stephen Sylvester lacked the necessary authority.

For the Northampton company to tackle *Saint Joan* at all was perhaps foolhardy, but Reeve seemed to compound his difficulties with unfortunate casting and bad timing. *Saint Joan* was the second production after the pantomime *Dick Whittington* in which June Ellis had played Alice Fitzwarren whilst rehearsing the important part of Nina for the twenty-first anniversary production of *His House in Order*, which preceded the Shaw revival. She was, therefore, playing a demanding part every evening during the hopelessly inadequate week's rehearsal for *Saint Joan*. June Ellis certainly earned her description as a "gallant little trouper", as she did the admiration and respect of her colleagues: "Only George Bernard Shaw and the Fair Maiden of Orleans was ever known to defeat her."[6] She returned, more happily, to Shaw as Eliza Doolittle in *Pygmalion* that March.

Alan Brown, a young actor with a long association with Northampton ahead of him, joined the company to play Brother Martin in *Saint Joan*. Brown recounted his experiences to Robert Young, who relayed them to Aubrey Dyas Perkins:

89

He told me something about St. Joan in which, he said, there was no production of the acting whatever. In the case of this stupendous play (done in five rehearsals!) there could not possibly be time for any real producing; but I understand that this weakness applies to all the plays. Probably the explanation is that such work is beyond the powers of the present producer.[7]

Young expressed his concern that "the N.R.T. is now a shop-window for the scenic artist", whereas "the company is not (or recently has not been) a strictly professional company". The *Chronicle and Echo* review had made the same imputation urging the board to make "the 'Rep' again a completely, or almost completely professional theatre".

Although Young had established his and the theatre's reputation within the constraints of twice nightly weekly repertory his recommended remedy was the introduction of fortnightly productions. The debate about fortnightly repertory was as hotly contested after the war as that about twice nightly performances had been before it.

Northampton's policy was pragmatic. *Lady Windermere's Fan* had earned its second week, as had *The Marquise* in September 1946. No doubt encouraged by this experience the board acquiesced to the introduction of fortnightly productions beginning with the revival of Drinkwater's *Abraham Lincoln* at the end of October 1946, but it was obliged to return to the weekly system in February 1947. The nub of the problem was that although the case for fortnightly productions was incontrovertible artistically, because it allowed a second week of rehearsal, there was simply not sufficient audience support in Northampton to sustain a second week regularly. There was however a solution in the offing, as the *Northampton Independent* suggested in its review of *The Marquise*, namely "a second subsidiary . . . in the district" (6.9.1946), a satellite theatre where each production would play its second week, thereby allowing two weeks' rehearsals, without the peril of a second week in Northampton.

The idea of repertory companies with a remit and region extending beyond a single town had gained currency during 1946 with the encouragement of the Arts Council, which had replaced C.E.M.A. as the state's agency for promoting the arts. Drama director Michael MacOwen and his deputy Charles Landstone had taken a direct interest in the development of the Midland Theatre Company, based at the College Theatre, Coventry and the Salisbury Arts Theatre Company which eventually extended to eleven towns in Wessex.[8]

When Northampton came to look for a subsidiary theatre there was one near at hand (in fact too near, a mere fourteen miles distant) in Kettering. There the Savoy Theatre had been opened in 1938 on the site of a former theatre/picture house in Russell Street, somewhat removed geographically from the town centre. With a capacity of 1,131 the Savoy was more suited in size and design to the showing of films and in 1944 it had been acquired by Clifton Cinemas Ltd.[9] Nevertheless with the burgeoning of repertory immediately after the war it had played host to the Reginald Salberg Repertory Company, run jointly by R. M. Salberg and his cousin, playwright Basil Thomas.

Salberg's company opened with J. B. Priestley's *How Are They At Home* in May 1946, but such was the local response that the initial trial period ran on into the next year. Responsible for many productions was Anthony Pelly, a former member of the Northampton repertory company. Through 1947 theatre-goers in the county had the choice of two repertory companies, whose repertoires were at times disconcertingly similar. Thus in May 1947 the Northampton company presented A. J. Cronin's *Jupiter Laughs* which revealed serious "casting limitations" (*NI* 9.5.1947) and in June 1947 the Kettering company presented "the most satisfying interpretation" (*NI* 27.6.1947) of the same play. One up to Kettering, which by then counted Geoffrey Lumsden, Noreen Craven (later Salberg's wife) and Maureen Reeve (Alex's daughter) in its number. Anna Quayle, aged only fifteen, also worked for the company.

Salberg had originally been on share terms with Clifton Cinemas, but towards the end of 1947 he and his brother took over the management of the Savoy. Even then the limitations of Kettering for a permanent repertory company were becoming apparent – the town's population of 37,000 was inadequate in relation to the size of the theatre, which was, in any case, ill-suited to live drama. Salberg's company returned for a short three week season in August 1948 and was well received: "*The Winslow Boy* scores. Great Production" (*ET* 10.5.1948), but its association with Kettering was drawing to a close.[10]

The year 1948 is assured a place in the annals of the theatre by virtue of the legislation which empowered local authorities to spend public money (max. of 6d. on the rates) on the arts. The *Northampton Independent* calculated that for Northampton this would amount to £20,000 per annum, though it hesitated "to suggest that these activities should be municipalised in the accepted sense of the word" (27.2.1948).

In acquiring Kettering as a subsidiary theatre the board of the Northampton Repertory Players was not motivated by the expectation of public subsidy. As the annual report dated 1 November 1949 (for the year ended 13.2.1949) stated:

> During the course of the year the Company was approached to take a lease of the Savoy Theatre at Kettering . . . After prolonged negotiations, a separate company was formed with a similar constitution to this Company, and a lease was entered into by that Company to take over the theatre.

The new company had in fact been registered on 6 October 1948 as the Kettering Repertory Theatre Ltd. "limited by guarantee, without share capital". There were fifty members of the company "each liable for not more than £1 in the event of winding up" (*ET* 11.10.1948). The directors were the same as those for the Northampton company (BM 6.8.1948).

The overriding motive for the Northampton board had been the realisation of fortnightly productions:

> to join in the policy of all high standard repertory companies in the country, and the Arts Council of Great Britain, in an endeavour to do away with an unsatisfactory system which allows only one week's rehearsal for a play. By presenting each production for a further week at Kettering, the burden on the players has been eased by a fortnight's rehearsal, and a consequent higher standard of acting and production has been achieved.[11]

The municipality of Kettering was keen to give the venture non-financial support. At the opening night on 12 October 1948 the Mayor, Alderman E. A. C. Woodcock welcomed this addition to the cultural life of the town, pointing out that "It was not a commercial venture, but one whose profits must be returned to the theatre for its improvement and the raising of its standards" (*ET* 13.10.1948).

In fact with profits still a distant, and in practice unattainable, prospect the new management had already been obliged to spend money on the Savoy to try to create a more sympathetic ambience:

> During only one week's closure for alterations the company has by the expedient of erecting a different proscenium arch on stage, successfully given the place the same intimate atmosphere that Northampton playgoers have enjoyed in Guildhall Road. (*C&E* 13.10.1948)

The opening production was Coward's *The Marquise*, perhaps chosen as a good omen after its successful two week run in 1946. The company for the opening production consisted of established Northampton actors (Dorothy Fenwick, Joan Charlesworth, Reginald Thorne, Nevil Whiting, Norman Bird and Arnold Peters) under Alex Reeve's direction. Osborne Robinson's set, the first of many to be re-erected in Kettering, "won a round of applause for itself" (*ET* 13.10.1948). *The Marquise* company had played in Northampton in the previous week and their place had been taken by the second company including John Scott and Margaret Denyer (both from the Harrogate Repertory Company), old-hand Franklin Davies, Noreen Craven (formerly in Salberg's Kettering company) and Christopher Rex (later better known for his television work as Rex Firkin). The play was another Falkland L. Carey première, *Knight's Move* about a H.M. Inspector of Schools with a past; it was jointly produced by Alex Reeve and Hugh Grant, but thereafter Grant, who had produced many of the Salberg company plays, was in sole charge of alternate productions in his capacity as associate producer. Grant's previous experience had included work with Sir Frank Benson and Bristol Repertory before the war. Following war service with the Intelligence Corps Grant had produced for several of Salberg's other repertory companies.

The logistics of the two companies were inevitably complex. Opening nights were staggered – Northampton's Monday, Kettering's Tuesday. The companies were not absolutely self-contained. A player would move from one to another if required thereby facilitating greater scope for appropriate casting. The greatest boon was, of course, the two weeks' rehearsal "the first . . . at the Northampton Drama Club . . . the second on the Repertory Theatre stage" (*C&E* 23.9.1948).

The immediate results were encouraging: "What a good company it is nowadays" wrote W.E.P. (*C&E* 12.10.1948) of the production of *Knight's Move* and for Constance Cox's adaptation of Thackeray's *Vanity Fair* he endorsed "an unstinting reception . . . for a work of art, for decor and production, for playing completely satisfying; for an adaptation retaining so much we love" (*C&E* 29.11.1948).

Unfortunately behind the scenes all was not well. In April 1948 the board had indicated that seat prices in Northampton would not rise, assisted by the theatre's exemption from entertainment tax (*NI* 16.4.1948). This position proved to be untenable. Early in 1949 the board of directors took the unusual step of publishing a leaflet explaining the financial position. Three trends were identified: (1) the decline in income from Thursday matinees from £60 to £30 per performance; (2) a falling-away in attendance in the unreserved seats, especially mid-week, amounting to £12 per week; (3) a substantial increase in costs "Our pre-war cost of production was £258 per week. The present cost of production is £560, an increase of 117%, and recent increases in authors' royalties and National Insurances have added a further £20 per week."[12]

Faced with this crisis the board judged that of the two courses open to it, "to cut costs or to increase prices", only the latter was consistent with maintaining standards. Accordingly prices were increased from 4s. to 5s. for orchestra stalls and dress circle and pro rata through the house except that the circle (2s. 6d.), the pit (1s. 6d.) and gallery (1s.) remained unchanged. Overall the new prices showed an increase of 76 per cent on pre-war figures (BM 1.2.1949).

The need to ensure the theatre's financial stability was enforced by the imminence of a new lease. Later that year the directors of the Northampton Repertory Players agreed to a twenty-one year lease for the Royal Theatre and Opera House with the Northampton Theatre Syndicate at an annual rental of £1,400. Interestingly one of the more unusual stipulations (30) read:

Not without the previous consent in writing of the Lessors to reduce the prices of admission to the Theatre . . . below those set out in the Schedule.[13]

A dispute about seat prices had arisen before the war, clearly the syndicate was safeguarding the New Theatre from undercutting by the repertory company.

In the January 1949 statement Mrs. Panther, as chairman of the board, had been at pains to make it "clearly understood that the increased costs are in no way attributable to the company's extended activities at Kettering, where the policy of the Board has been rewarded with the enthusiasm of the Kettering audiences for the high standard of our work and sufficient support to cover the costs of our productions in that theatre". Mrs. Panther herself executed a deed of covenant in favour of the company and her daughter Mrs. Butlin lent it £1,000 (BM 10.1.1950). After prolonged negotiations with the Customs and Excise Commissioners exemption from entertainment tax continued. In 1951 Mrs. Butlin donated £4,000 to the company (BM 18.7.1951).

The rent for the Savoy was £60 per week, which (at £3,120 annually) was over twice the amount payable for the Royal Theatre. Admittedly the capacity (1,131) at Kettering was larger, but with audiences settling down at 2,000 a week, instead of the estimated 3,000, the attendance was hovering around 25 per cent (*NI* 19.10.1951). The disparity in box office income between the two theatres is apparent from the chart for autumn 1950 (p. 202). Initially Kettering had contributed $33\frac{1}{3}$ per cent to production costs, but in January 1950 "it was resolved that the amount . . . must be increased to 40%" (BM 17.1.1950).

Despite Mrs. Panther's earlier protestations about the Kettering Repertory Company's financial independence the Northampton Repertory Players' annual report "for the Period from February 13th, 1949 to April 1st, 1950" (dated 27.11.1950) stated: "The higher standard of production achieved has resulted in a marked increase in this Company's income and under these circumstances the Board has decided that a grant should be made to Kettering Repertory Theatre Limited by this Company for the period to April 1st, 1950 . . . in the sum of £885."

It was indeed true that "Revenue from Box Office, Programmes, Bar Takings and Buffet" had amounted to £41,387 (compared with £29,358 in the previous year), showing, after the financial assistance to Kettering, a modest profit of £467.

A member of the combined acting company, if privileged with the sight of these figures, might have experienced some difficulty in reconciling them with his own recent experience. In the spring of 1950 all but two members of the company had agreed to a voluntary salary reduction of 15 per cent to take effect from 10 April and running until at least the following September. Artistes had accepted this course because the alternative was the closure of the Kettering operation with consequent job losses (*NI* 31.3.1950). In 1951 the total weekly expenditure for artistes was set at £150 (BM 18.7.1951).

Essentially therefore, although Northampton derived artistic benefits from Kettering that activity could only be sustained by financial support from the Northampton company, its actors (through reduced salaries) and subventions from the Arts Council and Kettering Borough Council.

At the meeting of the Kettering Town Council's Finance Committee on 26 April 1950 there was a unanimous vote in favour of awarding a grant of £750 (the equivalent of four-fifths of a penny on the rate under the 1948 Act) to the Kettering Repertory Theatre. The Arts Council had offered a subsidy of £1,000 conditional upon a favourable decision from the town council – an early example of the principle of matching funding (BM 7.2.1950). The Finance Committee's chairman Councillor H.J. Potter presaged the sentiments of many a local politician towards funding the arts when he said:

> We want to develop Kettering as a successful town . . . We are anxious to further drama as one of the social services – just as we spend money on band concerts, not only for our citizens, but to encourage people to come to the town and as an encouragement to young people. (*ET* 27.4.1950)

Another portent of the future was the Kettering Council's insistence that "assessors nominated by the Council should sit with the Board of directors of the theatre" (*ET* 27.4.1950).

Although Kettering renewed its grant in March 1951 the reprieve was only temporary and in October 1951 the closure of the Kettering Repertory Theatre was announced, the last production being *The Winslow Boy* in the week commencing 6 November. In fact the Kettering Repertory Company was kept in being until July 1965 (BM 26.7.1965).

There was little regret at the demise of the Kettering venture. Although it had given employment to more actors most of them fervently disliked the system and regarded their weeks in Kettering with foreboding. As Nevil Whiting recalled "Artistes have to be transported back and forth to the dreaded Kettering." Furthermore "the customers didn't come", committed theatre-goers in fact preferred the surroundings of Northampton's Royal Theatre, which had always prided itself on the extent of its catchment area.

Even without the local difficulties (population, distance, unsuitable premises) afflicting Northampton's intervention in Kettering, other satellite systems, upon which it was modelled, proved to be costly (£12,000 annual subsidy for Salisbury) and impractical. As an early exercise in cultural planning this was not a hopeful harbinger for the future.

Even the alleged rise in artistic standards was not consistently achieved. Cases of miscasting persisted within the larger pool of actors. In Coward's *Design for Living* three relative newcomers (Beth Hawkins, Christopher Rex and Alan Brown) were cast as the Fontaine-Coward-Lunt trio, "roles that demand above all things, experience and mature acting. Thus one feels that the fault does not lie with these youthful members of the company . . . but with the casting" (*NI* 20.6.1949). The critic's complaint struck a chord with "Permanent Seat-Holder, Northampton" who wrote: "It is about time that such obvious and recurrent mis-casting ceased" (*NI* 27.6.1949). Later Beth Hawkes, who was judged too inexperienced for Coward's Gilda had to play a septuagenarian in *Miss Mabel* (March 1950) and the spinster aunt in *Ann Veronica* (May 1950). John Scott was considered to be a frequent victim of miscasting and even Norman Bird "one of the most interesting young actors of his decade [with] . . . his meticulous attention to detail and characterisation" was all too often effectively asked "to return in twenty years' time", of which his performance as Pepys in *And So To Bed* (June 1950) was an example.[14]

In the right parts members of the company were capable of distinction as they had always been. Amongst those collecting their fair share of plaudits were: Margaret Denyer "triumphant", "faultless"; John Scott "impeccable", "excelling"; Reginald Thorne "ever-advancing stature"; Franklyn Davies "memorable", "amazing make-up"; Dorothy Fenwick "to perfection"; Joan Charlesworth "triumphal opportunity", Ronald Radd "unerring study", "a triumph"; with similar endorsement for Adrian Cairns, Arnold Peters, Christopher Rex, William Franklyn, Henry Marris-McGee, and, of course, Lionel Hamilton.

Actors are dependent upon the quality of the material at their disposal and, even with fortnightly rehearsals, there was still no relief from finding a suitable play for each week. Inevitably there was a fair amount of dross – R. F.

An Ideal Husband by Oscar Wilde 1947. (Royal Theatre Collection)

Delderfield's *The Queen Came By* "hardly approaches the foothills of high drama" (*NI* 19.8.1949); Denis Constanduros's *The Daughter of the Parsonage* deserved "dismissal out of hand as worthless" (*NI* 10.3.1950). Margaret Sharp's *The Foolish Gentlewoman* contained "some of the most loose and incompetent playwriting I have encountered [from an] undisciplined female pen" (*NI* 4.8.1950) and M. J. Farrell's and John Perry's joint effort *Treasure Hunt* lacked "even the elements of dramatic architecture" (*NI* 2.2.1951).

Although *Twelfth Night* had received a creditable production in March 1948, Shakespeare did not feature during the three years of the Kettering connection – a lost opportunity in view of the larger pool of actors. *The School for Scandal* was "a red-letter achievement" (*NI* 28.4.1950) with Lionel Hamilton as Sir Peter Teazle, Joan Charlesworth as Lady Teazle and Dorothy Fenwick as Mrs. Candour. In June 1951 a special Festival of Britain production of Gay's *The Beggar's Opera*, in collaboration with the Alexandra Theatre, Birmingham was a worthy success, with Nevil Whiting as Macheath. Following Wilde's immediate post-war popularity four years separated *An Ideal Husband* (May 1947) and *The Importance of Being Earnest* (August 1951). Shaw was represented only by *The Millionairess* in September 1949 with Margaret Denyer as Epifania.

Of contemporary dramatists Noel Coward was pre-eminent, followed by Terence Rattigan. New plays included three works by local authors: *The Fox Amongst the Grapes*[15] by Wellingborough-born journalist Jack Allcock (a personal success for Alan Brown as Shelley), Ernest Reynolds's version of *The Three Musketeers* (March 1951); and *The Heart Equation* by company actor Adrian Cairns (September 1951).

The tradition of staging adaptations of classic novels became firmly established, with Constance Cox (*Vanity Fair* November 1948, *Northanger Abbey* October 1949, *Fathers and Sons* – from Turgenev – February 1950 and *Mansfield Park* – with its local associations – October 1950) developing a special relationship with the theatre.

The strength of contemporary American drama was reflected in Arthur Miller's *All My Sons* (June 1949 with Reginald Thorne as Joe Keller), Tennessee Williams's *The Glass Menagerie* (December 1949 with Dorothy Fenwick as Amanda Wingfield and Joan Charlesworth as her daughter) and more unusually with *Deep Are the Roots* by Arnaud D'Usseau with a predominantly black cast in March 1949.

After the departure of Hugh Grant in spring 1950 Lionel Hamilton was appointed associate producer with responsibility for alternate productions. Lionel Hamilton had joined the Northampton company in 1946 having spent six years in the army latterly as a welfare officer in Italy with responsibility for between 4,000 and 6,000 combatants and prisoners. Before the war he had trained at the Guildhall School and gained experience at the Barnes Theatre and J. Arthur Rank documentary films. The impact of his skills as a producer was immediately apparent – "exquisite sense of fun", "characteristic finesse", "every telling detail", "smooth and nicely rounded production" and so on. The only regret was that he was less frequently seen on stage as an actor.

The Kettering experiment had again demonstrated Northampton's readiness to be in the vanguard of the repertory movement. The same spirit was evident in its contribution to International Theatre Week in November 1951 with the first British production of *My Little Obolinski* an English version of Marcel Achard's comedy *Nous Irons à Valparaiso* by Gilbert Wakefield. But when Christmas came to Northampton that year repertory audiences were denied the delights of the now customary pantomime, the cost of which was prohibitive, and had to settle for John Dighton's comedy *The Happiest Days of Your Life* – hardly an apt description for the years of the Kettering experiment.

Notes

1. Quoted in Richard and Helen Leacroft *The Theatre in Leicestershire*, 1986, p. 113.
2. Quoted in George Rowell and Anthony Jackson *The Repertory Movement* p. 84.
3. "Remembering Northampton" by Stephen Sylvester. This is one of several recollections by members of the company solicited by Lionel Hamilton. Sylvester married Reeve's daughter Maureen. In N.C.R.O.
4. Ibid.
5. Programme in Royal Theatre archives.
6. "Nev's Notions – Whiting's Writings". Recollections by Nevil Whiting in N.C.R.O.
7. Letter dated 3.2.1948 from Robert Young (living in Tunbridge Wells) to Aubrey Dyas Perkins, in N.C.R.O.
8. See Rowell and Jackson pp. 80–2; Charles Landstone *Off-Stage*, pp. 139–42; and J.B. Priestley *Theatre Outlook*, 1947.
9. *Cinema Theatre Association Bulletin* vol. 15. No. 1. Jan./Feb. 1981 "The Theatres and Picture Palaces of Kettering".
10. I am indebted to Reginald Salberg for information about his involvement with Kettering.
11. This and other annual reports cited in N.C.R.O.
12. *Northampton Repertory Theatre. An Announcement By The Board of Directors.*
13. Lease of Royal Theatre and Opera House, Northampton, dated 25.6.1949, in N.C.R.O.
14. Nevil Whiting op. cit..
15. Recalled in Michael Green *Nobody Hurt in Small Earthquake*, 1990, p. 45.

CHAPTER EIGHT

Landmarks 1952–60

DURING the remainder of the 1950s the Northampton Repertory Players passed several landmarks. Some of them were foreseeable – the twenty-fifth and thirtieth anniversaries of the company and the seventy-fifth of the Royal Theatre – others – notably the consolidation of Arts Council support and the Northampton Borough Council's acquisition of the Royal Theatre – can be seen as inevitable only with the benefit of hindsight.

Despite the passage of time there was still a remarkable degree of continuity in the affairs of the company. Mrs. Panther remained chairman of the board until April 1954, when she was succeeded by accountant W. H. Fox, who had been a director since 1944. Mrs. Panther's daughter Mrs. Irene Butlin joined the board in August 1951 and subsequently played a key role in safeguarding the theatre's future. The family's long-standing association came to a rather strained conclusion when mother and daughter resigned in February 1957 prompted, in part at least, by the board's ready agreement to Alex Reeve's departure in the previous summer. Reeve and Osborne Robinson had both become members ("executive directors") of the board in May 1948, an unusual and perhaps not entirely well-advised step for employees of the company.

The deaths of W. J. Bassett-Lowke and H. Musk Beattie created two board vacancies which were filled in 1954 by Aubrey Dyas Perkins and John Bennett, both of them future chairmen. Dyas Perkins, a solicitor, had been "connected with the Repertory Theatre for 26 years", long having been responsible for weekly programme notes on the forthcoming productions. He was the author (as Aubrey Dyas) of *Adventure in Repertory* (1948) which chronicled the history of the company to date. John Bennett, at thirty-three the youngest member of the board, was a director of the leather firm of Alsop Brothers Ltd., and, apart from war service, "had not missed a show at the theatre since 1937". Both men were actively involved in the Drama Club, but dismissed the "'round town' whispers that the elections were a Repertory 'move' to weaken amateur opposition in the town" (*NI* 7.5.1954).

In August 1958 the board was augmented by the appointment of Lady Hesketh, chatelaine of Easton Neston, and R. D. Enock, a county councillor and executive at Stewarts and Lloyds in Corby. Lady Hesketh, who had many cultural, historical and literary interests, remained a member of the board, latterly vice chairman, until 1990.

Although Alex Reeve was to serve as producer until the autumn of 1956 his tenure of office was interrupted by a period of several months as Visiting Associate Professor of Drama at Vanderbilt University, Tennessee from August 1953. During his absence Professor Joseph E. Wright came to Northampton as visiting associate producer. The exchange was arranged under the auspices of the Ford Foundation. Lionel Hamilton, already associate producer in the latter stage of the Kettering arrangement, became general manager of the Northampton theatre in 1954 and served as acting director of productions during Reeve's American sabbatical (BM 25.8.1953). Ever motivated by loyalty to the company rather than his own self-interest Hamilton was nevertheless the obvious "heir apparent" when Reeve recognised that the time had come (after thirteen and a half years) for him to move on. He returned to the United States as Associate Professor of Drama at Howard Payne College in Brownwood, Texas.

The retraction of the company following the demise of the Kettering subsidiary inevitably presented problems, primarily the consequent reduction of rehearsal time to one week. The need for the theatre to maintain its standards and appeal to local audiences was made all the more crucial by the increasing popularity of television. The number of licence holders in Northampton rose inexorably from 366 in 1949 to 19,795 in 1955 (*NI* 10.2.1956).

Apart from its attraction to audiences television also provided alternative employment for actors, but repertory remained the nursery for most young members of what was still an overcrowded profession. Equity claimed a membership of 9,900 "'legitimate' actors, singers and dancers" competing for about 6,000 jobs. Although the number of repertory theatres had declined since the post-war boom "established repertory theatres number 100–120, providing work for 1,000 to 2,000 according to the time of year" (*The Times* 30.1.1952). Charles Landstone put the figure for repertory theatres rather lower at eighty of which "about 25 . . . are run on a non-profit-making basis". Amongst these he included Northampton (drawing a veil over the Kettering experience), together with Liverpool, Sheffield, York, Oldham and Windsor, as being "entirely on the right side" financially, more significantly:

> Without wishing to make invidious comparisons Mr. Landstone selects Northampton, Ipswich and Windsor as three companies whose standard of performances is so high that the 'National Theatre' of any country would be proud to use them as a reserve team.[1]

Local pride in the theatre was more equivocal. The omission of the Royal Theatre from the final register of Northampton buildings listed for preservation prompted comment not only on the oversight, but also on the rather dated facilities offered to playgoers: "Patrons and productions will require better facilities, even if the charm of the old theatre is lost . . . let it be retained as a true theatre 'museum', complete with paint-shop, seats, gaslights and chandeliers" (*NI* 15.4.1952).

The theatre's period ambience was clearly a disadvantage, especially for young people, in the era of television. To one such it was "a bit bow-tie" and another was "so sick of seeing the same faces on the stage week after week" (*NI* 23.5.1952). The recent increase in seat prices also took its toll – "the sooner

Nine Days' Wonder by Constance Cox 1952. Lionel Hamilton as John Philip Kemble. (Lionel Hamilton Collection)

the management realise that 5s. for a two hour performance (often with long interval time) is too much to charge, then the sooner larger and younger audiences will be able to return" (*NI* 15.6.1952).

The programme for 1952 included two special silver jubilee productions. The first was Ashley Dukes's free adaptation of Nicolo Machiavelli's *Mandragola* in which H. Marris-McGee as "the arch-machinator", Lionel Hamilton as "the most pathetically gullible husband", Margaret Denyer as "the young wife" and Adrian Cairns as "the lover" combined with Osborne Robinson's "gloriously colourful Italian decor, with costumes to match" to create "this triumph of provincial production" (*NI* 9.5.1952). The second jubilee production, Norman Ginsbury's Regency play *The First Gentleman* with Norman Bird as the Prince Regent and Melanie Paul as Princess Charlotte, also drew plaudits *and* full houses:

> To have succeeded, with but a brief week of rehearsal and limited resources, in mounting such a brilliant and expensive show is an amazing achievement – it certainly amazed the author paying a special visit on Monday night! – and congratulations are due to all from Alex Reeve down to the lowliest "walk-on" with special laurels for Mr. T. Osborne Robinson, whose Chinese pavilion interior was a superlative triumph in paint and canvas. (*NI* 24.10.1952)

Trilby dramatised by Constance Cox. 1960 production. Lionel Hamilton as Svengali and Ann Kennedy as Trilby O'Ferrall. (Bryan Douglas Collection)

Ginsbury had already had a hand in an earlier success when his translation of Ibsen's *Ghosts* had been staged with Margaret Denyer giving a "performance of memorable intensity" as Mrs. Alving and Lionel Hamilton "perfectly secure as Pastor Manders, for this is, ideally, his part". Less secure was Ronald Radd "unfortunately cast out of type" as Oswald (*NI* 29.2.1952).

Another author who cultivated links with Northampton was Constance Cox, several of whose adaptations of novels had already been seen there. In February 1952 an original work from her pen *Nine Days' Wonder* was staged, providing the cast with the opportunity to embody a galaxy of theatrical legends from the past: Lionel Hamilton as John Philip Kemble, Adrian Cairns as Charles Kemble, Ronald Radd as Henry Betty and Margaret Denyer as Mrs. Siddons. Like Ginsbury, Miss Cox was overjoyed with the whole production, which had given Osborne Robinson another opportunity to display his flair for the Regency period. It returned a profit of £45 (BM 19.2.1952).

Miss Cox returned with what has proved to be the most enduring of her adaptations *Lord Arthur Savile's Crime* from Oscar Wilde's short story. The original cast included Adrian Cairns as the Dean of Paddington and H. Marris-McGee as Lord Arthur Savile, but it was Lionel Hamilton as the gentleman's gentleman Bains "who claimed the evening's laurels . . . Even to the subtlest shade his portrayal is faultless and is likely to go down as Mr. Hamilton's 'finest hour' at Northampton" (*NI* 14.11.1952). Later (1954 and 1960) Miss Cox provided Lionel Hamilton with another of his "finest hours" as Svengali, in her adaptation of George Du Maurier's novel *Trilby*.

To revert to 1952, a rich year for dramatists: John Whiting, formerly a member of the Northampton company, was accorded a production of his *A Penny for a Song*, originally seen at the Haymarket Theatre in 1951 under Peter Brook's acclaimed direction. Whiting's engaging English eccentrics were in good hands in Northampton: Arthur Pentelow as Sir Timothy Bellboys, Lionel Hamilton as William Humpage, Dorothy Fenwick as Hester Bellboys, Donald Churchill as Rufus Piggott and Melanie Paul as the ingenue Dorcas Bellboys. The setting "the garden before Sir Timothy Bellboy's house in Dorset, on a summer's day in 1804" might have been conceived for the benefit of Osborne Robinson.

The Northampton Repertory Players had observed their silver jubilee in fine style, but without benefit of the bard. In March 1954 *Much Ado About Nothing* was entrusted to Professor Wright as his valedictory production. The rigours of weekly repertory had been a revealing experience for the American academic, who confessed: "I had never produced a play in five 3-hr. rehearsals. I learnt fast. The actors were most helpful. They knew each other's strengths and weaknesses, and they were skilful in capitalising the former and hiding the latter."[2] Certainly the talent at Wright's disposal was remarkable: Lionel Hamilton as Benedick, Evangeline Banks as Beatrice, Tenniel Evans as Claudio, Donald Churchill as Borachio and Arthur Pentelow as Dogberry. Although some of the verbal comedy eluded the cast, the overall achievement was stylish and enjoyable.

The next Shakespearean offering, *As You Like It*, was presented for two weeks, but despite its title it did not commend itself to Northampton audiences. It was reported that during the first week "1,000 permanent seat-holders out of 1,800 cancelled their seats and attendances numbered 3,653 instead of the customary 4,000 and over. Happily the second week showed an improvement when there was quite a rush on the box office as the success of the production 'got around'." (*NI* 7.4.1955). In fact the box office returns were fairly consistent: £558 for week one and £573 for week two, with losses of £69 and £42 respectively.[3] Again the cast was impressive with established favourites: Mary Kenton (Godfrey's second wife) as Rosalind, Alan Brown as Oliver, Tenniel Evans as Touchstone, Arthur Pentelow as the Banished Duke and Lionel Hamilton as Jaques, being joined by Nigel Hawthorne as Orlando.

Many of the same team – "and a splendid team it is" – played in *A Midsummer Night's Dream*: Mary Kenton was "a lovely Titania", Alan Brown "an imposing Oberon", Nigel Hawthorne "suitably ardent as Lysander", with Tenniel Evans and Evangeline Banks (by then husband and wife) as Theseus and Hippolyta and Arthur Pentelow as Bottom leading the mechanicals, who included Richard Huggett as Quince: "All the magic and enchantment of this delightful play are here. It is imaginatively directed, extremely well acted, and magnificently dressed. Not a little of its success is due to the delicately beautiful scenery of Osborne Robinson" (*C&E* 14.3.1956). Box office income built up from £554 in week one to £695 in week two, but deficits of £169 and £40 were still recorded.

Lionel Hamilton combined producing *The Merchant of Venice* (assisted by William Sellars) and playing Shylock in March 1957. Tenniel Evans as Antonio and Arthur Pentelow doubling Morocco and the Duke of Venice were in their fourth consecutive annual Shakespearean revival. Anne Ford's Portia "did not quite convince", but eschewing over-implification, Lionel Hamilton rose to the challenge of Shylock: "His Jew is dignified and racially proud, and despite a shrewd head for ducats, there is undoubtedly a heart beneath his gaberdine which beats for his daughter Jessica (Sheila Kennedy looks lovely and speaks well as the latter)" (*NI* 15.3.1957). Long a devotee of Venice Osborne Robinson provided visually compelling sets.

Osborne Robinson's sets and Lionel Hamilton's Shylock were the key factors in generating an impressive box office take of £746 for the first week with a profit of £98, though this declined to £503 in the second with a resulting loss of £116. By now Lionel Hamilton was accorded the status of a repertory star, previously extended to Oswald Dale Roberts and Peggy Diamond. As one member of the 1950s company recorded "He had, and has, tremendous style, great presence and a wonderful voice".[4]

Peter Wyatt who had received lowly casting as Solanio in *The Merchant of Venice* was projected into the title role in *Hamlet* the following year, with Lionel

The Merchant of Venice by William Shakespeare 1957. Lionel Hamilton as Shylock, Arthur Pentelow as the Duke and Anne Ford as Portia. Osborne Robinson can be seen making a rare stage appearance on the Duke's right. (Bryan Douglas Collection)

Hamilton (also directing) as the Ghost and Alan Brown as Claudius. Dorothy Wheatley played Gertrude and Sarah Whalley Ophelia, with the youthful Edward Petherbridge combining Prologue and Luccanus, a Captain and A Priest. Hamilton confessed that "I regard the opportunity to produce this play as the most challenging thing that has happened to me since I came to Northampton in 1946" (PR 3.3.1958). He expressed envy for anyone seeing the play for the first time and accordingly (and probably without much difficulty) the *Northampton Independent* found "a junior editorial representative" who qualified. He professed himself impressed by Wyatt's Prince, not least in his soliloquies, and by Osborne Robinson's updated set and costumes. Robinson was, of course, no stranger to the play having designed the fabled Olivier/Guthrie Old Vic/Elsinore production in 1937, but this time he abandoned convention for a Victorian/Ruritanian style. The young critic considered it "daring" to mount such a production at a time when box office returns "are not all they should be" (*NI* 14.3.1958). His fears were sadly realised (first week £505, loss £220; second week £491, loss £291). Wyatt received £25 a week (BM 28.1.1958), £10 over his usual rate.

As the five Shakespeare productions between 1954 and 1958 show the acting company was relatively stable. Lionel Hamilton was, of course, the sheet-anchor, but other actors settled in the town for lengthy periods. Tenniel Evans recalled "we learnt our craft. I was in Northampton for four years, so I suppose I took part in upward of two hundred plays." Alan Brown, who was in Northampton "over three separate periods between 1948 and 1963 . . . performed in 271 productions, directed 17, and wrote the book and lyrics for 5 pantomimes."[5] Both men settled into married life, acquired property, produced children. They were part of the community. Each earned £15 a week (BM 26.6.1956).

Brown's acting achievements in Northampton show what a good actor could achieve within the constraints of weekly repertory. From Restoration comedy (*The Country Wife* "Mr. Brown handles his role [Horner] with credit" *C&E* 18.11.1957) to whodunnit (*Ten Minute Alibi* "Alan Brown gives his usual self-assured performance" *C&E* 26.11.1957) and psychological drama (*Dr. Jo* "Alan Brown scores another success as Dr. Alan Beresford" *C&E* 10.6.1958). One of his finest achievements was as General St. Pé in Anouilh's *The Waltz of the Toreadors* of which Janet Hargreaves, who played Mlle. Ghislaine de Ste-Euverte wrote: "Alan's General St. Pé . . . was a *tour de force* – imagine doing that in a week".[6] This view was endorsed by the local critic:

> Most of the verve and vitality of the play derives from Alan Brown, the ageing French general, a man with a fine military background, but equally proud of his life of romantic conquest. (*C&E* 19.8.1958)

As Heathcliff (in John Davison's adaptation of Emily Brontë's *Wuthering Heights*) Brown partnered Zoë Hicks as Catherine Earnshaw: "Once again the company is fortunate in being able to turn to Alan Brown for another powerful and fiery performance" (*C&E* 3.2.1959). A few months later Brown played Eddie Carbone, the Brooklyn longshoreman in Arthur Miller's *A View from the Bridge*: "He excels in this type of part and has given few better performances than this one" (*C&E* 2.6.1959). Alan Brown subsequently became a mainstay of the National Theatre (as actor and staff director) under all of its first three artistic directors.

Nigel Hawthorne's career has encompassed the heights of the National Theatre, the West End, Broadway and television. At Northampton initially he faced the recurrent difficulty of inappropriate casting, as in Ian Hay's *The Sport of Kings*:

> a newcomer Nigel Hawthorne plays [one of] the visitors to the Grange . . . the experience of Nigel Hawthorne is too meagre to enable him to play this leading part with conviction. (*NI* 6.8.1954)

Within months he was acquiring the experience:

Mr. Nigel Hawthorne, a newcomer who has recently proved his worth, reveals a delicious sense of comedy [in Arthur Watkin's *For Better For Worse*] in the role of the young, inexperienced and impetuous husband. (*C&E* 3.9.1954)

In Hugh Mills's *Angels in Love* "Mr. Nigel Hawthorne gives a beautifully restrained performance of Fauntleroy – a cross between Harpo Marx and Danny Kaye" (*NI* 4.3.1955). He risked comparison with everyone's personal image of Phil Archer in a stage version of the popular radio series *The Archers*. Within weeks in autumn 1955 he rang the changes from Captain Absolute in *The Rivals* to Able Seaman (Haggis) McIntosh in the hugely successful *Seagulls Over Sorrento* and from Fritz Wendel in John van Druten's *I Am A Camera* to Will Scarlet in *Babes in the Wood*.

Like Brown Hawthorne scored a personal success in an Anouilh piece, Christopher Fry's gossamer adaptation of *L'Invitation au Chateau*, *Ring Around the Moon* in the twin-roles of Hugo and Frederic:

In a vast, grotesque winter garden, like a private Crystal Palace, and at the centre of a collection of wonderfully mad people we find Hugo, a violet-gloved blue-blooded young man about town (Nigel Hawthorne), who by means of a carefully-staged party, is planning a complicated intrigue involving his sad soulful brother (a very different Hawthorne) a millionaire's daughter . . . and the millionaire's strident mistress. (*C&E* 24.1.1956)

Although the material at his disposal was precariously thin "Mr. Nigel Hawthorne, playing the dual role of the twin brothers with fine versatility . . . [was able] to collect acting honours" (*NI* 27.1.1956).

In later life Hawthorne testified to the excellent training he gained in repertory and recalled that "the standard achieved was quite high".[7]

Clearly the established company in the 1950s contained some notable developing talents, but nevertheless it was a recurrent policy to invite stars to augment it from time to time. No doubt this was partly conceived as an antidote to television which brought performers of the highest rank into the viewers' sitting-room.

It was apt that Freda Jackson and Sonia Dresdel, who had both established their reputations in Northampton in the 1930s, should return. In May 1954 Freda Jackson headed an all-female cast in *Women of Twilight* by Sylvia Rayman. In 1945 Miss Jackson had scored a personal triumph as Mrs. Voray in *No Room at the Inn* first at the Embassy Theatre and then at the Winter Garden. As one of her obituarists observed: "after her memorably repellent performance as Mrs. Voray she found herself doomed to specialise in harridans and sluts" (*Daily Telegraph* 23.10.1990). Nearly ten years after *No Room at the Inn* Sylvia Rayman sought to tap this vein yet again:

> Recalling her part in "No Room at the Inn" Miss Jackson uses every ounce of her fine histrionic talent to portray a woman who runs a "home" for young unmarried mothers and exploits her charges with diabolical cunning concealed under a suave, self-righteous exterior. This woman's cruelty is unbounded and Miss Jackson builds up a character which fascinates with its horror and repulsion. (*NI* 4.6.1954)

Box office returns of £740 with a profit of £129 testified to the appeal of this particular star.

When Freda Jackson returned to Northampton in July 1955 her choice of Marguerite Gautier in a new version of *The Lady of the Camellias* by Phyllis Hartnoll (editor of *The Oxford Companion to the Theatre*) indicated a desire to avoid stereotyping:

> in the leading part of Marguerite Gautier Freda Jackson presents us with a facet of her acting ability of which one had almost forgotten the existence. And although some vestiges of the virago still lingered in the first scene she

Photographed in later life Aubrey Dyas Perkins and John Bennett, who both joined the board in 1954 and subsequently served as chairman

The Eagle Has Two Heads by Jean Cocteau 1960. Sonia Dresdel as The Queen. (Bryan Douglas Collection)

shows us in this play that she can give a softer kind of part its full measure. (*C&E* 26.7.1955)

Perhaps Northampton audiences preferred the Freda they knew: box office returns showed sizable losses (week one £502, loss £142; week two £437, loss £217), but the midsummer timing of this production cannot have helped.

A further return in December 1959 was clearly intended to remedy the fact that "in recent months audiences have not flocked to see the Rep.'s strongest offerings". As Yvonne in Jean Cocteau's *Intimate Relations*, first seen in England at the Arts Theatre in 1951, Freda Jackson, in more familiar vein, "makes . . . the possessive and sick mother, an alarmingly unpredictable character. There can be few dramatic actresses on the English stage today who could extract so much from a part such as this. Miss Jackson makes it starkly effective, moving and, above all, exciting" (*C&E* 1.12.1959).

Sonia Dresdel chose lighter fare when she appeared as Maria Kararez, a retired opera singer, in *Come Live With Me* by Dorothy and Campbell Christie. As the "mercurial . . . temperamental, excitable yet always lovable woman" Miss Dresdel had "a made to measure part" in which she "exploits to the full her versatility and keen sense of comedy" (*NI* 8.2.1957). This exploitation was to good effect at the box office (£703, a profit of £85 which exactly matched Miss

Dresdel's fee). In May 1960 Sonia Dresdel followed in the footsteps of Tallulah Bankhead and Eileen Herlie as The Queen in Jean Cocteau's *The Eagle Has Two Heads*.

Other star visitors included Anona Winn in R. F. Delderfield's *The Orchard Walls* in May 1954; Avril Angers in Garson Kanin's American comedy *Born Yesterday* in June 1955 (box office £524, loss of £69); Binnie Hale in Royce Ryton's *Make Believe* in August 1956 (£690, profit £77); Leslie Henson in Rex Frost's *Small Hotel* in April 1957 (£665, profit £18 despite Henson's £100 fee) and Ralph Lynn in E. V. Tidmarsh's *Is Your Honeymoon Really Necessary?* in June 1957 (£728, profit £114). In March 1958 Frankie Howerd appeared as Freddie Cavendish, who is entrusted with the robot Ermyntrude (Sarah Whalley) the invention of Professor Belmon (Edwin Apps), in Wallace Geoffrey's and Basil Mitchell's *The Perfect Woman*. Howerd, already a veteran of the Palladium and recently seen at the Old Vic as Bottom, cut a rather lugubrious figure off-stage: "He was gloomy, and his ancient boxer dog was even more gloomy" recalled Janet Hargreaves, a member of the cast. But onstage "Frankie is a Riot":

> For the fun flows fast, and, at times, positively furiously as Mr. Howerd, with the backing of a team which plays up to him most unselfishly throughout, extracts every ounce from this most broad of farces. (*C&E* 25.3.1958)

Audiences responded well (week one £736, profit £91; week two £789, profit £143). Howerd's fee was £150, plus 20 per cent of box office over £1,400 (BM 4.2.1958).

Clearly stars did not come to Northampton to immerse themselves, rather less publicly than in London, in the new wave of so-called "kitchen-sink" drama. *Look Back in Anger* reached Northampton in October 1957 with Peter Wyatt as Jimmy Porter and Willis Hall's *The Long and the Short and the Tall* was staged in October 1959 with a cast which included Timothy West as the Japanese Soldier. That production also played a week at the Palace Theatre (Cinema), Wellingborough where, West recalled, "there were no dressing rooms and some of the all-male cast had to change in the ladies' lavatory".[8]

On the whole the Northampton repertoire still tended towards the french-windows rather than the kitchen-sink, but lest the worth of such work be dismissed out-of-hand the words of the then Secretary-General of the Arts Council Sir William Emrys Williams, writing in 1959, should be quoted:

> I write to say how much I enjoyed my evening at *Dear Charles* [by Alan Melville]. I see a good deal of the work of Repertory Theatres, and I can truly say that it is a long time since I was as deeply impressed by the presentation and acting of a play as I was last night at the Northampton Repertory. I know what difficulties you work under, yet that performance revealed no signs whatever of hastiness or rush. I think you have some exceptionally good talent in your company.[9]

The choice of plays, like the engagement of stars and the permanent company, had to be seen against the abiding backcloth of repertory theatre in Northampton – the need to survive. Press reports in March 1958 indicated just how strained the theatre's finances had become. A sixpence increase in seat prices was announced to counter costs which had risen from £31,500 in 1954 to £34,100 in 1957, "last year's costs work out at about £650 a week" (*C&E* 13.3.1958). The Arts Council calculated the weekly cost of running a repertory theatre at £550 in 1952 (AR 1951–2) rising to £589 in 1954 (AR 1953–4) by which time the weekly loss was £12 compared with a profit of £11 on a weekly expenditure of £255 in 1939.

During the 1950s the Northampton Repertory Players lived a hand-to-mouth existence. In the annual report dated 2 December 1952 (for the year ended 29.3.1952) H. Musk Beattie, director-secretary, reported:

> The lack of success at Kettering and the unexpected heavy loss at Northampton caused a crisis which gave the Board considerable anxiety. The crisis was surmounted by a magnificent gesture on the part of Mrs. Irene Butlin who came forward with a gift of £4,000 which relieved the Company of its immediate financial troubles.[10]

Mrs. Butlin's munificence is put into perspective when it is recalled that she was the major beneficiary of her father's £383,335 estate when Frank Panther died in 1944 (*NI* 3.11.1944).

In 1953 Mrs. Butlin paid half (of £3,000) for new stage lighting and in 1954 she lent the theatre £1,500 and "generously guaranteed the Company's Bank Account for a further £1,500 and supported this by a Deed of Covenant for seven years in the sum of £250 per annum. Without this help the activities of the Company could not have carried on" (A.G.M. 29.12.1954). The report, dated 28 November 1955, recorded the gift of "an extremely handsome drop curtain" by Mrs. Butlin and the Arts Council's contribution of £375 "towards the cost of providing combined bus and theatre tickets". The Arts Council's scheme had no doubt significantly enhanced attendance which had amounted to over 190,000 with "the highest box office revenue in the company's history", but this income was still unequal to the rising costs of running the theatre.

In February 1956 Aubrey Dyas Perkins presented the company's appeal against rates at the local valuation court. He submitted that the rates paid in 1955 amounting to £867 8s. 6d. were excessive, pointing out that:

> In 1951–2 there was a loss of £1,582; in 1952–3 a loss of £354; in 1953–4 a loss of £18; and in 1954–5 a loss of £415 – a total loss over four years of £2,369. (*C&E* 15.2.1956)

In effect the theatre had survived thanks to Mrs. Butlin. Nevertheless the appeal was turned down.

The mid-1950s were a watershed in the history of English theatre. Plays like *Look Back in Anger* introduced a radical new generation of writers, actors and directors who demanded a system very different from the minimum risk commercialism which had prevailed hitherto. Also in 1956 cheek by jowl with the Royal Court production of *Look Back in Anger* came the first visit to London by Brecht's Berliner Ensemble which opened English eyes not only to the artistic innovations of that company, but also to the resources which it enjoyed in terms of state subsidy. Entertainment tax on live theatre was abolished from 5 May 1957. Gradually local authorities were implementing their powers under the 1948 Act and the Arts Council, initially principally through its ticket/transport scheme, was assuming a growing role as the major subsidiser of culture. These developments could not ensure the survival of all theatres; there was, indeed there needed to be, a large-scale winnowing of the worthy from the worthless; closures were the order of the day. In neighbouring Leicester the Theatre Royal closed in 1957 leaving a city with a population of 300,000 theatreless. In 1959 at least twenty-seven theatres closed.[11] Television, especially after the opening of the Independent (commercial) network on 28 September 1955, was obviously a major contributory factor.

The two live theatres in Northampton remained the property of the Northampton Theatre Syndicate. During the mid-1950s the company managed to return a modest surplus: £1,385 for 1953 and £1,250 for 1954, but the death of Sir John Brown in April 1958 precipitated a crisis which was impending anyway. The New Theatre staged what was to be its last show (*Strip! Strip! Hooray!*) in August 1958 and early in 1960 the demolition men moved in.[12]

The foreseeable demise of the Northampton Theatre Syndicate (a liquidator was appointed in February 1960) and the prospect that Northampton's proud achievement of over thirty continuous years of repertory was in peril served to galvanise the local authority into action.

A special sub-committee of Northampton Borough Council's Finance and General Purposes Committee met at the Guildhall on 20 January 1959. Those present received reports from the Borough Architect, the Borough Treasurer and the Chief Fire Officer.[13] The import of these reports was that the Northampton Repertory Players (with total reserves of £1,107) could not afford to buy the theatre, indeed its immediate aim was to "spend an additional £2,000 per annum on salaries with a view to giving artistes a reasonable remuneration and to safeguard the standard of performance". The general condition of the building was judged to be "good", but "complete internal decoration is necessary" for which the cost was estimated at £6,000. The realistic, and in practice the actual, cost of purchase was put at £15,000, but it was recognised that the rental would have to be reduced and the council would have to support the theatre to the tune of £2,240 annually.

The repertory company's achievements were acknowledged: it "had

Twelfth Night by William Shakespeare 1959.
Lionel Hamilton as Malvolio. (Bryan Douglas Collection)

maintained its income very well . . . in spite of television" and its "expenditure has been well controlled during periods when prices have been rising". The spectre of Northampton contributing to the encircling gloom of theatreless towns was made all the more unacceptable as the fate of the New Theatre was sealed. As Lady Bracknell might have said "To lose one theatre may be regarded as a misfortune; to lose both looks like carelessness."

When the repertory company celebrated the seventy-fifth anniversary of the Royal Theatre and Opera House in May 1959 its survival was not completely assured. *Twelfth Night*, with which Edward Compton's company had opened the theatre in 1884, was revived under Lionel Hamilton's direction. Hamilton also played Malvolio (as he had done to acclaim in 1948) handling "this intensely comic – and yet tragic – character with feeling and a fine sense of fun" (*C&E* 6.5.1959). The strong cast included veterans of previous Shakespeare revivals – Alan Brown "striking the right note" as Orsino and Peter Wyatt "slipping into the role of his unsubtle suitor [Sir Andrew Aguecheek] admirably". Two young guest actresses Jennie Goossens (daughter of the distinguished oboist Leon Goossens) and Ruth Trouncer acquitted themselves well as Viola and Olivia respectively. As ever Osborne Robinson's set rose to the occasion, but the theatre carpenter Bryan Douglas was also to be seen on stage as an Attendant Lord and Second Officer. All were costumed for £50 (BM 10.3.1959).

In the auditorium the cream of Northamptonshire society assembled for the occasion: the Earl (Lord Lieutenant) and Countess Spencer, the chairman of the county council and the deputy-mayor of Northampton were ranged alongside visiting dignitaries (Sir William Emrys Williams from the Arts Council), past members of the company (Freda Jackson) and Fay Compton, daughter of Edward. In a speech from the stage, penned for her by Lionel Hamilton, Miss Compton asked "you the audience, to resolve by your untiring support now and in the future to ensure the continuance of the Opera House's distinguished history".[14]

Rarely can a theatrical anniversary have been so propitious. After such feting it would have been unthinkable for the Royal Theatre and its repertory company to be cast into oblivion. On 19 June 1959 the headlines of the local press read "BORO' MAY BUY REPERTORY THEATRE" (*C&E* 19.6.1959). The details discussed by the sub-committee in January were revealed, including a proposed reduction in rent to £700 annually.

After thirty years of uncertainty the Northampton Repertory Players had reached a well-deserved safe haven, made safer by the total abolition of entertainment tax in the summer of 1960 (*NI* 8.7.1960). By then the company was ensconced at the Playhouse Theatre, Oxford where its season included reprises of the two Cocteau pieces (*The Eagle Has Two Heads* with Sonia Dresdel and *Intimate Relations* with Freda Jackson). From thence it would return to Northampton to take possession of its refurbished home.

Notes

1. Landstone's article, originally published in *Adelphi*, was reported in *The Times* 20.5.1952.

2. Professor Wright's recollections of Northampton in N.C.R.O.

3. These and other box office and profit and loss figures cited in this chapter are from a list compiled by Aubrey Dyas Perkins in N.C.R.O. Although the list also gives amounts for Salaries and Artistes the basis upon which the profit or loss for a given week is arrived at is not clear. Nevertheless the box office figures do give some gauge of audience response.

4. "Nev's Notions – Whiting's Writings" by Nevil Whiting in N.C.R.O.

5. Recollections by Tenniel Evans and Alan Brown in N.C.R.O.

6. Janet Hargreaves's recollections in N.C.R.O.

7. Recollections by Nigel Hawthorne solicited by Lionel Hamilton in N.C.R.O. Hawthorne found the repertory discipline of learning a new part each week valuable training for his television series *Yes (Prime) Minister*.

8. Timothy West's recollections in N.C.R.O.

9. Letter to Lionel Hamilton dated 9.3.1959.

10. This and subsequent annual reports of the Northampton Repertory Players Ltd. in N.C.R.O.

11. See Lou Warwick *Death of a Theatre* 1960, p. 196.

12. Annual report of the Northampton Theatre Syndicate in N.C.R.O. For a full account of the history and closure of the New Theatre see Lou Warwick *Death of a Theatre*.

13. In N.C.R.O.

14. I am indebted to Lionel Hamilton for supplying me with a copy of the speech.

CHAPTER NINE

Promises and Threats 1960–75

DURING the fifteen years between 1960 and 1975 the Northampton Repertory Players learnt the difficult, though by no means original, lesson that those who pay the piper will want to call the tune. The twin fairy godmothers, the Arts Council of Great Britain and the Northampton Borough Council, gradually revealed themselves as exacting taskmasters. No suspicion of this was apparent in the lines, penned by Lionel Hamilton, spoken by Sir Gyles Isham, who had enjoyed a distinguished stage career before the war,[1] at the re-opening of the refurbished Royal Theatre on 6 September 1960. A splendid figure in full-bottomed wig and dashing Carolinian costume Sir Gyles declaimed:

Not Kings, as in our Charles' day
Assume the role of patrons here,
But Mayor and Corporation near
O'er this our House extend their sway.

What kindly overlords are these
That give full freedom to our Band
Their art to practice; understand
Their aim remains the Town to please.[2]

The curtain then rang up on Lionel Hamilton's production of Noel Coward's *This Happy Breed* with Alan Brown as Frank Gibbons.

Whether the body of repertory theatres could be so described in the early 1960s was debatable. The post-war proliferation of repertory companies had contracted and in 1960 the *Stage Yearbook* listed fifty-seven.[3] Commercial repertory had declined rapidly and most of the surviving companies were increasingly dependent on subsidy. As Arthur Brough of the Leas Pavilion, Folkestone put it: "*All* repertory companies must be subsidised either by the State or the local authorities if they are to maintain essential standards."[4] In Northampton weekly running costs were £650, requiring audiences in excess of 3,000 (*C&E* 7.9.1960).

During the 1950s television had been perceived principally as a rival for audiences, but by the 1960s the increasing opportunities of employment which it

Gala re-opening of the Royal Theatre in September 1960.
L-R Lord Hesketh, Major-General E. D. Fanshaw (High Sheriff), Lady Hesketh, Mrs. Fanshaw, W. H. Fox and Mrs. Fox (*C&E* 7.9.1960).

was offering to actors were making it difficult for repertory theatres to attract and retain a permanent company of quality. Quality was crucial as audiences could now compare the fare at their local theatre with two channels of entertainment available to them in their own homes. The supply of plays was also a problem. Longer runs in the West End reduced the flow of West End successes which could be brought on stream by repertory companies. The new school of "kitchen-sink" drama did not readily commend itself to the majority of provincial playgoers.

The widespread introduction of fortnightly repertory answered some of the problems. The grind of weekly repertory would have been an even less attractive alternative to television for actors. The two week run gave more time for rehearsal and thereby facilitated the achievement of higher standards. It also reduced the sheer quantity of plays needed to sustain a season.

Northampton finally, though initially only experimentally, introduced fortnightly repertory in August 1961:

It will mean an even higher standard of productions and a greater choice of plays, seeing that we shall have to find only 24 plays as against 40 . . . it removes that sense of urgency from our Director of Productions, and enables him to delve below the surface of the play and to attain a higher standard than he is able under the present system. (PR 19.6.1961)

117

In October 1961 author and critic Richard Findlater "had the pleasure of visiting what must surely be one of the most attractive, hospitable and best-run rep-theatres in the country". The play was Somerset Maugham's *The Noble Spaniard* "a curious period piece" (1909) which "makes rather confused demands on style which not everyone in the Northampton company can satisfy". Nevertheless his verdict was that "although the playing was at times uneven, the general standard was high – not 'considering . . .', but just plain high – under Lionel Hamilton's direction" (*Time and Tide* 26.10.1961). Findlater expressed anxiety that "Northampton's fortnightly experiment is in danger, because the company hasn't succeeded (in effect) in doubling its audience, and funds are pitifully low." He castigated the Chancellor of the Exchequer (Selwyn Lloyd) for reneging on his promise of the previous March to give more cash to repertory theatres and though he conceded that at 4s. 6d. the best seats were "a bargain" he doubted whether audiences would pay more.[5] *The Noble Spaniard* lost £113 on gross receipts of £1,154 (BM 31.10.1961).

By the spring of 1962 Lionel Hamilton observed that "People are beginning to realise now that the plays are on for two weeks and the theatre is filling up for the second week" (*C&E* 13.4.1962). In August he stated that "the standard of the plays produced has been maintained at a level not possible to reach under the breakneck pressure of weekly performance" and drew attention to a "better balance of plays" and "the younger element in the audience" (*C&E* 10.8.1962).

In fact every extension of the standard run raises the stakes for the selection of plays. The wrong choice for a fortnight is literally twice as disastrous as for a week, and so on. The fortnightly repertoire was still essentially cautious with Agatha Christie, John Chapman and Hugh and Margaret Williams alongside Oscar Wilde, Sheridan and Robert Bolt (*The Tiger and the Horse* in October 1961 and *A Man for All Seasons* in the following month).

Occasionally a production sustained a longer run as did Julian Slade's *Salad Days*, which ran for three weeks from the end of January 1962 and returned for a further two from 26 March. Such flexibility was very much in the spirit of the founding principles of repertory as well, of course, as making good financial sense. Nevertheless despite the success of *Salad Days* the year in which the fortnightly experiment had been introduced showed a loss of £624 (AR 1961–2).[6]

The board's commitment to fortnightly repertory was vindicated in the first full year:

> This radical change in policy would appear to have been justified by the fact that Box Office Receipts were not only maintained but increased. (AR 1962–3)

The cost of running the theatre was up by £5,618 but the nett surplus was £1,925.

A Passage to India, Anouilh's *The Rehearsal* and *The Rivals* provided ballast, but the key to success seemed to be "Murder" in the title – Agatha Christie's

Murder at the Vicarage, Simon Amberley's *Murder at Quay Cottage* and Frederick Knott's *Write Me A Murder.* The productions of the first two were entrusted to Kenneth Loach, the theatre's trainee director under a scheme financed by A.B.C. television. Loach also appeared as an actor (Mr. Burton-Fletcher in *A Passage to India* and Stanley Littlefield in *Guilty Party*), but he found his forte in a summer revue *All of A Twist* devised by Lionel Hamilton and himself in June 1962. The revue comprised sketches and short plays (Pinter's *Trouble in the Works,* John Mortimer's *Triangle*) performed by the resident company (Loach, Alan Brown, Jonathan Adams). Audiences were small (box office £1,175, loss £410 BM 10.7.1962), but the show "hung together well and changes of mood and tempo were smooth" (*C&E* 20.6.1962) - all good experience for Loach whose subsequent credits included the satirical television programme *That Was The Week That Was.*

Balancing the theatre's books was still like walking a tightrope. The annual report revealed that the first six months of 1963-4 had resulted in a deficit of £4,200 with such standbys as *The Circle* and *Rebecca* failing to draw audiences, but the situation was retrieved by the success of *A Christmas Carol, Robinson Crusoe* and Julian Slade's *Free as Air* and a surplus of £171 was shown on the year - a remarkable turnaround. Of course all surpluses (and deficits) were now inclusive of subsidies, without which the transition from weekly repertory could not have been achieved. The Arts Council grant was stable at £5,500 for 1962-3 and 1963-4, in addition to which the theatre made effective use of the transport subsidy scheme, designed to ease the costs for outlying audiences. Thus a travel grant of £750 "brought 13,000 more people to the theatre and an extra £3,000 to the box office" (*C&E* 18.10.1962). This form of incentive funding reflected the continuing emphasis on earned income. The national average for each £1 received by repertory theatres was 12s. 9d. through box office, 5s. 10d. from the Arts Council, a mere 1s. 1d. from local authorities and 4d. from other sources (*C&E* 18.10.1962). Despite the provisions of the 1948 Act local authorities were still making only a modest contribution, though Northampton Borough Council had agreed to make a grant of "a sum not exceeding £1,000" for 1963-4. The value of the A.B.C. Television trainee director bursary (in which Ronald Hayman succeeded Loach) was £750.

The transition to fortnightly repertory had coincided with a change in the chairmanship of the board. W. H. Fox resigned in February 1961; his expertise was recognised by his appointment to the drama panel of the Arts Council. He was succeeded by Aubrey Dyas Perkins. In September 1963 Lionel Hamilton resigned after seventeen years' association with the theatre, the last seven as director of productions. The theatre had been without the services of Osborne Robinson during 1962-3 when he was teaching at Vanderbilt University in the United States. Oliver Bayldon and John Page were scenic designers in his absence.

The new director of productions was Keith Andrews, who was appointed, from a field of fifty-four applicants at an annual salary of £1,250 (BM 22.7.1963). He came from the Marlowe Theatre, Canterbury, having trained at the Old Vic School and gained extensive repertory experience as an actor (*Stage* 22.8.1963). Andrews's impact on the repertory company during his two years in Northampton was salutary. Dyas Perkins in his annual report for 1964–5 identified "three vitally important spheres":

> In the first place, the plays were more diverse and of higher quality. Secondly, the Company of players was much stronger and better equipped than for some time. Thirdly, the support of the public responding to these two factors increased substantially.

Andrews combined Coward, Brighouse and Douglas Home with Shaffer, Shaw and Shakespeare; he assembled a company of actors whose talents and range were equal to this diversity. In November 1963 Joy Stewart, John Downing, Jonathan Adams, Kenneth Gilbert and Janet Henfry combined for a "first-rate" (*Stage* 24.11.1963) revival of Coward's *Present Laughter*.

Northampton rose to the challenge of Shakespeare's quatercentenary with the enterprising and apposite choice of *King John*. The Royal Theatre's stage "was enlarged with an Elizabethan apron which brought the action right out to, and almost among the audience". Osborne's Robinson's designs were supplemented with costumes from Stratford, but it was the quality of the acting that principally ensured success. Kenneth Gilbert as King John "thundered his wrath throughout the play; and his remorseless ambition gripped players and audience alike". As Constance Pauline Letts's "bursts of agony, as she cried aloud for 'her boy, her joy, her life, her widow's comfort and her sorrow's cure' was the most moving expression of a mother's sorrow that I have seen" (*C&E* 7.5.1964). Anthony Brown's Bastard ("a gentleman, Born in Northamptonshire") swaggered "with all the brash self-confidence of a son of Coeur de Lion" and the rest of the cast rose to the occasion magnificently: "It is a thousand pities that this notable production should be running for less than a fortnight" (*Stage* 14.5.1964). Although "witnessed by almost 5,000 people" the production resulted in a loss of £1,589 (AR 1964–5), but it was a notable *succès d'estime*.

David Tomlinson returned to Northampton in September 1964 to appear in a thin comedy *Trouble with Father* (his weekly fee was £100 BM 24.8.1964). By then the company had been augmented by the talents of Angela Down, Beth Harris and Ian Ogilvie all of whom appeared to advantage in a "first rate" production of Helen Jerome's adaptation of *Pride and Prejudice*, splendidly set by Osborne Robinson:

> *Pride and Prejudice* is a triumph for scenic designer Osborne Robinson. His settings are spectacular and make a fine background for the elegant

King Lear by William Shakespeare 1965. Kenneth Gilbert as Lear and James Wellman as the Fool. (Bryan Douglas Collection)

costumes of both men and women made in the theatre workshop by Emily Tuckley. (*Stage* 22.10.1964)

Over Christmas 1964 and the New Year audiences flocked in to see *Great Expectations*, *Aladdin* and *The Boy Friend* to a total of 37,000 patrons . . . "during the period 1st April 1964 to the end of March 1965, over 15,000 more persons paid for admission than during the similar period the previous year" (AR 1964–5). The year showed a surplus of £1,903, despite the fact that it included a second Shakespearean production *King Lear* in March 1965, though the loss for that (£509) was much more modest than for *King John*.

To cast *King Lear* from a repertory company is a formidable undertaking. Kenneth Gilbert as Lear portrayed "the petulant old man with a force which gains momentum as the play proceeds" (*Stage* 18.3.1965). James Wellman's Fool "was outstanding, just the right composition of wisdom and comedy" (*C&E* 10.3.1965); John Ringrose gave "a depth of feeling and sensitivity to his part of Gloucester" and Angela Down played "Cordelia with understanding and compassion" (*Stage*). The rest of the large cast (Paul Darrow as Edmund, Bill Johnston as Edgar, Jonathan Adams as Albany, Beth Harris as Goneril, Judy Dickinson as Regan down to Marcia Warren as a Lady-in-Waiting) acquitted themselves excellently: "This is Rep. in top gear – a piece of teamwork of which director Keith Andrews, keeping it fast [2½ hours] and taut, can feel justly proud" (*Stage*).

The respected critic Gareth Lloyd Evans hailed the "intelligent acting" and the "set of classical formality", which as for *King John* incorporated an apron stage – "At Northampton 'King Lear' is triumphantly Shakespearean . . . first-class" (*Manchester Guardian* 15.3.1965).

The principle of diversity was honoured with the next production, Agatha Christie's *Spider's Web*, which was followed by William Douglas Home's *The Reluctant Peer* which demonstrated the company's versatility:

> Kenneth Gilbert's Lord Cleghorn is a musical comedy lord; Marcia Warren plays his talkative wife well . . . Jonathan Adams . . . scores a parting success as the true-blue butler, Beecham. (*Stage* 15.4.1965)

When the National Council for Civic Theatres advanced a scheme for a theatre circuit Northampton was, naturally enough, included (*The Times* 5.5.1965), but shortly afterwards Beth Harris and Kenneth Gilbert announced their departures and much more critically Keith Andrews resigned in June to take up an appointment with A.B.C. Television (*Stage* 1.7.1965). Looking back on his short time in Northampton Andrews said that he had tried "to offer audiences a greater variety of good plays" though recognising that "Progress . . . is to a great extent dictated by what the audience will turn out to see" (*C&E* 18.6.1965). In the diversity of his play selection Andrews recognised that in a town of the size of Northampton the (only) theatre had to cater for a range of tastes. The quality of his work encouraged audiences to extend their playgoing beyond their usual preferences. In his all too brief two years in Northampton Andrews enlarged Northampton's capacity to respond to its theatre. In so far as any repertory producer can discover the elixir of success, Andrews had done so.

The fragility of any such formula was demonstrated during the following year when the theatre's place on the wheel of fortune was so dramatically reversed. "After consideration with the Arts Council of Great Britain the Board appointed Alan Vaughan Williams" (AR 1965–6), a Welshman who had begun his career at the Dublin Gate Theatre and subsequently worked in film and repertory, latterly in Lincoln (*C&E* 17.6.1965; *Stage* 1.7.1965). Only three members of Andrews's company remained (Paul Darrow, Bill Johnston and Marcia Warren) and Williams clearly had his own ideas about the sort of theatre he wanted to run.

On paper his choice of plays was not particularly innovative: Coward, Cooney and Christie still held their places, though Miller, Joan Littlewood, Albee, Anouilh (*Poor Bitos*), Behan and Thomas Dekker also appeared. It was the acting strength of William's productions which caused concern. He placed increasing reliance on guest players. In *Death of a Salesman* "John Justin joining the company . . . makes a very good job of this extremely difficult play", but although the production was "memorable in every respect" the perception of the rest of the cast as "supporting Mr. Justin" was in marked contrast to Andrews's team-work (*Stage* 23.9.1965), as was his fee of £150 (BM 23.8.1965).

With a cast of fourteen Williams mounted *Oh What a Lovely War*, originally staged by Joan Littlewood's Theatre Workshop Company. Maurice Merry provided the music and the cast showed itself equal to song and dance routines to create "definitely one of the best shows I have seen at the Rep" (*M&H* 5.5.1966). In March 1966 "a crowd of real shoemakers' apprentices from Northampton" lent support to "a production of great merit" of Dekker's *The Shoemaker's Holiday* with Sally Mates as the Shoemaker's wife "making shrewishness almost wistful" and Anthony Brown as her husband, making "bickering almost enviable". Williams's production had "racy efficiency" and the set by Osborne Robinson was "not only theatrically viable but a superb demonstration of how to modify Elizabethanism for this century" (Gareth Lloyd Evans in *Manchester Guardian* 3.3.1966). At the end of May Bill Johnston was entrusted with Albee's searing matrimonial drama *Who's Afraid of Virginia Woolf?* with Pauline Letts (Martha), Anthony Brown (George), Marcia Warren (Honey) and Norman Jones (Nick). Losses on these three productions amounted to £2,760 (BM).

The Shoemaker's Holiday by Thomas Dekker 1966.
Anthony Brown as Simon Eyre (the Shoemaker) and Sally Mates as his wife.
(Bryan Douglas Collection)

By then Alan Vaughan Williams's stewardship was a cause of concern. In his annual report for 1965-6 Aubrey Dyas Perkins wrote:

> Amongst other changes were numerous ones in the composition of the Company (which was never strong) through the special engagement of guest players, many for one production only. This gave no stability or continuity and tended to lower the quality of the acting, which on occasion failed to reach the standard customary at this theatre. In consequence there were many complaints from patrons and a serious falling-off of attendances resulting in heavy losses. The Directors felt deeply concerned regarding these aspects of the work of the Theatre, particularly as their recommendations to the Director of Productions went unheeded, even though the Arts Council intervened.

The Arts Council's subsidy had risen to £7,500, which enabled the board to show a surplus of £1,175 on the year.

Vaughan Williams expressed his own views on the theatre in interviews with the local press: "I haven't come here to produce Agatha Christie plays and nothing else. They are not the sort of plays I want to do" (*C&E* 31.3.1966). Nevertheless he conceded that of the fourteen plays he had done to date only five had been in "a serious vein". He considered that "We cater too much at the moment for those who like light comedy" and that the theatre relied "largely on coach parties. We are second in the country for coach parties after the Nottingham Playhouse. The organisers of these parties want light, jolly plays." The irony that as a star performer under the Arts Council's travel subsidy scheme the Northampton repertory theatre had locked itself into lighter rather than more demanding fare is inescapable, even though, as Williams pointed out, the purpose of the Arts Council's subsidy was to increase the ratio of serious plays to potboilers.

Williams returned to these themes in a further, uninhibited interview after his resignation in June 1966. He rejected the idea of compromising "between the artistically adventurous and the commercially viable" and defended his company and guest players. He deplored the lack of support from schools whose attitude was "thirty years out of date", but conceded that the size of Northampton was inevitably an inhibiting factor, compared with say Sheffield (*C&E* 1.6.1966). Mr. Williams moved on to be director-designate of the Greenwich Theatre. The verdict in the professional press was that he had "maintained an admirably venturesome policy at the delightful Guildhall Road theatre while still contriving to make a popular appeal" (*Stage* 16.6.1966).

After its recent failure to make an appropriate appointment the board was understandably cautious when it came to selecting Williams's successor. Initially Willard Stoker took over in a caretaker capacity. Stoker, already aged sixty, had

The Creeper by Pauline Macaulay 1966. Ivan Stafford as Holmes and Nigel Hawthorne as Edward Kimberley.
(Bryan Douglas Collection)

trained at R.A.D.A. and worked extensively in repertory and the commercial theatre as both actor and director. He had served on the Arts Council's drama panel from 1947 to 1950. For ten years he had been resident producer in Liverpool. At the beginning of September 1966, from a field of ninety-three applications, Stoker's appointment was made permanent at an annual salary of £2,000 (BM 5.9.1966).

Although Stoker professed himself "a keen Shakespearean" and fascinated by contemporary drama his basic philosophy was: "It is absolutely no use putting on a series of *avant-garde* plays if you are going to play to empty houses" (*C&E* 6.9.1966) – views which no doubt commended him to the board. With the board's backing Stoker with his undoubted "skill and experience . . . began to tackle the vital task of building up a strong permanent company". The, albeit only brief, return of Nigel Hawthorne (July to October 1966 at a weekly salary of £25 BM 25.7.1966) gave a fillip to the acting strength. His roles included Charles Condomine in *Blithe Spirit*, Arthur Winslow in *The Winslow Boy* and Edward Kimberley in Pauline Macaulay's *The Creeper*.

The Arts Council's role in monitoring its client theatres increased in proportion to the size of its subsidy, which for Northampton rose substantially from £7,500 in 1965-6 to £16,102 in 1966-7. In 1967-8 it went up to £18,882. Northampton Borough Council balanced its grant of £2,150 against its rental of £3,000, but in March 1967 it agreed to a new seventeen year lease.

Willard Stoker dealt effectively with the task of stabilising the theatre's fortunes. In his annual report for 1967-8 Aubrey Dyas Perkins welcomed "the marked all-round improvement", "a talented company" appearing in a diversity of plays, notably a modern dress *She Stoops to Conquer* and Sardou's *Let's Get a Divorce* as well as contemporary pieces such as Donald Howarth's *A Lily in Little India*, Ann Jellicoe's *The Knack* and Robert Thomas's *Trap for a Lonely Man*. Alan Melville appeared in his own play *Top Priority*, which justified extension to a third week. *Boeing-Boeing* (Marc Camoletti/Beverley Cross) having sustained three weeks in February 1967 returned for a further two in August. The first repertory production of the musical *How to Succeed in Business Without Really Trying* held the stage for three weeks early in 1968.

1968-9 showed an increase in box office of nearly £3,000, which helped to ensure that even with running costs at an unprecedented £58,486 there was a healthy surplus of £3,247. Central to this was the Christmas production of *Oliver* the run of which was extended from six to eight weeks to accommodate a total of 33,983 patrons – "the most successful [production] since our Repertory Theatre was launched 42 years ago" (AR 1968-9). Other highlights included Jimmy Thompson, the Scottish comedian, in a special adaptation of Goldoni's *The Servant of Two Masters*, and *Othello*. In *Othello* Michael Harbour, aged only twenty-three, "tackled the role of Iago . . . quite admirably" especially in "the scenes with Othello" (Keith Grenville) which "were conducted with demoniac fury as Iago's evil worked on the mind of the Moor". Sheila Barker was "an open, honest and innocent Desdemona". Osborne Robinson provided "a simple set", using the revolving stage (*C&E* 5.3.1969).

The installation of a revolving stage – initially one loaned from the Belgrade Theatre, Coventry and then a permanent structure at a cost of £1,645 (BM 4.8.1969)[7] was an attempt to update the aging theatre's facilities. In his report *The Arts in Northampton*, published in 1966, Sir William Emrys Williams, formerly long-serving Secretary-General of the Arts Council, had described the Royal Theatre as "this obsolete and inadequate building". Sir William had been

Oliver by Lionel Bart 1968. Gordon Faith as Fagin.
(Bryan Douglas Collection)

engaged "to survey the cultural needs of Northampton" in the context of the town's "proposed expansion . . . to approximately double its present size". In his report Williams recommended the construction of an arts centre, a replacement repertory theatre and a new art gallery and museum. Although Sir William advised against a large concert hall, the debate which led to the Derngate development nearly two decades later was underway.

The revolving stage provided enhanced opportunities for Osborne Robinson and his team, but the facilities for actors remained primitive: "Backstage is a shambles, wholly devoid of the simplest amenities, where the actors are packed into tiny ill-provided dressing-rooms as though they were a bunch of battery hens" (*C&E* 6.1.1967). Standard salaries edged up to a weekly maximum of £30 in 1968 (BM 27.5.1968). Guest players received more: Alan Melville £75, Adam Faith (for *Twelfth Night*) and Jess Conrad (*My Gentleman Pip*) £100 each and Jimmy Thompson £60 plus a percentage of box office takings.

In engaging guest players the theatre was trying to capitalise on the cult of personality which television and the world of popular entertainment promoted, but the other side of the coin was the reluctance of actors to commit themselves to long-term engagements which might prevent them from accepting lucrative offers of television work. The cases of two promising young actors – Michael Harbour and Maria Aitken – serve as examples. In December 1968 the board acceded to a request from Michael Harbour "to be released from his contract in order to take part in a Television Serial. The board approved, subject to Mr. Harbour promising to return to the theatre at the end of his engagement" (BM 2.12.1968). In March 1969 the board decided to cancel two performances of *The Right Honourable Gentleman* "due to Miss Aitken having a television engagement" (BM 10.3.1969). When the company for the autumn 1969 season was being selected the board bowed to the inevitable: "Miss Maria Aitken, Messrs Keith Grenville and Michael Harbour to be engaged whenever they were free and a suitable part available for them" (BM 19.5.1969). The process of erosion of one of repertory's basic principles – the permanent company – was underway.

The board's continuing involvement in what were essentially artistic matters such as the choice of artistes and plays became a source of contention. Certainly there had been little re-casting amongst the ranks of the board. As early as 1966 Lady Hesketh had proposed an increase in the size of the board from seven to nine. She also suggested that "more support" should be sought "from the educational authorities". The response from her fellow directors at the special meeting held to discuss the matter was not encouraging (BM 6.10.1966).

In May 1968 pressure for change came from another quarter, N. V. Linklater, an Arts Council drama officer, who "had expressed his concern that the Board was still understrength, also he warned that due to the financial situation, the Council did not see any hope of an increase in the Grant for the forthcoming year"

(BM 13.5.1968). The linkage of the criticism of the board with the prospects for subsidy could hardly have been fortuitous. Another Arts Council officer (Mr. Croft) reiterated the point in October (7.10.1968) and at the A.G.M. on 20 October Lady Hesketh's proposal for an increase in size to nine was approved, though the extraordinary meeting of the company which was required to make the change did not take place until 5 May 1969.

As a consequence two new directors were appointed – Eric Roberts, journalist and naturalist, and Michael Henley, Chief Education Officer for Northampton Borough Council (and later for Northamptonshire County Council). Clearly Henley's appointment was directly related to the theatre's objective of creating closer links with educational bodies. Alan Vaughan Williams's dismay at the lack of interest forthcoming from local schools was not unique. A youth theatre group had been set up in 1966, but this was essentially a voluntary organisation for individuals. With regard to his production of *The Tempest* in April 1967 Willard Stoker had protested that "not all the schools support such productions as they should", citing the case of one headmaster who said " 'But we always take them [the pupils] to Stratford every year' " (*C&E* 20.4.1967). Two years later "The poor school response for the production of 'Othello' was discussed and it was agreed that better liaison with the schools be discussed" (BM 10.3.1969). It was against this background that Michael Henley's appointment to the board took place.

Progress in forging educational links proved to be slow. For *Romeo and Juliet* in October 1971 one hundred first night tickets were issued free to teachers (BM 4.10.1971). In 1972 six hundred school children attended "The Making of a Play" during which members of the company explained the processes leading to the production of Constance Cox's adaptation of Jane Austen's *Mansfield Park* (*C&E* 25.11.1972). Despite these efforts the "poor attendances from the local schools" persisted for *Much Ado About Nothing*, in February 1973 but "Mr. Henley pointed out that he could not make the children attend performances" (BM 19.2.1973). In April the process was reversed when John Barton's compilation *The Hollow Crown* visited seven schools and was performed before about 1,300 students (*C&E* 7.4.1973). In May 1974 six hundred children attended the theatre for a programme of talks about *The Alchemist* (*C&E* 11.5.1974).

In May 1975 the entire production of *As You Like It*, having played for two weeks in Guildhall Road, was trundled out on six one night stands in schools in Corby, Rushden, Daventry, Wellingborough, Brackley and Weston Favell. The venture was organised by the theatre and the district councils, co-ordinated by the County Council's Leisure and Amenities Department. It was the product of bureaucratic aggrandizement rather than genuine need or demand. Willard Stoker, who had already announced his retirement, denounced the whole scheme:

129

> I think the idea was nonsense . . . The audiences we have had so far could
> have filled the gallery at one matinee. It is all political – an attempt to
> impress the Arts Council. It makes me angry because it is a gross waste of
> time, talent and ratepayers' money. (*C&E* 13.5.1975)

The folly of the *As You Like It* tour was symptomatic of what had been happening
to the repertory theatre over the preceding five years, during which it had come
under increasing pressure from the Arts Council and the agencies of local
government.

The Redcliffe–Maud Report of the Royal Commission on Local Government
changed the map of local politics, but in Northampton the creation of the
Development Corporation in 1968 had signalled that large-scale expansion and
change were underway. As early as November 1966 Osborne Robinson had
alerted the board to plans for a new theatre in the town (BM 21.11.1966). On 27
October 1969 the board meeting was preceded by one with Sir William Hart,
chairman of the Development Corporation: "In view of the information given by
him, consideration should be given to submitting plans for the improvement of
the present building rather than the construction of a new theatre" (BM). The
accidental demolition of the canopy at the front of the theatre by a lorry in
September 1969 seemed like an ill omen.

In 1970 a report entitled *The Theatre Today in England and Wales* was
published by the Arts Council presenting the findings of its Committee of
Enquiry under the chairmanship of Sir William Emrys Williams, who had been so
scathing about the Royal Theatre in 1966. Chapter IV "The Subsidised Theatre
Outside London" dealt with the fifty-two repertory companies funded by the
Arts Council on an average ratio of twenty-five per cent subsidy to seventy-five
per cent box office. Although it rejected the idea of a league table of theatres the
report made a distinction between the seven "three star theatres" and the rest.
Northampton was most emphatically amongst "the rest". The surge of new
theatre buildings in the 1960s (Guildford, Nottingham, Chichester etc), which
continued into the 1970s, encouraged the belief that good work was synonymous
with new buildings and inferior work with old ones. Northampton was singled out
for particular attention:

> We regret that one of the oldest established of the supported theatres is not
> in running for a new theatre. The Northampton Royal Theatre and Opera
> House is a handsome old theatre, but, like many old things, the building,
> particularly bad back-stage, is now worn out and should be replaced.
> (p. 36)

Apart from its demolition job on the old theatres the report also addressed itself to
funding:

The future of the theatre outside London will be mainly determined by the local authorities. Their partnership with the Arts Council is certainly stronger than it used to be, but their level of patronage still falls far short of what was envisaged in the Local Government Act of 1948. (p. 42)

Appendix C giving financial statistics for 1968–9 revealed that Northampton's Arts Council subsidy remained at just over £18,000 (3s. 2d. per seat sold) and its local authority grant at £2,650 (more than offset by the rental). With Arts Council subventions to the "three star theatres" in the range of £45–£50,000, Northampton was bracketed with Canterbury, Colchester, Leatherhead and Watford – modest company given its illustrious past.

Necessity and policy therefore combined to direct the Northampton Repertory Players to solicit support from the local authorities and Aubrey Dyas Perkins dutifully wrote to them. In his annual report for 1971–2 he recounted:

A Special Memorandum was prepared dealing with our work, general policy, Board of Management, attendances, finances and achievements. This appeal was submitted to 25 councils in Northamptonshire, Buckinghamshire, Bedfordshire and Warwickshire. The response was truly enheartening . . . The total sum received amounted to £4,275.

Northamptonshire County Council contributed £1,000, but Northampton Borough Council reduced its grant. The Arts Council, probably in recognition of these efforts, increased its subsidy to £21,500. By then inflation, the scourge of the 1970s, had increased expenditure by £13,279 in two years, so without these grants the modest surplus of £766 for 1972–3 would have been a considerable deficit.

The Northampton Repertory Players' instinct for survival was as keen as ever, but they now found themselves under pressure from the very quarter which had traditionally been supportive. In June 1973 N. V. Linklater, by then Arts Council drama officer, attended a board meeting at which he levelled several severe criticisms at the theatre:

Mr. Linklater was critical of the choice of plays . . . [he] stated that the Council considered that the Board "has lost its impulse and was in a rut" . . . Referring to the grant given to the theatre by Northampton Corporation, Mr. Linklater said that this was only 0.04 of one penny [new pence], and he felt that the Local Authority should do more to help the theatre. In view of the re-organisation of Local Government, he urged the Board to make a new application to the Local Authority immediately for an increased grant. (BM 25.6.1973)

Thus one erstwhile fairy godmother pushed the Northampton Repertory Players into the clutches of another, whose response was no more reassuring.

During February 1974 the local press abounded in reports that the Royal Theatre was to be demolished to make way for a great new entertainment complex. The Leisure and Recreation Advisory Committee of the newly constituted Northampton Borough Council had prepared a report on the development of an arts complex for consideration by the Town Expansion Committee. John Poole, chairman of the Advisory Committee, moderated the rumours by pointing to recent developments in Bristol, where the historic Theatre Royal auditorium had been preserved, but encased in new front of house and backstage facilities. The theatre board and such doughty supporters as Dr. Ernest Reynolds weighed in to defend "tooth and nail . . . this delicious Victorian playhouse" (*C&E* 18.2.1974). In the event the final report recommended the retention of the Royal Theatre auditorium within new facilities for the arts, but the theatre board remained vigilant in protecting its premises: "The Board of Management is unanimous in its desire to maintain the auditorium of the theatre" (BM 25.4.1974).

Although the future of the Royal Theatre seemed to be secure that of the company occupying it was still uncertain. Clearly the Arts Council was pressing hard for more local government involvement and the Northampton Borough Council, encouraged by the Development Corporation, saw a much more proactive role for itself. In June 1974 Aubrey Dyas Perkins reported on a meeting at which "Councillor Dilleigh stated that a recommendation to the Council to give the theatre a grant of £15,000 was under consideration" (BM 3.6.1974). Even larger sums (£20,000 and £30,000) had been mentioned, but progress was slow. A statement of policy was requested from the board, but the kernel of the matter was revealed in September 1974 when "The question of representation of Members of the District and Borough Councils on the Theatre Board was raised" (BM 23.9.74) – the principle was no ratepayers' money without representation. In the meantime the company's finances were deteriorating and approaches to the borough council brought no response until November when £3,000 was received.

In March 1975 the board, whose membership by then included Lou Warwick and John Kelly, considered Northampton Borough Council's proposals "to increase the number of Directors to 15 and allow a representation of 5 from the Council . . . To seek space for the theatre in the building adjacent to the Theatre" (BM 17.3.1975). On 11 April 1975 at an extraordinary meeting of the company the increase to fifteen directors was agreed. At the annual general meeting on 20 October five borough councillors were formally elected to the board, but "Mr. Aubrey Dyas Perkins did not seek re-election as Chairman". He was succeeded by John Bennett.

Mr. Perkins in fact resigned from the board altogether. The concluding years of his chairmanship had been as fraught as any in the company's history. He had had to contend with pressure from the Arts Council and Northampton Borough Council. For a time it looked as though the very building he had cherished for so long might be demolished. The effects of inflation were biting hard and his long-serving director of productions was approaching retirement. In April 1975 Northampton, which in 1961 had been included by Richard Findlater amongst his "Pick of the Reps", was the subject of sneering indictment in the magazine *Plays and Players*:

NORTHAMPTON REP, like the Northampton Town FC, is in the 4th Division and hence perpetually afraid of having to seek re-election. The recent sharp increase in costs and salaries has forced the theatre to endanger its box office returns by pushing up seat prices, the dearest seats by 30 per cent, the cheapest by over 50 per cent. Like so many other old-fashioned reps presenting revivals and recent West End successes, Northampton can't afford to go after the audiences that might ensure survival – in any case, it's doubtful whether the audience is there to be gone after.

In reply Aubrey Dyas Perkins pointed out that:

In the past year or so, we have staged Ben Jonson's *The Alchemist*, John Dryden's *Marriage à la Mode* (both rarely performed), *As You Like It*, *The Cherry Orchard*, *A Man for All Seasons*, *The Hollow Crown*, *Butley*, *Equus* in addition to four new plays.

It is also untrue that the increase in seat prices has endangered our box office returns since overall attendances are higher than during the similar period last year. (*Plays and Players* June 1975)

In his annual report for 1974-5 Mr. Perkins acknowledged that for the first time in the theatre's history seat prices had been increased twice in the same year, but the result was a £10,000 increase in box office income. This together with subsidies (Arts Council £28,500, Northampton Borough Council £15,350, other councils £3,000) had resulted in a surplus of £11,302. In fact Northampton Repertory Players had returned a loss in only three of Aubrey Dyas Perkins's fourteen years as chairman. Financial wellbeing is the chairman's overriding concern, but in Mr. Perkins's case this was balanced by a clear perception of what constituted a successful company – a varied selection of well-chosen plays, a strong permanent company and, as a result, good audience support and a buoyant box office income.

In fact as Perkins observed in his riposte to *Plays and Players* the theatre's repertoire had recently included many notable plays. Admittedly there had been some disasters too: Beatrix Carter's *Murder on Tape* was dismissed as "Agatha Christie given away with trading stamps on a bad day at the sale"

133

(*M&H* 23.8.1973) and Willard Stoker's own play *If It's Edna I'm Out* contained "a great deal of very loose writing . . . with a typically graceful gesture Mr. Stoker has placed the production of his play in the more than capable hands of Henry Knowles" (*M&H* 25.10.1973). One wonders whether Knowles perceived his task in those terms. However even amongst the lighter fare Stoker showed a deft hand with some of the better examples: *Boeing-Boeing* (February and August 1967), *Not Now Darling* (November 1970), *The Amorous Prawn* (April 1972) and *There's A Girl In My Soup* (October 1972).

True to the theatre's principles of offering a wide range of plays Stoker did not flinch from challenging work. In October 1969 he tackled O'Casey's *The Plough and the Stars* which "could hardly have been produced at a more opportune moment", or so it seemed then (*M&H* 2.10.1969). John Bott gave a creditable performance as Fluther Good, but the old problem of inappropriate casting surfaced with Michael ffoulkes's Peter Flynn, for which he was too young. In *Lady Windermere's Fan* Maria Aitken, who had charmed as the Hon. Gwendoline Fairfax in *The Importance of Being Earnest* in October 1968, jumped a generation to play the mysterious Mrs. Erlynne, and "her commanding appearance had the audience spellbound" (*M&H* 13.11.1969).

The sets for *The Plough and the Stars* and *Lady Windermere's Fan* were the work of Hugh Durrant. Osborne Robinson's personal distinction and long service to the theatre had been recognised by his appointment to the Arts Council drama panel in 1967 (BM 2.2.1967) and the award of the O.B.E. in June 1969. During the 1969–70 season he was at Stanford University in California as Guest Lecturer in Drama and Design. Hugh Durrant made a "stunning debut" with a style very different from Robinson's. His sets for *The Plough and the Stars* were "simple and crude, they grimly reflected the sad existence of tenement tenants of 1915 Ireland, without distracting from the impact of the action" (*M&H* 2.10.1969). His designs for *Lady Windermere's Fan* were in marked contrast to Osborne Robinson's much admired sets for previous Wilde revivals:

> [Durrant] has thrown tradition to the wind and come up with a brilliant design that incorporates the darkest corners of the stage. In deep purple and black the set has a richness without being cluttered. Mr. Durrant has steered clear of the miniscule tables and chairs that stunt movement in long, crinoline gowns, and has included a few functional chairs and flat benches. (*M&H* 13.11.1969)

Such a radical departure from tradition was too much for audiences inured to forty years of Robinson's style. The board, which had received "adverse comments . . . from Patrons concerning the new Designer's settings", was "strongly opposed to the work being done" (BM 1.12.1969). Durrant resigned, his departure coinciding with the retirement of Emily Tuckley the long-serving wardrobe mistress. His replacement Alan Miller Bunford reverted to a more acceptable style during the remainder of Osborne Robinson's absence, but then the delicate matter of what status to accord to the venerable designer arose. In October 1970 "Mr. Osborne Robinson was appointed to the newly created post of Head of Design" (BM 5.10.1970).

Alan Miller Bunford deployed the revolving stage to good effect for *Twelfth Night*, but the centre piece was Adam Faith's Feste to which he "brought a real understanding" and "a polished professional rendering of Feste's songs":

> All things considered a very commendable production – and one of the most polished first nights I have seen for a long time thanks to the painstaking direction of Willard Stoker. (*M&H* 5.3.1970)

At the end of the season Congreve's *The Double Dealer* was staged for a single week to coincide with the visit of C.O.R.T. by whose members it was received

Twelfth Night by William Shakespeare 1970. Grazyna Monvid as Maria, Roger Lloyd Pack as Sir Andrew Aguecheek, Adam Faith as Feste, Michael ffoulkes as Malvolio and Alan Meadows as Sir Toby Belch.
(Bryan Douglas Collection)

with approbation: "There are many notable performances, but none is more suave and sophisticated than Keith Grenville as the villainous Maskwell" (*C&E* 4.6.1970).

In 1971, as part of Northampton's Festival of Arts, Dryden returned to the Royal Theatre, albeit for one week only. *All for Love* featured Clare Ballantyne as a poised Cleopatra and David Beale as the lovelorn Antony with Rex Robinson as Ventidius and Philip Lowrie[8] as Alexas, the eunuch. Willard Stoker brought "swiftness and pace" (*M&H* 18.3.1971) to his production. Other contributions to the festival were John Whiting's *Marching Song*, which mystified audiences, and H. E. Bates's *The Darling Buds of May*.

The revolving stage received recurrent plaudits not least when Osborne Robinson returned to *Romeo and Juliet* with "an ingeniously constructed set, which used the revolving stage to full advantage. Six sets were built as one, and as the stage revolved, each set was revealed" (*M&H* 28.10.1971). Also revealed were Patrick Marley as Romeo, Jennifer Watts as Juliet, Andrew Manley as an admirably witty Mercutio and Elsie Winsor, a local favourite, as the garrulous Nurse.

Other highlights of the early 1970s included Michael ffoulkes leading a cast of nineteen in Peter Luke's *Hadrian VII*; Andrew Manley and Rex Robinson in excellent form in Arthur Miller's *The Price*; and Marc Crowley's controversial play *The Boys in the Band* "admirable direction . . . very competent all-male cast" (*M&H* 10.2.1972).

Marriage à la Mode by John Dryden 1973. (Bryan Douglas Collection)

In the autumn of 1972 Willard Stoker assembled a strong company: Henry Knowles, Leader Hawkins, Jill Johnston and Marjorie Bland. Knowles "making his debut as producer" with *Hindle Wakes* extracted "every nuance" to the extent that there was speculation that he was "the Crown Prince" (*M&H* 7.9.1972).[9] In the festival offering *Arms and the Man* roles were happily matched with performers - Majorie Bland as Raina, Elsie Winsor as Catherine Petkoff, Leader Hawkins as Major Petkoff, David Brierley as Bluntschli and Knowles as Sergius - all against Alan Miller Bunford's exquisitely Ruritanian sets. The return of Constance Cox with *Mansfield Park* found Stoker's direction lacking "nothing in elegance and style" with Marjorie Bland, as Mary Crawford, giving "her best performance of the season" (*M&H* 30.11.1972). Constance Cox's *Nightmare* was premièred in March 1974.

In spring 1973 Stoker proved that Shakespeare was still within Northampton's grasp with *Much Ado About Nothing* in Victorian costume. The "polish and timing of the gulling scene" (*M&H* 1.3.1973) found Knowles (Benedick) and Sheila Barker (Beatrice) at their best.

For the 1973-4 season the strength of the company was further augmented, not least by the return of Lionel Hamilton whose "extraordinary talent" was evident in the revival of Dryden's *Marriage à la Mode*:

I have never before been privileged to see a performance in the full magnificent "old style" of acting. Indeed there can be few exponents of this sadly fading art who still command its richness and vigour as does Mr. Hamilton. As the usurping King Polydamas with his sonorous pitch of voice, his astonishing ability to instil into the simplest line a miasma of prophetic doom, his overpowering presence and his glacial eye, he stands revealed as the true inheritor of the "high Roman" mantle of Sir Frank Benson. (*M&H* 20.7.1973)

Happily there was "no generation gap between a studied technique and the subtler portrayals of younger characters". Marjorie Bland was "beautiful and entrancing as Doralice". Bernice Stegers as Melantha the forerunner of Mrs. Malaprop, Henry Knowles as Palamede, Oz Clarke as the villain Argaleon, together with Leader Hawkins and Julian Fellowes, combined "for a production so outstanding that it must surely rank as one of the funniest in the Theatre's history". Continuity with the 1935 production was provided by Osborne Robinson whose designs were "in a lyrical melody of black, white and dove grey" (*M&H* 20.7.1973). The production, "an evening of sheer enchantment", was an entirely worthy contribution to the Festival of British Theatre.

In Henry Knowles's production of *Salad Days*, which as part of the Northampton Festival, was accorded a civic opening, Lionel Hamilton, requested by the director "because he was so popular as the Dame", played

137

"three singing roles: Sir Clamsby, a night club manager and Uncle Zed from out of space" (*C&E* 29.9.1973). In November Hamilton, who had directed the 1963 production of *Salad Days*, gave a reprise of another of his past successes – Sir Thomas More, in *A Man for All Seasons*.

The combination of a talented company and a strong leading man was evident in Simon Gray's *Butley*, the first Northampton repertory production seen by the present author. Marjorie Bland as the hapless wife Anne, Bernice Stegers as Edna Shaft, Oz Clarke as Reg Nuttall and Julian Fellowes as Mr. Gardner created an ensemble around Henry Knowles's "extraordinary talent" which rose to "a performance remarkable in its range and depth":

> For nearly two hours he dominates the stage. His technique is superb – every cadence is finely tuned, his voice is trained to magnificent effect, every move lends subtle power to speech. But all would be lost if he had not grasped Butley by the very soul. He lives Butley, he IS Butley. (*M&H* 22.11.1973)

The same company showed its versatility with the Christmas show *Chu Chin Chow* and in April Willard Stoker, returning after an illness, marshalled their talents in Ben Jonson's *The Alchemist*, a courageous choice for any repertory theatre. Jonson's "lesson on the frailty of human nature" had lost none of its freshness and potency – "the funniest play Rep. audiences have seen for months". Oz Clarke as Face was "the king pin". For "Bernice Stegers as Dol there can be nothing but the highest praise. Miss Stegers has so captured the common earthy, lascivious and grasping nature of the tart through the ages." In contrast Marjorie Bland as Dame Pliant exuded, at least the appearance of, innocence and Julian Fellowes engaged sympathy as the clerk, Dapper. Henry Knowles relished his long speech as Sir Epicure Mammon and Lionel Hamilton and Victor Woolf were "outrageous" as the puritans Tribulation and Ananias. The whole cast was to be "congratulated on a presentation which [was] exquisitely dressed and designed by Osborne Robinson" and showed that Willard Stoker's "wily hand has not lost its cunning" (*M&H* 2.5.1974).

1973–4 was a vintage year for acting talent which the company for the next season could not match. Nevertheless the productions of *Equus* in February and *As You Like It* in April 1975 showed that the principles of repertory casting could still deliver good performances. Jean/Jeannie Warren was "saucily charming" (*C&E* 26.2.1975) as the seductress Jill in *Equus* and as an enchanting Rosalind she deployed "the twinkle in her eyes and her cheeky gestures to accentuate the broad comic elements in the role" (*C&E* 16.4.1975). As Alan Strang Stephen Price was "superb"; but though his Orlando was "creditable and acrobatic" he was (still) prone to "gallop around the stage at a . . . furious pace". David Beale's Martin Dysart expressed "inner tensions and frustration, balanced with growing

The Alchemist by Ben Jonson 1974. Costume Designs for Tribulation Wholesome (Lionel Hamilton) and Ananias A Deacon (Victor Woolf) by Osborne Robinson. (Author's Collection)

empathy – even envy – towards his patient". He mastered the character's long monologues – good experience for Jaques whose "Seven Ages of Man" speech he "recited with memorable eloquence". Osborne Robinson's hand had not lost its cunning and he produced two contrasting sets: "functional" for Shaffer and "riotous colours" for Shakespeare, both of them making effective use of the revolving stage, especially for Alan Strang's orgiastic midnight ride.

Though many of Osborne Robinson's sets still displayed the distinctive, colourful exuberance which had characterised his work from the beginning he showed himself capable of innovation in his use of the revolving stage and the recreation of the Elizabethan-style apron-stage as well as his sparer sets for some modern plays.

Aubrey Dyas Perkins's resignation as chairman of the board and Willard Stoker's retirement came after a troubled period for the theatre, but both men could take pride in their achievements to the end. Fourth division repertories do not even contemplate staging *Marriage à la Mode* and *The Alchemist*, let alone make of them resounding successes.

Notes

1. For Sir Gyles Isham's stage career see: Richard Foulkes "The Acting Career of Gyles Isham" *Northampton Independent* May 1979, pp. 42–5, and Richard Foulkes "Gyles Isham: Shakespearean Actor" *Northamptonshire Past and Present* VI. 3, 1979, pp. 165–75.

2. I am indebted to Lionel Hamilton for a copy of the prologue and for his extensive help in providing information.

3. Jackson and Rowell *The Repertory Movement*, p. 90.

4. Article in the *Stage* 4.5.1961. Other repertory managers/artistic directors (including Reginald Salberg at the Salisbury Playhouse) expressed similar views.

5. *The Noble Spaniard* was toured to the Little Theatre, Leicester, one of several productions to play there in the 1960s when the city was without its own professional theatre.

6. Annual reports for this period now deposited in N.C.R.O., but originally in Aubrey Dyas Perkins's collection of theatre papers. Unfortunately I was unable to talk to Mr. Perkins about his long involvement with repertory in Northampton. I am grateful to his son, Mr. John Perkins, for making his late father's papers available to me.

7. Northamptonshire County Council holds board minutes from October 1966 onwards. I am grateful to Alan Claridge for putting them at my disposal.

8. Northampton-born Lowrie was best known for his role of Dennis Tanner in *Coronation Street*. He played several roles in 1971 receiving the standard pay of £30 per week (BM 22.2.1971).

9. The board (BM 10.12.1973 and 4.2.1974) considered Knowles's appointment as assistant director of productions, but lacked the necessary funds.

CHAPTER TEN

Turbulence and Calm 1975–81

A LARGE number of applicants is no guarantee that the job for which they have applied will be filled satisfactorily. Fifty-six aspiring candidates responded to the advertisement for director of productions, but "the Committee did not feel that any of the applicants was suitable for the post, so *Spotlight* had been approached and had submitted a list of a dozen names, these had been considered by the Committee and reduced to a short-list of four" (BM 9.6.1975).

Aubrey Dyas Perkins, fulfilling his last major duty as chairman, conscientiously informed the Arts Council drama director (N.V. Linklater) of the process, but the Council's representative failed to attend the interviews on 4 June. Linklater subsequently expressed his disappointment "that there has been less consultation between us over this appointment than is usual", though he stressed that "I am not questioning your Board's choice of Christopher Denys, whom I hope will suit you very well."[1]

Denys, aged thirty-eight, was yet another Lancastrian, born in Oldham, though he grew up in North Wales, where he began his career as assistant stage manager at the Grand Theatre, Llandudno. After national service he became stage director at the Nottingham Playhouse with Val May, with whom he moved to the Bristol Old Vic in 1961 as associate director, remaining there six years. He took over as director of productions at the Connaught Theatre, Worthing in 1967 and stayed until 1971 when he became director of productions at the Pitlochry Festival Theatre. Since 1972 he had combined the associate directorship at Pitlochry with free-lance directing and writing (PR 2.8.1975).

Denys's arrival coincided with – indeed probably precipitated – several important changes in personnel. W. Bland Wood, the long-serving general manager, announced his retirement from October 1975, though he was to continue as secretary to the board. His successor was Norman Florence, a forty year old ex-actor. Kevin Ricketts, an Australian who had been working in England for four years, was appointed assistant director and John Friend Newman took over as company and stage manager.

Alan Miller Bunford, who had worked alongside Osborne Robinson since 1969, resigned in September 1975 after a disagreement with the new director of productions. The work-load was clearly too onerous for the veteran designer alone and Christopher Denys proposed Helen Wilkinson, with whom he had previously worked, but she "would only come as Head of Design" (BM 15.9.1975). This condition posed a problem over Osborne Robinson's function, but the board's resourcefulness in conjuring up suitable designations prevailed and he became "Design Consultant".

Denys and his fresh team seemed to be poised for an effective start to a new era. His first season of plays (August to Christmas 1975) was approved at the board meeting on 22 July and the next month he presented a statement of policy, which included more work for schools and the (re-)establishment of a Theatre Club (Playgoers) with a junior section. Denys methodically drew up a comprehensive chart detailing casting for a nineteen week season, amounting to a total salary bill for actors of £11,690 (individual wages ranged from £25-45) with an average weekly cost of £616.[2]

The Lion in Winter, James Goldman's historical comedy about Henry II and his troubled and troublesome family, which Denys had directed at Pitlochry in 1970, made a favourable impression: "produced with taut and crackling excitement by Mr. Christopher Denys . . . the pristine director of productions . . . [it] augurs well for the future" (*M&H* 7.8.1975). A revival of Bernard Miles's Mermaid Theatre success *Lock Up Your Daughters* exhibited a large and polished cast in good voice against the background of Osborne Robinson's last set as head

A Midsummer Night's Dream by William Shakespeare 1975.
(Bryan Douglas Collection)

142

of design. In *A Midsummer Night's Dream* Helen Wilkinson made "an auspicious debut" with interiors which reflected the cosy warmth of the auditorium and exteriors replete with rustling trees and the sound of a waterfall. Gilbert Wynne (previously Richard Lionheart and Ramble), doubling Theseus and Oberon (almost *de rigueur* since Peter Brook's epoch-making 1970 revival), delivered Oberon's speeches "with an eloquence worthy of Stratford". Simon Merrick (previously Henry II and Squeezum) was a bumbling Bottom not above a certain amount of "hamming it up" (*C&E* 15.4.1975).

The Great Northampton Fire . . . And After devised by Christopher Denys was a perhaps rather over-hasty attempt on his part to engage with the local community through a documentary drama in the vein of Peter Cheeseman's highly regarded work at the Victoria Theatre, Stoke-on-Trent. In practice the scope of the piece "between 19th September 1675, and the day after tomorrow" was too great and much of the material "could as easily apply to any ancient, and presently expanding town in the country as to Northampton" (*M&H* 30.10.1975).

Joe Orton's *Loot* was found to have lost much of its lustre and capacity to shock, but *Joseph and the Amazing Technicolor Dreamcoat*, the Christmas

Tom Osborne Robinson 1904–76. (Bryan Douglas Collection)

production, was greeted with "vociferous approval", especially Gilbert Wynne's Pharaoh, a "King [Elvis] Presley . . . in dazzling gold embossed white, complete with fetching sideboards and darkling sultry leer . . . a gloriously funny impersonation of the folk hero of the Fifties" (*M&H* 23.12.1975).

Denys's opening months had produced a varied bill of fare, but had not commanded popular support - *Lock Up Your Daughters* had made a heavy loss and 1976 opened with a deficit of £15,000 on the preceding quarter (BM 12.1.1976). The death of Osborne Robinson in January 1976 seemed to symbolise the disintegration of the theatre which he had cherished for so long. Thereafter off-stage dramas eclipsed anything to be seen on the theatre's boards. Helen Wilkinson was "released" in February to undertake free-lance work (BM 2.2.1976); in March Norman Florence resigned after a series of accusations and counter-accusations, which necessitated an unprecedented Sunday meeting of the board at chairman John Bennett's home on 14 March. Press and public speculation was rife - the *Northants. Post* (27.3.1976) chronicled "an explosive behind-the-scenes drama" which included a staff petition demanding the manager should go; police called in to witness money being put in the safe and keys handed over; the dismissal of the front of house manager; the resignations of the production manager and the box office manager. Christopher Denys assumed overall responsibility for the management of the theatre, but inevitably he did not escape untarnished.

On stage Ben Travers's antiquated farce *Thark* had been followed by Edgar Wallace's "lamentable piece . . . *On the Spot* . . . really the most appalling stuff" (*M&H* 19.2.1976) and even the guest appearances by Eleanor Bron and Maurice Kaufmann could not disguise the shortcomings of Donald Cotton's new play *Love Between Friends*. The ever-dependable Noel Coward came to the rescue with *Private Lives* (Philip Lowrie and Alice Fraser "exceptionally attractive [as the] pair of mismatched lovers" *M&H* 14.3.1976) which also toured some outlying venues within and beyond the county.

Brecht's *The Threepenny Opera* was a bold choice for Northampton. In "Backstage with Brecht" Des Christy observed Christopher Denys at work with his cast. With only two weeks in which to rehearse this ambitious piece Denys was fully stretched - "Time is the worst enemy of all repertory companies" he complained as he put the company through their paces from 10.30 am to 10.45 pm on the day before the production opened. Having witnessed the effort involved Christy confessed to "a disappointment [at the first night] that I expect those who were involved in the production may have felt. What could Chris, his cast, his musicians and his technical staff have achieved with more time?" (*C&E* 3.4.1976).

Linal Haft gave Macheath "a neat blend of suave cruelty and comic charm" (*C&E* 1.4.1976). He came to Northampton immediately after appearing at Bottom, with Mia Farrow as Puck, at the Leicester Haymarket Theatre.

Coincidentally Michael Bogdanov had recently also staged *The Threepenny Opera* at Leicester's Phoenix Theatre. The overlap in repertoires between the two towns was fortuitous, but after its years as a theatrical desert neighbouring Leicester was now the "big brother" with levels of subsidy vastly exceeding those for Northampton.[3]

Haft remained to play Macbeth with Alice Fraser as Lady Macbeth. A virile and powerful Thane he fell short, like most of the cast, in his verse-speaking, delivering "the magnificent and moving eulogy for his wife as if it were a grocery list" (*M&H* 12.5.1976). Denys's production emphasised the thrills and melodrama of the play, but it was encumbered by Ray Lett's dense, gloomy and cramped set of logs and ladders which lumbered around on the revolving stage.

The season ended with ill-chosen plays: *So Who Needs Men?* a university comedy by American John Briley and David Halliwell's *Little Malcolm and His Struggle Against the Eunuchs* which toured for a week before arriving at the Royal Theatre. *Little Malcolm* has since assumed legendary status as the all-time nadir in the repertory company's fortunes. Kevin Ricketts's production received "well deserved applause . . . from the first-night audience" (*C&E* 16.6.1976), but it took only £742 in two weeks and attendance sank to eleven at one performance (*C&E* 31.8.1978).

The experience of *Little Malcolm* did not help the case for changing to a three weekly production schedule, which Denys presented to the board on 26 July 1976. He argued that actors and actresses would be more likely to accept engagements on a three weekly basis. As with the previous change to fortnightly productions rehearsal time would be extended – the desirability of which was evident from Des Christy's account of staging *The Threepenny Opera*. The board agreed to the change, but asserted its right to be consulted over the selection of plays.

The opening plays of the autumn 1976 season showed some deference to public taste: Anthony Shaffer's two-hander *Sleuth*, Alan Ayckbourn's *Absurd Person Singular* and Oliver Goldsmith's perennial comedy *She Stoops to Conquer* with Arnold Peters and Kay Trembley as the Hardcastles, Jacquey Chappell an engaging Kate, Antony Linford as the painfully shy Marlow and Robin Bowerman as the unlovely Tony. The box office returns for *She Stoops* were 43 per cent for week one, 40 per cent for week two and 51.4 per cent for week three (BM 18.10.1976). Thus although the third week had proved to be the most popular (audiences tend to wait until the end of a run whatever its length) the total attendance could easily have been accommodated in two weeks.

By then Christopher Denys was on the point of departure (BM 20.9.1976). Finances were in a parlous state. At the April meeting Denys had reported that the theatre "was unable to pay bills at the moment" (BM 26.4.1976) and at the June meeting that it was not possible "to present the regular production 'Profit and Loss' sheet showing the running cost and receipts for each production and the current financial position" (BM 7.6.1976). The budget for the future season was similarly elusive (BM 24.5.1976). None of this encouraged confidence amongst the providers of subsidy whose support was more crucial than ever. The Arts Council's grant was £32,000 and Northampton Borough Council's £15,000, but in July Northamptonshire County Council made a contribution of £15,662 in response to the deficit of £12,850 (*C&E* 8.7.1976).

The arrival of a new general manager Makki Marseilles was no solution since Denys "stated that under no circumstances would he work with Mr. Marseilles" (BM 6.9.1976). When the "accounts for the first quarter of the current financial year" emerged in September they revealed "a complete loss of £31,817" (BM 20.9.1976).

Denys's final selection of plays did nothing to alleviate the situation. Under the forbidding umbrella title of "Three Feminist Plays" he scheduled his own *Lilian* (commissioned by the Bristol Old Vic to celebrate the centenary of Lilian Baylis in 1974), Ibsen's *Hedda Gabler* and Jay Presson Allen's *The Prime of Miss Jean Brodie* (from Muriel Spark's novel). "The lamentable *Lilian* . . . was vastly overlong, tiresomely ragged, rambling and repetitive" (*M&H* 14.10.1976) and above all it had no appropriateness whatsoever to Northampton. Kay Gallie, specially engaged to undertake this trio of leading roles, foundered with the eccentric Lilian, but as Hedda she gave "a lovely shimmering performance" (*M&H* 4.11.1976) under David Gilmore's direction. As Miss Brodie (directed by Kevin Ricketts) she "perfectly captures the excruciating elegance of the refined provincial [in] a splendid if trifle over-mannered performance" (*M&H* 25.11.1976).

Christopher Denys's brief tenure as director of productions recalls that of Alan Vaughan Williams – as their subsequent careers showed both men possessed undisputed talent, but they were disinclined to tailor their tastes to those of Northampton. After a promising start Denys's flair faded, no doubt partly because of the off-stage difficulties for which he could not be personally exonerated. On the credit side he introduced three weekly runs, developed work with schools and revived the Playgoers' Club. His persistence with the policy of touring main house productions through the county perpetuated an ill-advised scheme the futility of which had earlier become all too apparent to Willard Stoker.

As the board contemplated the future (closure after Christmas 1976 seemed a real possibility) Councillor Alwyn Hargrave, a Northampton Borough Council nominee since July 1976, proposed that when selecting the new director of productions "consideration be given to a person who would have more interest in the theatre and the town rather than one who would be out to present an *avante-garde* programme" (BM 18.10.1976). Upon the selection of such a candidate the future wellbeing – existence even – of the Northampton Repertory Players depended.

The post of director of productions again attracted a large field (sixty-seven) of candidates from whom David Kelsey was selected at interviews held on 5 January 1977. A forty-three year old Yorkshireman Kelsey had been artistic director of the Marlowe Theatre, Canterbury (1968–72), followed by eighteen months as director of the Kenya National Theatre in Nairobi, returning to England as associate director of the Northcott Theatre, Exeter.[4] In the interim before Kelsey could take up his full duties Philip Anthony and Lionel Hamilton directed Wilde's *The Importance of Being Earnest* and William Douglas Home's *The Dame of Sark* respectively.

Despite all the difficulties of the preceding year the board had been preparing for the Northampton Repertory Players' golden jubilee in January 1977. Dr. Ernest Reynolds, with his remarkable knowledge of and enthusiasm for Victorian theatre and architecture, had written a booklet on the history of the Royal Theatre and Opera House which was published in November 1976. In February 1977 the board put into motion the commissioning of a new act-curtain by local artist Henry Bird. This magnificent and intricate piece of work was installed in July 1978 and remains a splendid adornment to the auditorium.[5]

The principal golden jubilee celebration was a dinner at the Saxon Inn on 10 January 1977 at which Lord Donaldson, Minister for the Arts, was guest of

The Importance of Being Earnest by Oscar Wilde 1977. Freda Jackson as Lady Bracknell. (Lionel Hamilton Collection)

147

honour. Other speakers included board chairman John Bennett, Lady Hesketh and actor Tom Baker who had recently filmed an episode of the television series *Dr. Who* at the Royal Theatre. Lord Donaldson's speech was indicative of current thinking on arts funding – he drew attention to the Association of Business Support for the Arts and recommended that "The business support for the Arts should be enormously extended" (*C&E* 11.1.1977).

During the jubilee week the theatre was occupied by the Christmas show *The Owl and the Pussycat*, but in February one of the Royal Theatre's most distinguished alumni, Freda Jackson returned for a commemorative production of *The Importance of Being Earnest*. She delivered Lady Bracknell's celebrated "handbag" speech "rather as an expression of honest bewilderment than a crescendant cry of outraged horror". Lionel Hamilton "inspired casting [as Canon Chasuble] achieved a triumph . . . Was ever prelate so coy, so demure, so given to vapours, so divinely unctious yet so radiantly full of benevolence and tender subtlety?" (*M&H* 10.2.1977). Hamilton's talents were to be stretched even further when Freda Jackson became ill and he took over as Lady Bracknell, thereby earning himself a place in the history books.

In accordance with Lord Donaldson's injunctions to seek support from

The Importance of Being Earnest by Oscar Wilde 1977. Lionel Hamilton as Lady Bracknell and Antony Linford as Algernon. (Lionel Hamilton Collection)

Members of the board seated in the balcony.
Alwyn Hargrave, Lou Warwick, Michael Henley, Gordon Gee, Rowan Mitchell, John Poole O.B.E., Eric Roberts, Janet Dicks, Vincent Halton.

business *The Importance of Being Earnest* was sponsored by the National Westminster Bank. Though this trend predated the election of a Conservative government in May 1979 it gathered pace thereafter with the creation of a special sub-committee, chaired by Councillor Cyril Benton, in October 1979.

In March 1977 the conduct of the Northampton's repertory company was the subject of a pamphlet – *The Northampton Repertory Theatre Some Questions and Suggestions*[6] compiled by Richard Foulkes and some of his drama students at the University Centre. The pamphlet considered: organisations and management; finance; repertoire; the company; publicity; box office and concessions; and transport facilities, but it was its observations on the composition of the board that attracted most attention in the local press. The pamphlet asked "whether some system might be introduced whereby nominations to the Board might be proposed by people who are not already on it" (p. 4). Existing board members defended their position, but later in the year a major shake-up took place.

In June chairman John Bennett indicated that he would not seek re-election to the board (BM 13.6.1977). By July his intentions were known to the press who speculated that his reason was increasing local authority involvement in the theatre. Councillor Alwyn Hargrave, who was "tipped as hot favourite" to succeed Bennett, observed that "The advent of political animals like myself may have hastened his departure" (*NP* 23.7.1977). Hargrave was duly elected chairman at the A.G.M. on 3 October 1977 after which Bennett became less circumspect:

> The very disturbing feature of the year has been the further wearing away of the independence of the board . . .
> It is because of this attitude of the local authorities that I have decided to stand down as a director of this theatre. I find that a board that has to toe the line in order to get the finance it requires is not to my liking. (*C&E* 4.10.1977)

Of the repertory company's paymasters the Arts Council and Northampton-shire County Council had raised their subventions significantly: the former by 30 per cent to £47,500 and the latter from £11,000 to £20,000. Northampton Borough Council's grant remained £20,000 (*NP* 30.7.1977). The local authorities proferred support in kind:

> The County Council had offered the services of the County Secretary's Department to provide secretarial and legal services to the Board, and the Borough Council had suggested that the Borough Treasurer should assist in the production of a forward budget and other matters of budgetary control . . . (BM 28.3.1977)

The county council had also recommended an interest-free loan to cover the current deficit and the use of a committee room in County Hall for future meetings of the board. At the August meeting the board decided to accommodate county council representatives within the existing membership of fifteen and that the Playgoers' representative should attend as a co-opted member (BM 8.8.1977). These proposals were put into effect at the A.G.M. (BM 3.10.1977) when Councillors W. G. Gee and J. Poole O.B.E. took their places as the county's nominees.

Increasingly important though subsidy was becoming box office income, which after all is the true expression of the patrons' support, was as vital as ever. In fact Kelsey's regime got off to an uncertain start. The revival of Northampton's favourite Shakespeare play *Twelfth Night* as a fiftieth anniversary production culminating in a gala performance on the bard's birthday (23 April) was undoubtedly apt. The setting (in 1877) raised some questions – was Feste (Antony Linford) really meant to suggest Queen Victoria's Highland servant John Brown? On the credit side the cast included Jenny Oulton's ironic Olivia, Heather Ramsay's captivating Viola, Richard Gale's understated Malvolio and Lionel Hamilton's bravura Sir Toby. Ray Lett provided an attractive period set and

Martin Waddington, a versatile member of Kelsey's new team, composed an harmonious musical score.

Kennedy's Children, Robert Patrick's exploration of the effect of President Kennedy on six ill-assorted citizens of the United States, initially received three late-night performances (11 pm) after the Gilbert and Sullivan Society's production of *The Yeoman of the Guard* – a curious juxtaposition by any standards – and then continued for two weeks at conventional times. A play which "fell like a dull, sickening thud" at its off-Broadway première in 1974 (*C&E* 26.4.1977) was hardly calculated to bring in the traditionally conservative Northampton audience. The Anthony Newley and Lesley Bricusse musical *The Roar of the Greasepaint – the Smell of the Crowd* offered "a pearl unknown to our Gadarine age, that of a shining lustrous hope" (*M&H* 19.5.1977), but audiences were hesitant and bemused.

The verdict on Kelsey's debut was that:

> The new regime began in an uncertain way and Kelsey put on several plays – "Kennedy's Children" and "The Roar of the Greasepaint" – that were as unconventional and nearly as unsuccessful as what had gone before. (*C&E* 31.5.1978)

By the time he came to decide upon the 1977–8 season Kelsey had begun to get the measure of Northampton and to formulate his own policy. Early on he had signalled his intention "to gradually change the image of the repertory and in particular to eliminate the name of repertory from the title, he would like the theatre to be known as the Royal Theatre" (BM 17.1.1977). He was committed to the principle of a permanent company, wanted to develop "After Dark Theatre", Sunday performances and touring (gradually changing to specific touring productions rather than sending main house productions on the road). In the pursuit of these aims the services of a marketing manager were seen to be crucial – Jane Adams was appointed in September 1977 and succeeded by Andrew Thompson in November 1978. In November 1977 Nick Allott, who had been recruited – initially as assistant stage manager – from Exeter by Kelsey, took over as general manager (almost certainly the youngest in the country).

Kelsey was more fortunate and skilful than his predecessor in his appointments and during his tenure an air of convivial comradeship pervaded the theatre. Nevertheless the essential ingredient was the work on stage. The autumn 1977 season began with two repertory standards: Coward's *Present Laughter* and Rattigan's *The Deep Blue Sea*. In the former, under the direction of Martin Waddington, who combined directing with his gifts as a musician (he had been resident musical director at the Northcott Theatre, Exeter), Kelsey revealed his acting talents to Northampton for the first time, giving an accomplished performance as the egotistical actor Garry Essendine. Jenny Oulton (Liz

151

Present Laughter by Noel Coward 1977. David Kelsey as Gary Essendine and Francis Lloyd as Roland Maule. (Royal Theatre Collection)

Essendine), Rosamund Shelley (Monica Reed) and, especially, Susan Colverd as the eccentric domestic Miss Erikson gave excellent support. As director of *The Deep Blue Sea* Kelsey elicited a "fine sensitive performance" from Jenny Oulton as Hester Collyer and Lionel Hamilton "personified dignity blended with kindliness in his interpretation of Sir William Collyer. His scenes with Jenny Oulton are very touching" (*C&E* 25.8.1977).

The box office response was slow. *Present Laughter* achieved only 35 per cent, *The Deep Blue Sea* 39 per cent (BM 12.9.1977) and Alan Bennett's *Habeas Corpus*, the run of which was extended for an extra week, attracted only 50 per cent though it showed a surplus on budget of £4,305, raising the average on the three plays to 43 per cent (BM 3.10.1977). Certainly Bennett's play which Kelsey described as "a hilarious, full-bloodied, very English farce" (PR 30.7.1977) showed Kelsey's exuberant skill as a director of comedy to advantage with a talented cast including father and daughter Brian and Jenny Oulton – appearing together for the first time – as Arthur Wicksteed and Constance Wicksteed and Martin Waddington following in Alan Bennett's footsteps as Mrs. Swabb.

Susan Colverd got her opportunity as Vicky in Charles Laurence's *My Fat Friend* with Kelsey directing and appearing in the Kenneth Williams role of Henry. After such favourites as *Charley's Aunt*, *Hobson's Choice* and Lionel Hamilton's adaptation of Charlotte Brontë's *Jane Eyre* (Jane Hayward in the title role, Malcolm Mudie as Rochester) Kelsey returned to anarchic modern comedy with Joe Orton's *What the Butler Saw* in May 1978. Sporting a Hitlerian moustache, black wig and German accent Kelsey gave a *tour de force* performance as the inspecting psychiatrist Dr. Rance and the rest of the company was in fine form: Malcolm Mudie as the libidinous Dr. Prentice, Clare Welch as his nymphomaniac wife, the delectable Glynis Barber (who later achieved television fame in *Dempsey and Makepeace*) as Geraldine Barclay, Francis Lloyd as her quick-change brother Nicholas and John Dixon as the dim Sergeant Match. Stuart Kerr's production maintained a frantic pace.

The season ended on an elegiac note with Christopher Fry's *Ring Round the Moon* (from Anouilh's *L'Invitation au Chateau*). Compared with the Orton play this seemed "pretty tame and tedious . . . much too long", but two young members of the company showed their developing talents to advantage: Simon Templeman in the twin-roles of the brothers Hugo and Frederic and Glynis Barber "wistful and charming" as Isabella, the ballet dancer. Ray Lett's set for the Winter Garden was an exquisite creation in pale green and John Heywood arranged some enchanting dances. Despite his reservations about the play Dick Murray wrote "'Ring Round the Moon' rings down the curtain of a very successful season at the Royal Theatre" (*C&E* 25.5.1978).

In its first two weeks *Ring Round the Moon* had taken ten times the box office revenue of the fateful *Little Malcolm* (£742 in two weeks). Board chairman Alwyn Hargrave described his own contribution as "Discipline and an ability to balance the books"; for his part David Kelsey had refrained "from excessive artistic experiment" and concentrated "on getting back the theatre's traditional audience" (*C&E* 31.6.1981). With a gradual rise in attendances (and income), including the first full houses for three years, chairman Hargrave and director of productions Kelsey had turned around the theatre's fortunes.

For his second full season David Kelsey felt that he could afford to be more adventurous: "I have tried to encompass regular and irregular tastes in modern and classical drama . . . [in the] most ambitious programme for many years" (*NP* 1.7.1978). In fact the opening play Alan Ayckbourn's *Table Manners*, part of the *Norman Conquests* trilogy (with Simon Templeman as Norman) drew disappointing support perhaps because audiences sensed that they were getting an incomplete menu. Another factor may have been that the autumn season still opened in late July though the traditional industrial summer closure was progressively giving way to family holidays stretching to the re-opening of schools in late August.

The next offering "Two of a Kind" ingeniously paired Rattigan's *The Browning Version* with Peter Shaffer's *Black Comedy*, two contrasting pieces which enabled the company to display its versatility – none more so than Kelsey himself, whose desiccated classics master Andrew Crocker-Harris achieved pity through his denial of self-pity and whose Colonel Melkett breathed pink gin. Clare Welch combined the bitchy Mrs. Crocker-Harris with the lost soul Miss Furnvil, becoming oddly touching in her tipsy speech addressed to her dead father. Simon Templeman, Glynis Barber and Malcolm Mudie appeared in well-suited duos and newcomer Marie Tempest Whiteley, a strikingly beautiful actress, played the mischievous Clea in *Black Comedy*.

The touring production of Donald Cotton's musical *The Ballad of Mrs. Beeton* was launched in the main house directed by George Peck, who as assistant director combined occasional acting with responsibility for touring productions. Daphne du Maurier's *Rebecca* (Glynis Barber as Mrs. de Winter, Clare Welch as Mrs. Danvers and Malcolm Mudie as Maxim de Winter) proved as dependable as ever and justified an additional week, which reduced the run of one of the greatest rarities ever seen at the Royal Theatre, Addison's *The Drummer*.

Adapted by Lionel Hamilton as *The Drummer of Love*, the piece was originally staged in 1716 and enjoyed consistent popularity through the eighteenth century. It fully merited its revival and the cast's evident enthusiasm spread to audiences. As Lady Truman Mary Tempest Whiteley assumed an alluring disguise until her restoration to her husband Sir George (Malcolm Mudie). Glynis Barber was the winsome Melinda Lorn disguised as Lieutenant Feignwell and Simon Templeman took the title role: Fantome, the Drummer. Will Yeomans supplied period music at the harpsichord.

Sheila Mathews, whose experience included several West End musicals, joined the company to play Blanche Dubois in Tennessee Williams's *A Streetcar Named*

The Drummer of Love by Joseph Addison adapted by Lionel Hamilton 1978. Glynis Barber as Melinda Lorn disguised as Lieutenant Feignwell. (Royal Theatre Collection)

Desire and Antony Linford returned at three days' notice to play Archie Rice in Osborne's *The Entertainer* (set in Northampton) alongside Lionel Hamilton's consummate performance as Billy Rice.

Through 1979, 1980 and into 1981 David Kelsey continued to show a sure hand in play selection. Noel Coward (*Hay Fever* with Sheila Mathews as Judith Bliss), Terence Rattigan (*In Praise of Love* with Kelsey and Anne Jameson as Sebastian and Lydia Cruttwell) and Joe Orton (*Entertaining Mr. Sloan* with Anne Jameson as Kath and Antony Linford as Kemp) were dramatists whose attraction to Northampton audiences could be relied upon.

Novel adaptations continued to hold their appeal with Lionel Hamilton rendering (at Kelsey's suggestion) an effective version of Wilkie Collins's *The Woman in White* with Jane Hayward (previously seen in the title role in Hamilton's *Jane Eyre*) giving excellent accounts of Anne Catherick, the mysterious fugitive from a lunatic asylum and as the heroine, Laura Fairlie, trapped in a loveless marriage. In Emily Brontë's *Wuthering Heights* (adapted by Donald Cotton) Catherine Hall played Cathy Earnshaw and James Healey Heathcliff.

New plays were conspicuously lacking from this period – the exception being Lionel Hamilton's less than satisfactory whodunnit *Quartet to Murder* – but Kelsey gave Northampton audiences judicious revivals of recent London successes: Shaffer's *Equus* (again); Alan Ayckbourn's *Bedroom Farce*; Peter Nichols's *Privates on Parade* (Kelsey as Major Giles Flack and Antony Linford as Acting Captain Terri Dennis); James Saunders's *Bodies*; Charles Dyer's *Staircase* (Kelsey and Linford striking a balance between comedy and pathos as the homosexual barbers) and Brian Clark's West End hit *Whose Life Is It Anyway?* (with Peter Denyer as Ken Harrison).

Amongst repertory stand-bys were *Boeing-Boeing*, *Dial M for Murder*, *Ghost Train* and *Arsenic and Old Lace*, which was given a new twist by casting Antony Linford and James Wooley as Martha and Abby Brewster, the inveterate, veteran murderers. The time-honoured theatrical pseudonym Walter Plinge was pressed into service as Mr. Gibbs.

Classical revivals were infrequent, but in March 1979 Kelsey, in the best tradition of repertory, gave a young actor the opportunity to play Hamlet:

> In choosing the play I had to be sure we had an actor who possessed the skill and merit to take on this demanding role. SIMON TEMPLEMAN has been with the company for over twelve months. In that time he has gained considerable confidence in the first year of his professional career as well as having captured the interest of our regular patrons in a series of performances. (PR 28.2.1979)

Kelsey recalled the advice of a much revered elderly actor who told him (prior to

156

Hamlet by William Shakespeare 1979. Simon Templeman as Hamlet, Clare Welch as Gertrude. (Royal Theatre Collection)

Kelsey's appearance in the play) to read it fifty times (Kelsey read it fifty-three) and to "take 'advice to the Player's speech', drink Guinness before the fight, and die down centre" (PR 21.3.1979). More speculatively Kelsey saw the play as "beseeching us to recognise our moral obligations" a timely reminder prior to "the forthcoming election" (PR 28.2.1979). Templeman was physically well-suited to the Prince and though his inexperience showed he compensated for it with a shining, radiant sincerity. Far from being mad he appeared the sole possessor of sanity in a lunatic court, partly due to the uneven and sometimes wilful performances of the rest of the cast: a Claudius (Peter Spraggon), who sounded like Ted Heath and an Ophelia (Jane Egan) reduced to an over-painted sixth-former in dementia. Antony Linford (a witty, gritty Polonius) and Clare Welch (a ravaged Gertrude) salvaged some honour. David Kelsey was a worthy Player King, but his directional touch lapsed in manifesting the Ghost through hi-fi, which suggested that the spirit was hovering about with astonishing rapidity. *Hamlet* played to 43 per cent which still kept it within budget (BM 9.4.1979 and 21.5.1979).

The next year guest director Stuart Kerr achieved "the best thing the theatre has done for a long time" with Chekhov's *The Seagull*, bringing out "some first class acting from the company" (*C&E* 29.10.1980). Sheila Mathews gave a delicate touch to the aging stage beauty Madame Arkadina, David Kelsey was the raffish author Trigorin, Christopher Brown the frustrated Konstantin and Catherine Hall a spirited Nina. Audience resistance to such fare was still apparent and attendances were not good.

The form of entertainment with which Kelsey stamped his mark upon Northampton was the musical: *Guys and Dolls*; *Joseph and the Amazing Technicolor Dreamcoat*; in a lower key the spoof whodunnit *Something's Afoot*; Cole Porter's *Kiss Me Kate* and *Godspell*. His revival of *Guys and Dolls*, in February 1979, predated Richard Eyre's acclaimed production at the National Theatre. He cast mainly from the existing company with Clare Welch as Miss Adelaide and Antony Linford as Nathan Detroit. Musicals are demanding on repertory resources and attendances for *Guys and Dolls* fell below 50 per cent at some performances.

When Kelsey turned to another classic American musical, *Kiss Me Kate*, in February 1981, the box office achieved 62½ per cent, short of the 67 per cent target (BM 16.3.1981) and the theatre resorted to extensive "papering" disposing of 420 complimentary tickets (BM 14.4.1981). Public response had not been helped by what the board regarded as an unconstructive review in the *Chronicle and Echo* (BM 23.2.1981) in which John Gilbert considered that "*Kiss Me Kate* was not quite ready last night for its opening night. It was too long and uneven in quality." The company was supplemented by Norma Dunbar as Lillie, Sally Brelsford as Lois Lane and Tano Rea as Freddie Graham, but it was regulars Antony Linford and Derek Ware as the two gangsters, who nearly stole the show with their rendition of "Brush Up Your Shakespeare" (*C&E* 13.2.1981).

Whatever Northampton's reservations about Kelsey's *Kiss Me Kate* it attracted the attention of some American impresarios who, having seen it, offered him the job of directing a largescale Broadway-bound musical *Gold in the Hills*. As he prepared to leave Northampton after four and a half years Kelsey reflected on his achievements.[8] He had found the theatre – "the invalid of the Midlands" – playing to 33 per cent average houses and accumulating a daunting deficit. Through his judicious choice of plays he retrieved and enlarged the traditional audience. Of fifty-seven productions he had directed forty himself and appeared in five (*C&E* 15.6.1981). Kelsey's accomplished and versatile performances helped to give a public face to the theatre and undoubtedly encouraged the rest of the company. He was adroit in his selection and deployment of actors and

Kiss Me Kate by Cole Porter 1981 Derek Ware and Antony Linford "Brush up Your Shakespeare". (Royal Theatre Collection)

nurtured young talent (Templeman, who later joined the R.S.C., and Glynis Barber in particular) in the best tradition of repertory. His management team (Martin Waddington, Nick Allott who left to join Cameron Mackintosh for *Cats* in March 1981, George Peck and Andrew Thompson) was young and enthusiastic. He introduced "After Dark Theatre" and Sunday performances and encouraged the theatre's touring wing (with some enterprising work including Webster's *The Duchess of Malfi* and *Pericles*). For three years (1979–81) Kelsey was artistic director of the Ludlow Festival which, as well as raising his own theatre's profile, gave increased opportunities to the Northampton company and attracted new performers thither (Jan Harvey, for instance, who played Rosaline in Ludlow's 1979 *Love's Labour's Lost* and then came to Northampton as Myra Arundel in *Hay Fever*).

By leaving when he did Kelsey was aware of the fact that he would lose out on the challenge of the construction and opening of Derngate, the multi-purpose entertainment complex planned for the site adjacent to the Royal Theatre in Guildhall Road. Throughout the late 1970s and into the 1980s the board and management of the Royal Theatre had been increasingly preoccupied with the proposals for Derngate and the renovation of the Royal Theatre. In October and November 1979 meetings were held between the board and the Derngate architects.

On 18 June 1980 Northampton Borough Council issued a press statement outlining the Derngate project. At current costs the new multi-purpose hall was priced at £5 million "with a budgeted final contract figure of £8 million", funded partly through the realisation of assets and "deferred purchase". The list of possible functions was described as "almost unending", but significantly it did not include drama or pantomime. Indeed the document stressed that "the uses of the two auditoria (the new hall and the Theatre) should complement each other". With Cyril Benton as chairman of the Derngate committee and Alwyn Hargrave as his deputy there was significant overlap between its membership and that of the Royal Theatre's board of directors.

In August 1980 the board of the Royal Theatre and the Northampton Borough Council jointly authorised "a study in order to investigate the future financial needs of the Theatre and the Derngate Project". By the spring of 1981 a "Study Workbook" appeared in several drafts listing projects and costs which, at their most ambitious, totalled £1,600,000. By this stage the London-based Wells fund raisers were being consulted and their representatives attended board meetings on 29 April and 11 May 1981, at the latter of which it was unanimously agreed to engage Wells. The target was to raise £400,000 within two years, so that the Royal Theatre would be refurbished by the time its new neighbour opened in 1983.

Notes

1. Letter dated 25.6.1975 to Aubrey Dyas Perkins in N.C.R.O.

2. In N.C.R.O.

3. For 1975-6 Northampton received £32,000 from the Arts Council compared with the Birmingham Repertory Theatre's £172,000, the Bristol Old Vic's £162,000 and Leicester Haymarket's £135,942 (Arts Council annual report).

4. Ludlow Festival programme for *Love's Labour's Lost* 1979.

5. See Ernest Reynolds *Northampton Repertory Theatre* 1976 and Henry Bird *The Sipario Dipinto* 1978.

6. Richard Foulkes ed. *The Northampton Repertory Theatre Some Questions and Suggestions* published by University (of Leicester) Centre, Northampton, March 1977.

7. An exhibition Osborne Robinson His Life and Work opened at the Central Art Gallery, Northampton on the same day.

8. Kelsey also featured in an article on regional theatre in the *Stage* 24.7.1980 in which his unflattering remarks about local councillors were quoted.

CHAPTER ELEVEN

A Steady Hand 1981–92

BUILDING on success is probably a greater challenge than recovery from a low ebb. From the thirty-seven applicants to succeed David Kelsey the board selected forty-four year old Michael Napier Brown. His experience ranged from West End appearances as an actor (*The Four Musketeers, Show Boat*) to directing in repertory, latterly at the Derby Playhouse and the Everyman Theatre, Cheltenham at both of which he had been associate director.

Michael Napier Brown's autumn 1981 season began with two echoes from the past: Brian Oulton returned to play the harassed husband-of-convenience Victor Keene in Ben Travers's *The Bed Before Yesterday* and Lionel Hamilton appeared as the Dean of Paddington in Constance Cox's adaptation of Wilde's *Lord Arthur Savile's Crime*. Rudolf Besier's pre-war costume drama *The Barretts of Wimpole Street* proved to be a more resilient piece than many would have expected thanks largely to Napier Brown's skilful direction of a cast of fifteen (including John Bott as Edward Moulton-Barrett, back in Northampton after eleven years away) and a dog (Flush/Ayesha).

West End plays followed: Alan Ayckbourn's *Absent Friends*, Simon Gray's *Stagestruck* (Janet Hargreaves returning after twenty years), Ronald Harwood's *The Dresser* and Tom Kempinski's *Duet for One*. In *Absent Friends* Vilma Hollingbery (Mrs. Napier Brown) gave an outstanding performance as the anguished Diana, who arranges a reunion tea party for her bereaved friend Colin (Antony Linford, then associate director). In March 1982 Michael Napier Brown made his Northampton acting debut as Sir, the old-style actor, in *The Dresser* with Vilma Hollingbery as Her Ladyship and Antony Linford as Norman.

Michael Napier Brown took to the stage again as the psychiatrist Dr. Feldman in *Duet for One*, Kempinski's two-hander about a violinist Stephanie Abrahams (Helen Bourne) suffering from multiple sclerosis (based on Jacqueline du Pré). Neither of these pieces particularly attracted Northampton audiences, but by the end of his first season Napier Brown had begun to gauge local tastes. Uniquely the season had included two Agatha Christie plays: *And Then There Were None* and *Spider's Web*. Far from condescending to the whodunnit Napier Brown's direction of *Spider's Web* was "thorough and sure-footed and the general standard of performance and presentation was very high" (*C&E* 20.5.1982). He was rewarded with 78 per cent attendances (AR 18.10.1982) including around

162

sixty organised parties (BM 28.6.1982). Lest the new director felt himself sentenced to a life of directing Agatha Christies more encouraging evidence was forthcoming from his revival of William Gibson's *The Miracle Worker*, which "in its final week broke all box office records" (PR 19.5.1982). Alexa Povah played the blind governess Annie Sullivan and Valerie Whittington (shedding eight years) was her ten year old deaf, mute and blind pupil, Helen Keller. Napier Brown's direction traversed "the emotions from laughter to tears . . . superlatives seem almost an insult" (*M&H* 18.2.1982). A workshop on the production was attended by 350 children (BM 8.3.1982).

Another governess Miss Giddens, played by Joanna David, featured in the opening production of the autumn 1982 season: *The Innocents*, William Archibald's adaptation of Henry James's enigmatic ghost story *The Turn of the Screw*. Her charges, Miles and Flora, were played by local schoolchildren (Daren Gardiner aged eleven/Gian Sammarco aged ten and Gina Lander aged ten/Lindsey Stagg aged twelve) the selection of whom was good publicity for the theatre and whose performances revealed a particular skill of the director's. The production drew "the audience to the edge of the seat and kept them there until

The Innocents adapted by William Archibald from Henry James 1982. Joanna David as Miss Giddens, Lindsey Stagg as Flora and Darren Gardiner as Miles. (Royal Theatre Collection)

the end" (*C&E* 26.8.1982) – and audiences there were in abundance, an amazing 97.8 per cent (BM 13.9.1982). No-one was more amazed and puzzled than public relations officer Andrew Thompson who wrote "we can always conjure reasons why theatres are empty", but found success more difficult to explain. Amongst likely factors he listed early planning combined with a later opening, increased publicity across a wider area, media coverage (B.B.C.'s local radio station had opened earlier in the year and Anglia Television devoted a six minute slot to the production), the casting of Joanna David recently seen on television in Daphne du Maurier's *Rebecca* ("responsible for the last 30% of the Box Office") and Michael Napier Brown's "quality production" (board paper 18.10.1982).

Given his faith and skill in handling young performers it was not surprising that Michael Napier Brown's first Shakespearean offering should be *Romeo and Juliet*, with the title roles going to two young assistant stage managers straight out of drama school – Jonathan Docker-Drysdale (aged twenty-five) and Yolanda Vazquez (aged twenty-one). Raw emotion was to the fore "Romeo pouts, shouts and flings himself about, Juliet rants, sobs and shrieks" (*C&E* 8.10.1982), but if the young leads lacked subtlety they were ably supported by Vilma Hollingbery's garrulous Nurse, Kim Wall's uncompromising Mercutio and Lionel Hamilton, eloquent as ever, as Escalus/Chorus. Ray Lett's set (for which he had a budget of £900 plus £1,300 for costumes *M&H* 30.9.1982) was "quite beautiful and created a real feeling of Renaissance Italy" (*ET* 8.10.1982). The production achieved a creditable 58 per cent of capacity (BM 20.12.1982).

The story of another ill-fated teenager, Anne Frank, caught the imagination of Northampton, in the dramatisation of her diary by Albert Hackett and Frances Goodrich – *The Diary of Anne Frank*. In the title role Mary Roscoe "was charming and completely convincing" especially so in the touching scene with her first date Peter Van Daan (John Goodrum). Despite the sombre subject Michael Napier Brown brought out "the play's considerable stock of humour" (*C&E* 28.10.1982).

Ian Mullins's adaptation of Charles Dickens's *David Copperfield* provided the opportunity for Gian Sammarco and Gina Lander to return to the stage as the young David Copperfield and Agnes Whitfield whom they played with aplomb. The novel abounds in wonderfully theatrical characters who were embodied by a cast of twenty-two including "Vilma Hollingbery, looking like an affronted female showjumper, superb as Aunt Betsey" (*Guardian* 5.2.1983). Ray Lett created "a fascinating set . . . a skeletal wooden creation that conjures up anything from the Peggotty's nautical dwelling to the Steerforths' patrician home, even magically including the wrecked schooner in which Steerforth dies" (*Financial Times* 7.2.1983). Extra performances were scheduled and attendance reached 86 per cent (BM 28.2.1983).

The Royal Theatre took to the road with Charles Dyer's 1962 comedy *The Rattle of a Simple Man*, which, after six performances (94 per cent) in Guildhall Road, visited ten venues within and beyond (Bedford, Chipping Norton,

Loughborough) the county for which East Midlands Arts provided a grant of £6,000. The tour attracted 1,716 (BM 16.5.1983). Unusually a play had been found that was equally suitable for the main house and touring. Peter Denyer's direction was assured and there were "two first class performances from Barbara Morton as the prostitute Cyrenne and Glynn Sweet as Percy, the simple Mancunian soccer fan of the title" (*C&E* 16.3.1983). Another play which would have fulfilled the dual demands of the main house and touring was Willy Russell's two-hander *Educating Rita* (Cindy O'Callaghan as Rita and Antony Linford as Frank) which followed its success elsewhere with 86 per cent attendance. The educational theme recurred in Emlyn Williams's *The Corn is Green* with Dilys Hamlett, whom the author had greatly admired as Ophelia at Stratford in 1956, as Miss Moffat and Robin Davies as Morgan Evans. Miss Hamlett also exercised her skills as a director with Arthur Miller's *All My Sons* in which Michael Napier Brown and Vilma Hollingbery made the first of several impressive appearances in modern American drama.

During the first two years at the Royal Theatre Michael Napier Brown had established a remarkable affinity between his own strengths as a director (particularly of young people) and local tastes. To a large extent he had done the

David Copperfield dramatised by Ian Mullins 1983. Vilma Hollingbery as Aunt Betsey, Paddy Ward as Mr. Dick and Gian Sammarco as David Copperfield. (Royal Theatre Collection)

sort of work which he wanted to and carried the public with him. This, of course, resulted in healthy box office income, but that was not without its hazards for, although grants rose (the Arts Council's from £72,750 in 1980–1 to £86,000 in 1982–3) the theatre nevertheless turned in a loss of £2,771 in 1982–3 (AR). The margins were very narrow and the reliance on box office imposed its own restraints.

Self-help was the order of the day as far as the refurbishment of the Royal Theatre was concerned. Whereas in 1960 Northampton Borough Council had footed the bill its priority now lay with Derngate and the onus was on the tenants to finance improvements. The Royal Theatre Development Trust under the chairmanship of Peter Hulmes, managing director of the Robert Marriott Group Ltd. and consisting of twenty-eight members drawn from industry, commerce, local government and the board produced a glossy brochure and set about its task with the professional support of Wells's John Telfer. By April 1984 three-quarters of the £400,000 target had been raised, but the assistance of the local authorities (in the form of interest free loans) had to be sought for the remainder (BM 18.4.1984).

As the new Derngate structure rose inexorably alongside the Royal Theatre anxiety increased as to whether it would dwarf its neighbour not only physically but also artistically. Practicalities such as the box office (shared computerised facilities) and the bars had to be ironed out, but fears about the Derngate repertoire surfaced in June 1983, when within a couple of months of its opening the assurance that it would not compete with drama was reversed. There was no objection to Francis Durbridge's *Night Cap* (with Nyree Dawn Porter) or to the star-studded (Joan Plowright and Frank Finlay) revival of Chekhov's *The Cherry Orchard* in August, since the Royal was closed then, but the prospect of Peter Shaffer's hugely successful *Amadeus* (which Napier Brown wanted to stage himself) with Keith Michell as Salieri from 31 October was regarded as a serious threat (BM 28.6.1983).

Against this background of competition within its own sphere, the renovations, undertaken during a complete closure between 4 June and 28 September, took on even greater significance if the Royal was to retain its audience. At the A.G.M. on 17 October 1983 Alwyn Hargrave, who in December became a foundation director instead of a local authority representative, outlined "the most comprehensive refurbishment programme in [the theatre's] 99 year history". It encompassed "brand new dressing rooms, workshop and side stage" and the reseating (with the loss of thirty-seven seats in the stalls), re-carpeting and redecoration of the auditorium, together with total rewiring and a new heating system.

The show with which the Royal Theatre reopened signalled its intention to assert its profile: only the second regional production of the Andrew Lloyd Webber/Tim Rice musical *Jesus Christ Superstar*. It was an ambitious choice at any time, but especially so in the context of last-minute building work. Michael Napier Brown conceded that the first night on 29 September was "an unmitigated disaster" (*M&H* 8.10.1983). The performers (sixteen of them), the set and lighting were just about up to scratch, but "the sound problems" were not even up to the standard of "a badly run amateur talent competition" (*C&E* 3.10.1983). The problems were resolved and despite the adverse reviews *Jesus Christ Superstar* played to 16,529 patrons, 87.4 per cent of capacity (*C&E* 20.3.1984).

Happily critical and popular taste were in step with Bernard Pomerance's *The Elephant Man* in which the deformed John Merrick, the object of Victorian medical and side-show curiosity, was played by Timothy Weston who had made his professional debut in *Jesus Christ Superstar*. The twenty-one year old actor conveyed the Elephant Man's deformities without make-up, having sought inspiration at Fawsley Park where Merrick had enjoyed the hospitality of the Knightley family in 1887 and 1889. The local associations may have contributed to the play's surprising success (84 per cent BM 21.11.1983), despite the competition of *Amadeus* at Derngate.

James Roose-Evans's adaptation of Laurie Lee's nostalgic autobiography *Cider with Rosie* with Rex Robinson as the Narrator almost literally filled the theatre in February 1984 (91.7 per cent *C&E* 20.3.84). By then no excuse was needed for home-grown nostalgia for the centenary of the Royal Theatre was at hand. With Lady Hesketh taking a leading role (as she had with the Development Trust) a celebratory programme of events had been planned including a service in All Saints Church, an entertainment in words and music involving past and present members of the company (both on Sunday 29 April), a talk (in fact cancelled) by Arts Minister Lord Gowrie and a lecture on Charles Dickens by Professor Philip Collins.

The latter was occasioned by the centrepiece of the Royal Theatre's centenary season, an adaptation of Dickens's *Great Expectations* by Vilma Hollingbery. In the *Guardian* Gareth Lloyd Evans wrote of "the enthusiasm and skill" on show – from Miss Hollingbery as adapter and actress (Miss Havisham) to veteran Lionel Hamilton's "pompously regal Pumblechook" and Antony Linford's Jaggers through to Gian Sammarco the youngest of the three embodiments of Pip:

> All possess that bright-eyed honesty and vulnerable gullibility, but . . . the youngest has an indefinable quality. I am willing to bet that this quality may lead to stardom. (*Guardian* 5.5.1984)

Sammarco went on to fame as Adrian Mole in the television version of Sue Townsend's *The Secret Diary of Adrian Mole*.

On the evening of Saturday 5 May Her Royal Highness Princess Alexandra and the Hon. Angus Ogilvie attended the performance of *Great Expectations* and a reception afterwards. On previous royal visits by H.M. the Queen in November

Royal visit November 1982.
Her Majesty The Queen, The Mayor of Northampton (Councillor Reg Harris),
Mrs Joan Benton, Alwyn Hargrave, Mrs Joy Hargrave.

1982 and Princess Anne in November 1983 the Royal Theatre had been included on the itinerary only by virtue of its proximity to Derngate.

The rest of the centenary season was less successful. With the recent high level of public support "Now, Michael says, he feels confident enough to throw caution to the winds and put on something different" (*C&E* 20.3.1984). Ted Tally's *Terra Nova* did not stir the emotions despite its epic subject of Scott's expedition to the Antarctic. Peter Durrant's *The Brylcreem Boys* about a Second World War R.A.F. bomber crew, a rewrite of his 1979 television drama, failed to take off. Bernard Slade's Broadway comedy *Tribute* was touching and amusing, but could not restore amends. In his report to the A.G.M. on 16 October 1984 Alwyn Hargrave speculated that failure was "because the plays generally appeared to have more male appeal than female". Whilst Michael Napier Brown was entitled to be bold in his choice of plays for the centenary season the pity was that not one was of sufficiently high calibre to compensate artistically for the financial losses, which were compounded by extended runs of three and a half weeks. In the game of theatrical snakes and ladders the centenary season had been an abrupt reversal of fortunes for the Royal Theatre.

Whatever the significance of 1984 for Northampton, a new order in state subsidy of the arts was heralded by the Arts Council's publication of *The Glory of the Garden The Development of the Arts in England A Strategy for a Decade* on 30 March. In his preface Sir William Rees-Mogg, chairman of the Arts Council, quoted a talk on B.B.C. radio in July 1945 in which Maynard Keynes outlined the priorities of the newly established Council of which he was the first chairman. The first priority was "to decentralise and disperse the dramatic and musical and artistic life of this country, to build up provincial centres and to promote corporate life in these matters in every town and county"; the second "to make London a great artistic metropolis" (p. iii). Rees-Mogg considered that the second objective had "been achieved, to a degree even beyond what he [Keynes] envisaged", but that the first "has not been adequately realised" (p. iv). Whilst safeguarding the capital Rees-Mogg set about the task of improving regional provision through the "devolution of assessment and funding to the Regional Arts Associations" and enhanced partnership with local authorities (p. v).

The section of *The Glory of the Garden* devoted to drama proclaimed:

The purpose of the programme is to enable the major, existing building-based companies . . . to achieve two broad objectives: to sustain the highest artistic standards of theatrical performance and to bear a much greater responsibility than they have had in the recent past for enriching the theatrical experience of the wider community in the whole of their region. (p. 16)

To this end "the Council will be spending £2 million on new developments in Drama in the initial stage of its strategy: £1.5 million for the expansion of the regional repertory companies' responsibilities and £500,000 for other purposes" (p. 18). Although any new money was welcomed by the theatrical community, anxiety was expressed about how it would be dispersed, especially under a system in which the more generously subsidised (and supposedly more prestigious) regional theatres would continue to be funded direct by the Arts Council and only the lower tier be devolved to the Regional Arts Associations. In the East Midlands the Haymarket Theatre Leicester and the Nottingham Playhouse remained with the Arts Council; Derby Playhouse, the Royal Theatre Northampton and the Perspectives Theatre Company were to be devolved to East Midlands Arts. A scheme of partnership between theatres in the two tiers was envisaged but not realised.

The board, not surprisingly, "were unhappy with the proposed two-tier approach and felt that Northampton had been 'relegated to the second division'" (BM 8.5.1984). Michael Napier Brown produced a document *The Royal Theatre. Northampton Repertory Players Ltd. Stagnation or Progression? To Perish – or Flourish?* expressing the case for "substantially increased funding . . . from 1985". He drew attention to the company's long history and its recent fund-raising initiative which had resulted in improved facilities but also higher (estimated £30,000 annually BM 8.5.1984) running costs. He wrote of the need to build up new audiences and identified two linked goals: "the formation of a Theatre-in-Education and Studio Theatre company". For the financial year 1985-6, in which devolvement to East Midlands Arts took place the Royal Theatre received £20,000 development money bringing its subsidy up to £115,500 to which East Midlands added a further £6,500 from its own budget, specifically for Theatre-in-Education on the condition of a matching response from the local authorities (BM 11.3.1985 and 16.4.1985). *The Glory of the Garden* had scattered some new seed in Northampton. Jenny Cann was appointed director of T.I.E. from 29 July 1985 (BM 25.6.1985).

In the large format programme for *Annie* Michael Napier Brown wrote ("Tomorrow" at the Royal) of the "project . . . [which], apart from its intrinsic educational value, will help to spread the word to upcoming potential theatregoers that theatre is exciting, fun, stimulating, provocative – and necessary". The choice of the musical *Annie* to launch the autumn 1985 season accorded well with the establishment of T.I.E. affording, as it did, tremendous scope for Michael Napier Brown to deploy his flair with young performers.

Through the summer the search for prodigies and canines generated excellent publicity. In May two hundred aspiring Annies were auditioned from whom Gina Lander now aged thirteen and Hayley Palmer aged eleven were selected to alternate in the role; in June a call was put out to dog owners as a result of which Snoopy, an old English ("Dulux") sheepdog and Kelly, a rather indeterminate terrier were chosen. The casting of such old favourites as Vilma Hollingbery (Miss Hannigen), Antony Linford (President Roosevelt inter alia), Clare Welch, Glynn Sweet and Alexa Povah was newsworthy as was John Larsen's visit to the barber's to acquire a shaven head for his portrayal of Daddy Warbucks. The importance of an imaginative and energetic publicity officer (Andrew Thompson) was amply demonstrated.

Annie collected unanimous plaudits in the local press: "Enchanting *Annie*" (*C&E* 28.8.1985); "Annie Just Magical" (*M&H* 31.8.1985); "Annie You're a Winner" (*NP* 29.8.1985). Michael Napier Brown's direction tempered the musical's sentimentality with wry humour and elicited excellent performances from professionals, children ("As a showcase for local talent, this production is a winner" *ET* 27.8.1985) and quadrupeds alike. Even the illness of Gina Lander was turned to good effect with her replacement twelve year old Maria Carrington hitting the headlines: "Maria Steps into Stardom" (*M&H* 7.9.1985). The board had been hesitant about extending the run of *Annie* to over six weeks, but the quality of the production and the audience response (77 per cent capacity) completely justified the decision and the outlay of £110,000.

Another, very different, musical held the stage in November 1985 – Willy Russell's *Blood Brothers* which was brought back following its phenomenal

Annie 1985. John Larsen as Daddy Warbucks surrounded by Karen Galloway, Maria Carrington (Annie), Nicola Crouch, Rachel Lewin, Natalie Conant and Helen Thompson. (Royal Theatre Collection)

success in April/May 1985. On both occasions Reina James played the mother of twin sons who are separated at birth – Eddie to a privileged upbringing, Mickey to one of deprivation. The first night in April had been greeted by a standing ovation (a rare if not unique occurrence in Northampton) and the magic was recaptured in the revival.

Following the success of *Annie* Lionel Bart's *Oliver* must have seemed a natural choice for the opening of the autumn 1986 season. Again there was good publicity surrounding the casting of Oliver (Paul Arnold aged nine and Andrew Young aged eight), the other boys and the dog Bullseye ("Max, the ale-swilling, peppermint-crunching hound from the Crown and Anchor in Victoria Road" *C&E* 8.7.1986). Martin Friend was cast as Fagin and Heather Page as Nancy, though she had to be replaced by Tracy Sweetingburgh when she succumbed to a throat infection after the first night. Dickens's powerful story line and Bart's memorable score (under the musical direction of Maurice Merry) held audiences "torn between exhilaration and deep pity" (*Mirror* 18.8.1986). Ray Lett's set design "brought a whole new dimension to the Royal's stage – St. Paul's and London Bridge tower over the underworld, an intricate series of steps and a revolving stage present endless possibilities for dramatic chase scenes" (*ET* 10.9.1986). As usual Ray Lett's method was "to conceive the set full-size FIRST in order to build the miniature. That way any inaccuracies are scaled down rather than blown up. It is then easier to construct the full-size set, having visualised it to start with" (*Northamptonshire Image* October 1986). Like *Annie*, *Oliver* sustained a run of over six weeks (76 per cent BM A.G.M. 2.11.1987).

Unfortunately musicals of the quality and appeal of *Annie* and *Oliver* are in short supply. The Melvyn Bragg/Howard Goodall saga of a Cumbrian family between 1898 and 1925 *The Hired Man* (autumn 1987) drew on the English folk tradition, but the large cast was never fully energised in the rather cramped permanent stone wall set. In August 1989 Michael Napier Brown returned to the formula of using local children, thirty-five of whom made up the cast of *The Ragged Child* a musical about the work of the Earl of Shaftesbury, but the impression created was of an amateur show. It achieved only 45 per cent attendance instead of the estimated 60 per cent (BM 2.10.1989). Willy Russell's *Our Day Out* a stage version, with music, of his television play about a school trip heralded the autumn 1991 season.

An enterprising musical choice *Seesaw*, based on *Two for the Seesaw* by William Gibson (author of the Helen Keller plays) was staged in April 1987 with much interest attached to the casting of former pop star Helen Shapiro as the love-struck Gittel Mosca (played by Shirley MacLaine on film). Expectations ran high ("The West End is buzzing with excitement to see if the Royal can make a success of a musical new to these shores" *C&E* 21.3.1987) and several national critics beat their way to Northampton. Martin Hoyle commended "Ray Lett's stylised cityscape . . . Christopher Wren's choreography" and Helen Shapiro's performance and vocal technique – "she deals splendidly with the songs" – and judged *Seesaw* "A decided feather in Northampton's cap" (*Financial Times* 14.4.1987). The hoped for West End transfer did not materialise.

It was in the sphere of recent American drama that Michael Napier Brown raised the Royal Theatre's profile to at least the verge of national prominence. In June 1986 he secured the rights for the regional première of John Pielmier's Broadway success *Agnes of God*. The cast of three comprised Katharine Schlesinger (the twenty-three year old niece of film director John Schlesinger) as the young nun Agnes, Fiona Walker as the psychologist Dr. Livingstone and Vilma Hollingbery as Mother Miriam. The unravelling of personality and events following the discovery that Agnes had given birth to a baby, strangled by its umbilical cord, more than compensated for the play's lack of action.

In July 1987 the Royal Theatre staged another regional première James Duff's *The War at Home*, about the return of a Vietnam conscript to his family in Texas for Thanksgiving Day 1973. Again putting his trust in youth Michael Napier Brown cast Anthony Leete as the disillusioned soldier and he made "a stunning professional debut" (*M&H* 3.7.1987). As his sister Karen, Kate Napier Brown's (Michael's daughter) "vocal and emotional range, her timing and physical bearing all combine to make hers an unforgettable performance" (*ET* 27.6.1987). Tony Caunter was the short-tempered father; Barbara Morton the dominating mother. Despite the offer of three hundred free tickets for new playgoers at the performance on Monday 6 July the overall attendance only mustered 31 per cent, but the production went on to play a week at the Richmond Theatre, where it collected further plaudits.

Frank Gilroy's *The Subject Was Roses* in October 1988 also revolved around the return of a soldier, this time Timmy (Bill Neville) back from the Second World War to confront his dominating father (Jon Croft) and possessive mother (Barbara New). Though the pace was slow the tension gradually built up, but not before audience attention had begun to waver.

Thematically both *The War at Home* and *The Subject Was Roses* owed a debt to Arthur Miller's *All My Sons* in which Michael Napier Brown had made the first of several impressive appearances in classics of the modern American stage. In April 1985 he and Vilma Hollingbery played George and Martha in Edward Albee's *Who's Afraid of Virginia Woolf?* under the direction of Richard Olivier (son of Laurence Olivier and Joan Plowright) who spent a season as a trainee at the Royal. As the battling George and Martha the Napier Browns excelled themselves: "Vilma Hollingbery confirms beyond doubt that she is one of our great dramatic actresses and when on stage with real life husband Michael Napier Brown, the result is stunning" (*M&H* 9.3.1985). With experienced performers in such fine form it was difficult to apportion credit to their young director, though both Michael Napier Brown and Vilma Hollingbery were generous with their praise.

Arthur Miller's *Death of a Salesman* followed in 1986 with Michael Napier Brown as Willie Loman giving "a magical performance as the road weary salesman" powerfully supported by Vilma Hollingbery as his long-suffering wife Linda (*Bedfordshire on Sunday* 16.11.1986). Helped by prime scheduling in November and the husband and wife casting the production played to an impressive 80 per cent (BM A.G.M. 2.11.1987).

As the hammy actor James Tyrone in Eugene O'Neill's *Long Day's Journey into Night* Michael Napier Brown was partnered by Diana Fairfax as his drug-

Who's Afraid of Virginia Woolf? by Edward Albee 1985. Vilma Hollingbery as Martha, Tilly Tremayne as Honey, Michael Napier Brown as George and Timothy Block as Nick. (Royal Theatre Collection)

dependent wife Mary, with Kim Wall and Bill Neville as their sons. The production was by Mark Clements, for a time associate director and thereafter a regular guest director. Michael Napier Brown delivered a *tour de force* as Tyrone, capturing "perfectly that testy Irishness that doesn't need the brogue to bring it out, and [he] has a way of looking hopelessly dejected whilst still carrying himself as a matinee idol"; Diana Fairfax showed "profound insight into the harrowing role of Mary . . . the mask of normality; the madness which is more harrowing for being contained" (*Guardian* 6.5.1989). All these productions provided ample substance for lecture–discussions, which from the early 1970s had become a regular feature of the adult education programme at the University Centre.

In his performances as Joe Keller, Willy Loman, George and James Tyrone Michael Napier Brown achieved the status of a repertory star, as did Vilma Hollingbery in hers as Kate Keller, Linda Loman and Martha. Significantly *The Crucible* in June 1988 without the benefit of these performers was disappointingly supported despite excellent reviews.

The American tradition was upheld with Chris Sergel's dramatisation of Harper Lee's novel of racial discrimination *To Kill a Mocking Bird* with which the autumn 1988 season opened. The sweltering heat of Maycomb, Alabama pervaded the set which was populated by a cast of eighteen including Alan Dobie, quietly dignified as the lawyer Atticus Finch and Hildegard Neil as his daughter Jean Louise narrating the incident in later life. The part of the young Jean Louise (Scout) was played by Penny Gonshaw, who with Nick Raggett as her brother Jem, almost stole the show. The director was Chris Hayes, who after experience in Europe and a spell as artistic director of the Marlowe Theatre, Canterbury, had founded North Bank Productions in 1984. *To Kill a Mocking Bird* was a joint production destined for a seven month tour after Northampton and it in fact ultimately reached London's Mermaid Theatre. The pros and cons of co-productions with commercial managements are finely balanced. The repertory company's production budget is enhanced and the commercial company gets its show on the road more cheaply. The repertory company achieves a longer life for its production (though at the cost of losing the services of the cast for the rest of the season), it extends its reputation and hopefully accrues extra revenue. In the case of *To Kill a Mockingbird* these objectives were by and large achieved. A Northampton production was eventually seen in London and the theatre received "£7,500 since the production left the main house" (BM 4.9.1989).

Other similar ventures were less successful. A production of J. B. Priestley's *An Inspector Calls* in January 1988 benefited from the West End set and the presence of Helen Ryan, Michael Craig and Reginald Marsh in the cast, but Westminster Productions' tour foundered, making a loss of £20,000. Thus far from receiving extra money the theatre's finances were depleted by the base estimate of £4,000 from the tour which had been built into the budget (BM 14.6.1988). This experience did not deter the Royal Theatre from engaging in similar ventures including Lionel Hamilton's adaptation of *Jane Eyre* (with Richard Warwick and Charlotte Harvey) and Willis Hall's *The Long and The Short and The Tall*, both in conjunction with North Bank in the autumn of 1989. In January 1991 Jeffrey Archer's West End success *Beyond Reasonable Doubt*, having played to 83 per cent (BM 4.3.1991) in Northampton, was launched on its first national tour with Francis Matthews and Barbara Murray lending starry lustre to the cast and Ray Lett's sets enhanced by a more generous budget.

The search for a new play, which will bring distinction and/or financial rewards, is the repertory theatre's equivalent to the alchemist's stone. William Gibson's *Monday After the Miracle* proved to be a worthy successor to *The Miracle Worker* with Alexa Povah returning to her role of Annie Sullivan and blind actress Ailsa Fairley mastering the vocal peculiarities of the now almost adult Helen Keller. Credit reflected on the Royal Theatre: "[it] is obviously placed high on the list of provincial repertory theatres to claim the right to stage the British première of such an ambitious play" (*NP* 8.2.1986).

In lighter vein Richard Everett's *A Bride Too Far* in March 1987 was trumpeted as a play with West End prospects, but these were summarily dismissed even by the local critics. In October 1988 the same author's *Happy Event*, though not a première, was attended by similar expectations which again proved to be ill-founded. Earlier that year London managements were said to be "expressing interest" in *The Murder Factory of John George Haigh* a world première by John Peacock, whose *Children of the Wolf* (first seen in Cheltenham in 1971) had been successfully revived at the Royal in May 1987. Peter McEnery, an actor equally admired for his stage (including R.S.C.) and television (currently *The Mistress* with Felicity Kendal) work, was enticed to Northampton, protesting – perhaps too much – that he unexpectedly had "an available slot". McEnery's promotional appearance on B.B.C.'s Wogan chatshow was frustrated by re-scheduling, but the local press found additional stories in the casting of the distinguished actress Maxine Audley as Olivia, Haigh's intended victim, and Frazer Corbyn a thirteen year old Wellingborough schoolboy as the young Haigh. Peacock's attempt to reveal the child as father of the man failed to provide the clue to the multiple murderer's psyche. Although local critics were more indulgent, the *Guardian* judged the play "an ungainly piece", Michael Napier Brown's direction "clumsy" and the stars "wasted" (6.4.1988). Again Northampton's hopes for a metropolitan transfer were dashed.

National, indeed international, attention was directed at the Royal Theatre in the summer of 1990 when the world première of *Is This The Day?* by Vilma Hollingbery, with Michael Napier Brown, was staged. The play was based on *Jean's Way* in which journalist Derek Humphry related how he had helped his terminally ill first wife end her life. The *Guardian*'s choice of Ludovic Kennedy as its reviewer was symptomatic of the tendency to concentrate on the moral issues rather than the quality of the play. There was however uniform praise for the two

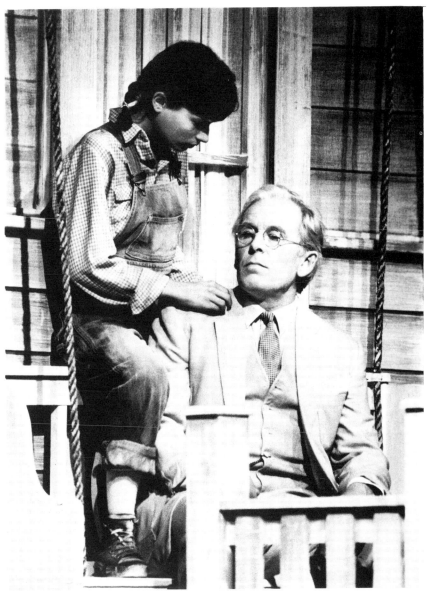

To Kill a Mocking Bird dramatised by Christopher Sergel from Harper Lee 1988. Alan Dobie as Atticus Finch and Penny Gonshaw as the young Jean Louise. (Royal Theatre Collection)

central performances: David Hargreaves as Max presented an uncannily accurate portrait of Derek Humphry and as Jane Polly James, an actress best known for television comedy, was "magnificent. Insisting on her toughness, she draws her audience's tears while holding mawkishness at bay" (*Independent on Sunday* 13.5.1990). *Is This The Day?* received the Eileen Anderson Central Television Drama Award and was staged in Berlin in November 1991.

With new plays such an uncertain commodity adaptations of well-known novels combined the encouragement of new writing with the reassurance of familiarity. Dickens featured with a hugely popular (88 per cent BM A.G.M. 2.11.1987) adaptation of *A Christmas Carol* by Vilma Hollingbery in the 1986 pre-Christmas slot and David Horlock's rather sprawling version of *A Tale of Two Cities* (with Kim Wall as Sydney Carton) was staged in April 1989 to coincide with the bicentenary of the French Revolution. By far the most effective Dickens adaptation was Stephen Jeffrey's four-handed *Hard Times* which received a studio production in November 1990, but that was not original to Northampton.

Local novelist H. E. Bates's *Fair Stood the Wind for France* (in an adaptation by Gregory Evans) was premièred in the presence of his widow in April 1986. The dramatic opening scene of the crashing bomber was effectively rendered and thereafter the touching love story of the young pilot Franklin (Kim Wall) and his French nurse Françoise (Katharine Schlesinger again showing her great promise) held powerful sway. Thomas Hardy's *Far From the Madding Crowd* stretched

Is This The Day? by Vilma Hollingbery 1990. Polly James as Jane and David Hargreaves as Max. (Royal Theatre Collection)

Vilma Hollingbery's skills as an adapter – "Drawn-out classic maddened the crowd" (*NP* 3.7.1986). A more interesting choice, especially for a theatre in the middle of England, was Richard Llewellyn's *How Green Was My Valley*, adapted by Shaun McKenna for the opening of the autumn 1990 season. As with many family sagas three actors were required to portray the character of Huw from childhood to old age, the later teenage years being embodied by Aled Jones embarking on an acting career after achieving tremendous fame as a treble soloist. Geoffrey Beevers's skilful adaptation of George Eliot's *Adam Bede* was staged in autumn 1991, with Katharine Schlesinger returning to play Hetty Sorrel. In April 1992 Aled Jones was back in Northampton in the title role of Martin Chuzzlewit in an adaptation of Dickens's novel by Lynn Robertson Hay.

For an artistic director remaining in post for a considerable length of time the choice of plays becomes increasingly difficult, especially at a time when financial constraints militate against large casts. West End successes which transferred successfully to Northampton included: *84, Charing Cross Road*, Nell Dunn's *Steaming*, Michael Frayn's *Noises Off* and Peter Shaffer's *Lettice and Lovage*. There was more resistance to Pam Gem's *Piaf* (Lorraine Brunning "*magnifique*"), Sharman McDonald's *When I was a Girl I Used to Scream and Shout* and Tom Kempinski's *Separation*. Though easily incensed by bad language (*When I was a Girl . . .*) Northampton audiences found the warning of stage nudity (*Steaming* and Mike Stott's *The Fancy Man*) irresistible. The supply of whodunnits, traditionally so beloved in the town, was halting, though *Wait Until Dark* (with Liz Crowther) and Ira Levin's *Deathtrap* were up to standard, unlike Anthony Shaffer's *Murderer*. Agatha Christie had been banished.

Four authors proved themselves almost banker-proof: Alan Ayckbourn; Willy Russell; Alan Bleasdale; and John Godber. In *Intimate Exchanges* Kim Wall and Alexa Povah so successfully peopled the stage with a range of typical Ayckbourn characters that some members of the audience could not believe their eyes when only two performers took a bow. Richard Cheshire's lively production of Godber's three-handed *Teechers* struck a common chord with the public and encouraged Michael Napier Brown to mount *Bouncers*, a racy tale of teenage club life, under Mark Clements's direction.

Of the earlier generation of standard repertory authors only J. B. Priestley (*When We Are Married, An Inspector Calls* and *Laburnum Grove*) and Noel Coward (*Hay Fever* and *Blithe Spirit*) continued to hold sway. One surprisingly successful rediscovery was Shelagh Delaney's *A Taste of Honey*. True classic revivals were very few, the cost of larger shows outweighing the absence of authors' royalties. *Macbeth* was accorded a further revival in autumn 1987 with Michael Irvine as the Thane and Liz Crowther as his wife. In June 1990 Richard Cheshire (on leave from his post as drama lecturer at the University of Wales, Aberystwyth) showed that a major classic was still within Northampton's range with a stylish production of Congreve's *The Way of the World*. Haydn Gwynne

Statements After An Arrest Under The Immorality Act by Athol Fugard 1988. Roy Lee as The Man (Errol Philander) and Shenagh Govan as The Woman (Frieda Joubert). A studio production. (Royal Theatre Collection)

(recently seen on television in David Lodge's *Nice Work*) was a captivating Millament, Paul Spence her Mirabell and R.S.C. and National Theatre actress Janet Whiteside a vigorous Lady Wishfort. Alison Ashton's scenery and costumes were a delight. Here was a production to stand comparison with the best of regional, even national, theatre.

A cast of fourteen, period sets and costumes and low box office expectations put plays like *The Way of the World* beyond the range of Northampton except very occasionally. The operation of a studio theatre was seen as an outlet for less commercial work, inexpensively staged, as an alternative to the inescapably box office orientated main house. The experiment of staging occasional studio productions in the functions suite at Derngate was initiated with *The Kiss of the Spider Woman* in Spring 1987. Although productions have been intermittent – only three or four a year – the opportunity to see more experimental work (Athol Fugard for instance) has been created and new, younger audiences attracted. Alas this facility came to an end in 1992. Meantime Derngate's own programme consisted of an increasing number of plays, including latterday examples of the fare that W. H. Holloway disparaged as part of his campaign to create a repertory theatre in Northampton. It is ironic that Northampton Borough Council should have spent millions of pounds to house the likes of *Ladies' Night*, *Last Tango in Whitby* and *Home and Away* (all summer 1991), with "net spending by the authority on the centre" amounting to "more than £2 million" in 1990–1 (*Stage* 20.2.1992).

The fortunes of the Royal Theatre came under the scrutiny of a review by the drama panel of East Midlands Arts which published its recommendations in May 1989. These included: "at least parity funding between the Association and the combined local authorities", "a senior administrative appointment", a review of the board structure, the establishment of sub-committees for programming and T.I.E., and the development of community touring and studio work. Board chairman Alwyn Hargrave welcomed the review in his annual report (2.10.1989) and pointed out that "The recommendations made were implemented almost before the Report appeared". Anthony Radford, a Cambridge graduate, became administrative director in autumn 1989 and Gavin Stride combined a lively T.I.E. programme with successful community touring (*Rosie Blitz*, *These Things Do Happen*, *Grimaldi*), even extending into Leicestershire. New appointments have been made to the board: Roy Atkinson (County Chief Education Officer), Richard Foulkes and Jane Harari, who replaced Lady Hesketh when she resigned in October 1990 after thirty-two years' service.

The publication of the Wilding Report in September 1989 advanced the devolution to the Regional Arts Associations begun by *The Glory of the Garden*. After much lobbying and debate and a rapid turnover of Arts Ministers (Richard Luce, David Mellor and Timothy Renton)[1] the restructuring of East Midlands Arts was completed with the prospect of Leicester's Haymarket Theatre and the

Board of directors

Left to right: Michael Boss, Eric Roberts, David Hughes, Richard Foulkes (Vice-Chairman), Cyril Benton, Richard Morris, Roy Atkinson, Alan Maskell (Honorary Treasurer)

Seated: Jane Harari, A. J. Hargrave (Chairman), John J. Gardner B.E.M.. Michael Henley

Kneeling: Tony Parker (Secretary).

Nottingham Playhouse being devolved to it, thereby ending the invidious two-tier system. The Northampton Repertory Players were required to draft a three year business plan (January 1990, updated March 1991) the key proposals of which included a studio theatre and the introduction of a subscription scheme. The subscription scheme was a response to the fickle conservatism of Northampton audiences which resulted in attendance ranging from 26 per cent to 79 per cent cash capacity over a short period in 1990. The achievement of over 2,000 subscribers meant not only money in the bank, but also an assured core audience for less popular plays. The Friends of the Royal Theatre, a reincarnation of the Playgoers, continued to provide support, extending to the sponsorship of the studio production of *Hard Times* in 1990.

In March 1991 Michael Napier Brown was confirmed in his post as director of productions until 1995, by which time he will have become the longest serving occupant of that post. Alwyn Hargrave's tenure as board chairman has already overtaken that of all his predecessors save Mrs. Panther. Together these two men have steered the fortunes of the Northampton Repertory Players adroitly. In his annual report (2.10.1989) Alwyn Hargrave reiterated the policy which historically has served Northampton so well: "to provide a varied diet of plays, to appeal to a broad spectrum of tastes . . . I certainly hope and expect that all our productions are productions of quality".

Michael Napier Brown's capacity to gauge and stretch the theatre-going habits of Northampton has held firm. His own skills as a director (like Kelsey he did a stint at the Ludlow Festival) and talent as an actor are recognised and appreciated. His particular flair with young performers (professional and amateur) has been put to good account. The principle of a permanent company has lapsed, but regulars such as David Neal, Kim Wall, Alexa Povah, Glynn Sweet, Clare Welch and of course Vilma Hollingbery and happily, the now octogenarian, Lionel Hamilton are welcomed back. The spirit of the times is evident in the pursuit of sponsorship (£23,500 in 1990-1) and co-productions with commercial managements. However the inevitably uncommercial work of T.I.E., community touring and studio production has been safeguarded, though the provision of a permanent studio remains unrealised.

The Royal Theatre stands proudly near the top of the national league table for audiences as a percentage of capacity, but though box office returns are an important measure of success, Northampton depends also upon its grant-aiding bodies for the maintenance and development of its impressive standard and range of work. It remains true, as Alwyn Hargrave wrote in response to *The Glory of the Garden*, that "when compared with most other comparable regional theatres the Royal Theatre has, historically, suffered a relatively low level of public funding" (BM A.G.M. 16.10.1984).[2]

Notes

1. Following the April 1992 general election the Department of National Heritage was formed with David Mellor as minister.

2. The East Midlands Arts grant for 1991-2 was £165,290 compared with £258,970 to the Derby Playhouse. Grants represented approx. 31 per cent of total income; attendance target 58 per cent throughout the year (BM A.G.M. 11.11.1991).

CHAPTER TWELVE

There is Nothing Like a Dame: Pantomime

IN an article in the *Guardian* on 24 December 1988 Matthew Engel reported on the preparations for and opening of *Cinderella* at Northampton's Royal Theatre. Northampton had been selected because of its reputation as a bastion of traditional pantomime. The first pantomime to be performed at the Royal Theatre was *Robinson Crusoe* in 1888 in which Vesta Victoria, the celebrated music hall star, played the Clerk of the Weather.

When the Northampton Repertory Players contemplated their first Christmas entertainment in December 1927 the view of the *Northampton Independent* was that "a back-slang and possibly vulgar pantomime" (10.12.1927) would be inconsistent with the theatre's new artistic aspirations. Instead Rupert Harvey staged Shakespeare's *A Midsummer Night's Dream* with a cast that included James Hayter as Puck.

For Christmas 1928 Herbert Prentice presented his own *Alice in Wonderland* (from Lewis Carroll), which was distinguished by Curigwen Lewis's performance as Alice – "Perhaps she could not be paid a bigger compliment than to be told that the Alice of our book acquaintance was not nearly as *ingenue*, as sweet, and as brightly curious as she is" (*NDC* 26.12.1928). James Hayter was the White Rabbit, Noel Morris a dignified King of Hearts, C. T. Doe a rounded Cook and T. G. Saville gave three nicely contrasted performances as the Mock Turtle, Humpty-Dumpty and the Walrus. All of the cast recalled the Tenniel drawings and Osborne Robinson supplied settings in keeping with the best traditions of pantomime. The first night was not without incident as Osborne Robinson recalled forty-eight years later:

> It was a Christmas Eve opening and can only be described as a Christmas nightmare one likes to forget. At the beginning of the performance Alice was supposed to be falling down the hole and one of the men lowering her shouted "All right miss, we got you!" As if that wasn't enough the White Rabbit in his mask turned downstage instead of up, headed into the orchestra and ended up in the first row of the stalls. The curtain had to go down and we had to begin again. (*NI* Dec. 1975)

The next four Christmas productions were *Raffles* (1929), *The School for Scandal*

Sinbad the Sailor 1935. Designs by Osborne Robinson for Sinbad (Patrick Crean) and Mother Antimacastra (Olga Murgatroyd). (Programme 16.12.1935)

(1930), *Nothing But The Truth* (1931) and *Tons of Money* (1932). Seasonal associations were not entirely denied and *The School for Scandal* was hailed as a "Charming Christmas Production" which reached "the peak of achievement" (*NDC* 23.12.1930).

The repertory company's first traditional pantomime was *Jack and the Beanstalk* by Margaret Carter, presented in 1933 for matinees only, under the direction of Robert Young with sets by Osborne Robinson and special music by Marian Wilson. Patrick Gover was Jack, Oswald Dale Roberts Peterkins, Donald Gordon Rufus, Sheila Millar Mother Grubble, Zillah Grey Lady Flavia and Doris Littell Azelle. Two young members of the company made their mark: Freda Jackson as First Weaver and Errol Flynn as a dashing and handsome Prince Donzil. Osborne Robinson's designs for the thirteen scenes included a bean plant that grew and grew and the giant's kitchen with its "monster copper, the six-foot bottle of 'Phizic', the tremendous packet of bird seed for the hen that laid the golden eggs . . . There was not a vacant seat in the house, and many people had to stand or sit on the gangway steps" (*C&E* 28.12.1933).

Following this success pantomime returned with Margaret Carter's scripts being used for *Cinderella* (1934), *Sinbad the Sailor* (1935) and *Dick Whittington* (1936). The tradition of making the costumes, settings and properties in the theatre was firmly established and happily reproductions of some of Osborne Robinson's costume designs for *Sinbad the Sailor* survive. For *Dick Whittington*, which was "set in the Richard II period", Osborne Robinson used "tons of paint

185

and yards of material", the latter consisted of his favoured fabric, felt, from which the wardrobe mistress Mrs. Fred Pratt made thirty-seven dazzling costumes (*C&E* 27.12.1936). Over the years Osborne Robinson put his friendship with the sales manager at Liberty's to good effect to acquire material at bargain prices.

Latterly pantomime has become a major money-spinner, but the early experience was mixed: *Jack and the Beanstalk* showed a profit of £97; *Cinderella* one of £105 10s. 9d. but *Sinbad the Sailor* was in credit to only £21 5s. 8d. (BM).

This financial downturn probably influenced the abandonment of pantomime for the next decade, much of which was affected by the shortages of war. A seasonal flavour was provided in 1941 with a large cast (forty named characters) production of *Pickwick* with William Brookfield in the title role, Edwin Morton as Sam Weller, Lawrence Baskcomb as Buzfuz, Franklin Davies as Tupman, George Roche as Jingle and Florence Churchill as Mrs. Bardell. Wartime restrictions hampered preparations and Osborne Robinson recalled "we couldn't work at night because of the Blackout – we had a glass roof which it would have been too expensive to cover up" (*NI* Dec. 1975).

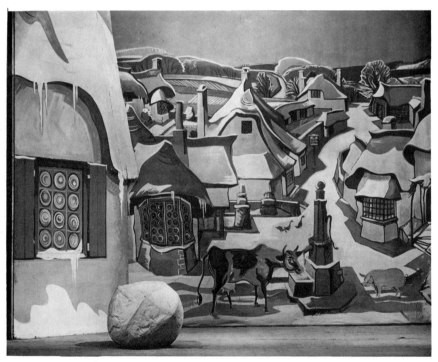

Dick Whittington 1936. Design by Osborne Robinson. (Royal Theatre Collection)

186

Cinderella 1946. Lionel Hamilton as the Ugly Sister Diaphenia. (Lionel Hamilton Collection)

187

Reginald Arkell's *1066 and All That*, which had originated at the Birmingham Repertory Theatre, was staged in 1943; *The Scarlet Pimpernel* in 1944; and in 1945 Alex Reeve and Osborne Robinson devised *Command Performance*: "The whole thing is like a well-filled pre-war Christmas stocking; it contains songs and dances, a Nativity play, an old fashioned melodrama, and some superb pieces of sheer clowning . . . The company . . . put everything into it . . . Alex Reeve also acts as compere" (*C&E* 27.12.1945).

Traditional pantomime returned in 1946 with *Cinderella*, Northampton's favourite, in a version by Alex Reeve. Beryl Robinson was Cinderella, Arnold Peters the Demon King and Ronald Radd as Buttons, who "showed just how well the audience and the players were getting on together. He asked the children to answer 'Hello Buttons' every time he called 'Hello Children'. The response he got each time was magnificent". The high point was Lionel Hamilton's performance as Diaphenia, one of the Ugly Sisters: "Funniest scenes are perhaps those in which the Ugly Sisters (Lionel Hamilton and Mary Russell) appear." Lionel Hamilton's Dame remained a major attraction for years to come. Tradition was embodied in the retention of the harlequinade in the history of which Osborne Robinson was deeply interested. This constituted the penultimate scene (before the wedding) and was "lively, attractive and amusing" (*C&E* 31.12.1946).

In 1947 Lionel Hamilton delighted as Dick's Mum ("A Boy's Best Friend is His Mum") in *Dick Whittington* and in 1948 as Mrs. Baba in *Ali Baba* "a dame in the high tradition . . . She is the new look welded to a very old and knowing look, and deserves the reception she gets" (*C&E* 28.12.1948). Reeve's team included Stephen Sylvester who wrote the songs and Molly Mayhew (who had appeared as the Fairy Godmother in the 1946 *Cinderella*) with her corps of young dancers.

By now the company was also operating in Kettering and in 1948 it realised the formidable achievement of staging pantomimes in both theatres. *Cinderella* was revived at the Savoy with a cast which included "admired Repertory players, augmented by some new, and some entirely local talent". Mary Chester "a fairy tale unto herself" was Cinderella, Peter Mizzen Buttons, Franklin Davies and Arthur R. Webb Brokers men, Dorothy Fenwick and Norah Williams the Ugly Sisters and Arnold Peters repeated his Demon King: "He it was who introduced and danced in a delightful harlequinade, with Molly Mayhew, a dancer not only to her toes, but finger-tips as well" (*ET* 28.12.1948). Osborne Robinson's sets were on view at both theatres, but the strain of mounting two pantomimes was excessive and in 1949 a visiting production filled the Savoy.

The New Theatre in Northampton also staged an annual pantomime, at this time under the management of S. H. Newsome in association with Emile Littler "perhaps our best known chief of pantomime". *Little Bo Peep* was very much a show business affair, with speciality turns in the style of variety: "The Tiller Girls and the Du Garde Babes are both well-trained dancing groups, while that exciting and beautiful turn Eugene's Flying Ballet, adds its quota to the spectacular side"

(*ET* 28.12.1948). In the face of such competition the repertory company wisely stuck to tradition.

The two pantomime companies joined forces for a special pantomime service held at the New Theatre. In 1951 the Rev. Louis A. Ewart (theatre chaplain and Vicar of Earls Barton) was responsible for the arrangements with proceeds going to the Actors' Church Fund. Against a brightly patterned stage-set the Bishop of Peterborough (Dr. Spencer Leeson) preached the sermon, Reginald Thorne (Royal Theatre) and George Moon (New Theatre) read the lessons, the Marshman Singers and the St. Giles's Church choir performed, Joan Burden sang "Ave Maria" and Miss Hannah Watt recited two of her own poetic compositions. The New Theatre orchestra under William Griffith led the singing of hymns (*NI* 9.2.1951).

An annual pantomime ball was also held to which the managers of the Ritz and Plaza Cinemas lent their support in 1953. Music at the Salon-de-Danse was provided by Jimmy Wooding and his Band with special displays of ballroom dancing by "the Northampton experts, Stanley and Keeler" (*NI* 23.1.1953).

Traditional pantomimes continued to hold sway during the 1950s with Lionel Hamilton's Dame and Osborne Robinson's sets and costumes eagerly awaited. Members of the permanent company threw themselves into the annual seasonal offering with enthusiasm – *Babes in the Wood* (1955) included Nigel Hawthorne as Will Scarlet, Alan Brown as Little John, Arthur Pentelow as Much-the-Miller, Tenniel Evans as Baron Blique Prospect, Dorothy Fenwick as Lady Eleanor (of the Royal Court), all alongside Lionel Hamilton's Dame Crawfoot (Nanny). Casts were sizable ranging from twenty-six to thirty with between ten and fifteen scenes. The number of performances increased from thirty-four in 1954 to fifty-one in 1959. Expenditure inevitably crept up – from £3,298 in 1954 to £5,723 in 1958 – but so did attendances from 20,636, to 26,311. The margin of profit was adequate – £316 for *Dick Whittington* in 1954, £938 for *Babes in the Wood* in 1955, £608 for *Jack and the Beanstalk* in 1956 and £360 for *Cinderella* in 1957, but in 1958 *Aladdin* returned a loss of £10, due more to high expenditure than low income.[1]

In 1959 Alan Brown provided the script for *Dick Whittington*, which still included the harlequinade as the penultimate scene. He followed this with *Puss in Boots* (for the first time) in 1960, *Cinderella* in 1961 and *Babes in the Wood* in 1962. Henry Marshall supplied *Robinson Crusoe* in 1963 and *Aladdin* in 1964 and in 1965 theatre historian V. C. Clinton-Baddeley's version of *Dick Whittington* was used: "skilfully produced by Alan Vaughan Williams, artistically staged and costumed by Osborne Robinson . . . with the Maurice Merry Trio, providing a major part of the show's success". Marcia Warren as Dick's faithful cat had "the audience jumping up and down in their seats with excitement" (*Era* 6.1.1966).

Excitement could get out of hand and behaviour in the balcony on the last night of the pantomime recalled an earlier more unruly age of theatre-going:

Dick Whittington 1959. Lionel Hamilton centre as Dick's mother. (Lionel Hamilton Collection)

> In view of the disturbances in the Balcony on previous last nights of the Pantomime, it was agreed that the services of two policemen be engaged in stand by in case of more trouble. (BM 8.1.1968)

The pantomime on that occasion was Willard Stoker's *Sinbad the Sailor*, but as the sixties drew to a close the taste for novelty exerted itself and Stoker broke with tradition to stage Lionel Bart's musical *Oliver*. Gordon Faith played Fagin; Angela Eaton was Nancy; John Bott was Mr. Sowerby and Gerald Davis undertook Oliver, with the customary amount of press interest being heightened when he left the cast for an engagement in *Mame*, with Ginger Rogers at Drury Lane. He was replaced as Oliver by John Hicks. The production, extended from six to eight weeks, was seen by 34,000, making it "the most successful play to be staged at the theatre for 42 years" (*C&E* 17.2.1969). *Oliver* was the occasion for the introduction of a revolving stage. Osborne Robinson recalled "It was a hand-turned revolving stage which we borrowed, but without it the quick changes in the complicated scenes would never have been possible" (*NI* Dec. 1975). An attempt to follow the *Oliver* formula with *My Gentleman Pip* (based on Dickens's *Great Expectations*) in 1969 fell far short of comparable success, despite the casting of pop singer Jess Conrad as Pip.

Jack and the Beanstalk 1991. Felicity Goodson as Jack, Michael Kirk as Rapscallion Runner Bean and Mark Carey as Minor.

After *Cinderella* in 1970 Willard Stoker turned to A. A. Milne's *Toad of Toad Hall* in 1971 which Osborne Robinson recalled with particular affection:

> My most nostalgic memory of Christmas in the theatre is undoubtedly that of 'Toad of Toad Hall', when the little animals of the wood and river bank sang Christmas carols outside badger's front door. It was on Boxing Day when the curtain rose to a crowded house of children and all the work put in by all and the anxieties we had melted away into laughter and delight. (*NI* Dec. 1975)

A reprise of *Dick Whittington* followed in 1972, then in 1973 Willard Stoker staged "perhaps the most spectacular Christmas show of all . . . *Chu Chin Chow*", Oscar Asche's First World War "Musical Tale of the East" (*NI* Dec. 1975). With a talented cast including Oz Clarke, Bernice Stegers, Henry Knowles (as Ali Baba), Marjorie Bland and Julian Fellowes and Osborne Robinson's exuberant costumes and sets the run was extended until 9 February 1974. A dissenting note was sounded in a *Chronicle and Echo* editorial:

> When Chu Chin Chow finally folds his tent and silently steals away, there will be discreet sighs of relief on both sides of the curtain. (24.1.1974)

Further departures from tradition followed – *The Wizard of Oz* in 1974, *Joseph and the Amazing Technicolor Dreamcoat* in 1975, *The Owl and the Pussy Cat* in 1976 – before it was restored by David Kelsey in 1977 with a version of *Cinderella* by himself and Martin Waddington. The same team was responsible for *Dick Whittington* in 1978 and Kelsey alone for *Aladdin* in 1979. Donald Cotton delivered *Mother Goose* in 1980.

After using the Myles Ridge/John Gould *Jack and the Beanstalk* in 1981, Michael Napier Brown instituted the still unbroken tradition of entrusting the pantomime to Vilma Hollingbery with *Babes in the Wood* in 1982. The familiar stories of *Cinderella* (1983 with Maurice Merry and 1988), *Dick Whittington and His Cat* (again with Merry in 1984), *Aladdin* (1987) and *Robin Hood* (1990) were interspersed with *Sleeping Beauty* (1985) and *Beauty and the Beast* (1986) with both of which Michael Napier Brown collaborated on the script. In 1991 *Jack and the Beanstalk*, the first pantomime ever staged by the repertory company, returned.

Of her approach to writing pantomime Vilma Hollingbery said:

> For me pantomime has to be traditional . . . Children love to be involved in the story. They love to feel that they helped beat the villain or brought *Mother Goose* to the land of eiderdown or whatever. As I write I'm always checking to make sure I've involved the youngsters as much as possible, is there a line I can put in that will give them a chance to respond? (*ET* 2.1.1990)

As Vilma Hollingbery observed the Royal's pantomimes, for all their traditionalism, are "invariably big productions; a large cast, lots of costumes, lots of scene changes" (*ET* 2.1.1990). Ray Lett, the long-serving head of design, has maintained the traditions and standards of scenery established by Osborne Robinson. For *Dick Whittington and His Cat* audiences were transported "from London to London, via Paradise Bay, Morocco and a visit to King Neptune in his underwater grotto" (*C&E* 11.12.1984). The underwater transformation scene used gauze and other techniques dating back to the Victorian theatre.

Indeed the Royal Theatre is still very much functioning with late-nineteenth-century apparatus:

> this is one of the last theatres in England where the scenery is controlled by brawny lads hauling on ropes instead of using modern counterweight mechanisms. Weekes Baptiste, the lord of the Flies, is aloft in a gallery not unlike the rigging of a galleon. There are 52 fly-cues in this production [Cinderella] and 17 full scene changes. (*Guardian* 24.12.1988)

The pressure to get the show ready in three weeks (without incurring prohibitively expensive overtime) is intense and Matthew Engel's description of the first night of *Cinderella*, when a torn backcloth prolonged the interval to twenty-five minutes, recalls the false start to *Alice in Wonderland* in 1928. Stage superstitions are upheld (as befits a theatre with its own "Grey Lady" ghost)[2] with the exchange of first night "prezzies" and the disclosure of the final line, which is always kept a secret until the last minute.

Not that tradition and folk-lore should obscure the sheer business side of pantomime. As Michael Napier Brown revealed in the *Guardian* article the pantomime takings constitute about one fifth of the annual box office income. *Robin Hood* in 1990 was a particularly testing case since that year the Royal Theatre faced direct local competition, for the first time since the closure of the New Theatre, from Derngate's *Snow White and the Seven Dwarfs* featuring Letitia Dean of television's *Eastenders*. The production opened early – on 10 December – with a view to getting established ahead of the competition, and ran for seven weeks. Attendance reached 27,800 with a box office income of £131,308, but at 63 per cent it fell short of the estimated 68 per cent, thereby reducing the surplus from £61,231 to £52,636 (BM 4.3.1991).

Pantomime is important to the Royal Theatre, not only financially, but because it attracts non-regular theatregoers and introduces the audiences of tomorrow to the magic of theatre. As Matthew Engel put it:

For 10 months a year theatre here represents an uneasy compromise between the artistic aspirations of the company and the tastes of the local people, who don't much like "headache plays". At Christmas there is a truce. Everyone loves the panto. Don't you? . . . a bit louder this time . . . That's better.

Notes

1. Figures compiled by Aubrey Dyas Perkins, amongst his papers in N.C.R.O..
2. Osborne Robinson and Bryan Douglas (stage carpenter, photographer and latterly front of house manager) were amongst those convinced of the Grey Lady's existence. (*C&E* 16.3.1989). Further sightings were reported in *NH&P* 14.11.1991.

Epilogue

'tis true that a good play needs no epilogue . . .

Rosalind *As You Like It*

IF the title of any Shakespeare play can serve as a motto for repertory in Northampton it must be *As You Like It*, for over the Northampton Repertory Players' history to date the taste of the town's theatre-going public has been an overriding consideration. Dr. Johnson's adage

The drama's laws, the drama's patrons give . . .

has been amply illustrated.

Much has changed in the sixty-five years since 1927. The town's population has risen from 90,000 to over 160,000 with the surrounding villages expanding proportionately. From the 1960s the M1 has traversed the county – a major artery for north–south mobility; after the ravages of the Beeching cuts, which left only five railway stations, the increase in commuters since the 1970s has resulted in improved services to London. The predominance of shoe-manufacturing has given way to diversification into light and service industries. Belatedly provision of higher education came in the form of the University of Leicester Centre (1967) and the creation of Nene College (1975). The opening of Derngate in 1983 provided the town with an impressive and versatile entertainment complex.

In terms of the repertory company gone are the days of twice nightly weekly productions with an annual turnover of forty-plus plays, each of them receiving a mere week's rehearsal. Instead there are less than ten productions a year with commensurately extended rehearsal time. It would be fascinating to be able to compare, say, Herbert Prentice's 1930 production of *The School for Scandal* with Richard Cheshire's 1990 revival of *The Way of the World* – both of them highly praised – to assess the standards achieved under the two systems. The principle of a permanent company has given way to *ad hoc* casting. The exigencies of making ends meet have been tempered by substantial (though still inadequate) subsidies from the Arts Council/East Midlands Arts and the local authorities, who are now represented on the board. A range of satellite activities – T.I.E., touring and studio – has grown up to complement the main house. Facilities, especially backstage, have been improved. Annual income now exceeds £1 million, as, of course, does expenditure.

Despite all of these changes the essential character of theatre in Northampton has altered remarkably little. C. J. Phipps's gem of a Victorian playhouse still exerts its charm, but the constraints of its stage and the ambience of its auditorium impose their own limitations. Audience taste remains resistant to "headache plays" with the preference for lighter fare (comedies, whodunnits, latterly musicals and of course pantomime) as pronounced as ever. The *avant-garde* is as alien in the form of Brecht or feminist drama as was expressionism in the 1930s. Classical plays occupy an even smaller part of the repertoire now than they did in the early days. In sixty-five years the Northampton Repertory Players have not brought into existence a single new play of enduring worth, but the same is true of most repertory companies. Adaptations from novels have been a more productive seam, with the work of Constance Cox setting an example for others to follow.

Stage design has been a remarkable strength thanks to Osborne Robinson's outstanding forty-eight years' service, and the tradition has been honourably upheld by his successor Ray Lett. Northampton has produced its fair share of famous players, with vintage companies in the 1930s (Max Adrian, Vivienne Bennett, James Hayter, Bertram Heyhoe, Noel Howlett and Curigwen Lewis – all 1930 – and Lois Obee, Oswald Dale Roberts, Donald Gordon, Freda Jackson and Errol Flynn), the 1950s (Nigel Hawthorne, Donald Churchill, Tenniel Evans, Alan Brown and Arthur Pentelow), and the early 1970s (Henry Knowles, Oz Clarke, Bernice Stegers, Marjorie Bland and Julian Fellowes). Lionel Hamilton's personal record from 1946 to 1991 has been a benchmark for repertory acting.

Of the successive artistic directors Herbert Prentice and Robert Young were men of national distinction, but they, like their more successful successors Lionel Hamilton, Keith Andrews, David Kelsey and Michael Napier Brown, balanced their artistic integrity with the tastes of the town. The experiences of Bladon Peake, Alan Vaughan Williams and Christopher Denys demonstrated the futility of trying to impose more adventurous fare on Northampton.

The board (originally five in number but totalling seventeen by 1992) has been criticised for being too static and limited in its membership, but on the credit side there has been continuity with four chairmen (Mrs. Panther, W. H. Fox, Aubrey Dyas Perkins and Alwyn Hargrave) accounting for fifty-seven out of sixty-five years between them. The board has conscientiously safeguarded the theatre's financial security without which nothing can be achieved. This has of course been inseparable from a generally cautious artistic policy, but to jettison that would be to abandon not only economic wellbeing but also audience loyalties.

Above all the Northampton Repertory Players have survived, making them the longest continuously running repertory company in the country. Longevity is not an end in itself, but "Master N.R.P.", born into this world in 1927, now looks forward to the future with undiminished confidence and enthusiasm. Through how many of his seven ages he has now passed only the future will tell, but in his time to date he has played many parts and long may he continue to bring the world's stage to appreciative audiences in Northampton.

Chairmen of the Board

Sir James Crockett	1927–30
W. H. Horton	1930–2
Mrs. Helen Panther	1932–54
W. H. Fox	1954–61
Aubrey Dyas Perkins	1961–75
John Bennett	1975–7
Alwyn Hargrave	1977–

Producers/Artistic Directors

Max Jerome	1927
Rupert Harvey	1927
Herbert Prentice	1928–32
Robert Young	1932–5
Bladon Peake	1935–8
William Sherwood	1938–40
William E. Brookfield	1940–2
George Roche	1942
Arthur Leslie	1942–3
Alex Reeve	1943–56
Lionel Hamilton	1956–63
Keith Andrews	1963–5
Alan Vaughan Williams	1965–6
Willard Stoker	1966–75
Christopher Denys	1975–6
David Kelsey	1977–81
Michael Napier Brown	1981–

Sample Seasons

Programmes for autumn seasons at five yearly intervals, giving size of cast (M – Male, F – Female) and box office information where available.
★ indicates a significant number of additional (children/amateur) performers.
P – Première.

1930 Producer: Herbert Prentice				Box Office Income £	Profit/ Loss £
Aug. 4	*Spring Cleaning* – Frederick Lonsdale	6M	5F	299	+ 95
Aug. 11	*Diversion* – John van Druten	5M	6F	242	+ 47
Aug. 18	*Skin Deep* – Ernest Enderline	2M	5F	258	+ 44
Aug. 25	*The Soul of John Sylvester* – Eric Barber	7M	3F	129	– 81
Sept. 1	*And So To Bed* – J. B. Fagan	8M	8F	335	+105
Sept. 8	*And So To Bed* – J. B. Fagan			332	+108
Sept. 15	*Water* – Molly Marshall-Hole	7M	3F	182	– 18
Sept. 22	*The Last of Mrs. Cheyney* – Frederick Lonsdale	7M	6F	342	+129
Sept. 29	*The Last of Mrs. Cheyney* – Frederick Lonsdale			247	+ 41
Oct. 6	*Misalliance* – Bernard Shaw	6M	3F	242	+ 35
Oct. 13	*A Hundred Years Old* – Adapted by Helen and Harley Granville-Barker from Bros Quinter	6M	6F	225	+ 11
Oct. 20	*The Moving Finger* – Sir Patrick Hastings K.C.	6M	4F	230	+ 21
Oct. 27	*Canaries Sometimes Sing* – Frederick Lonsdale	2M	2F	296	+ 75
Nov. 3	*The Witch* – Adapted by John Masefield	8M	5F★	215	– 23
Nov. 10	*Ask Beccles* – Cyril Campion and Edward Dignon	10M	2F	261	+ 39
Nov. 17	*March Hares* – H. W. Gribble	4M	5F	193	– 22
Nov. 24	*The Letter* – W. Somerset Maugham	12M	7F	244	+ 19
Dec. 1	*Murder on the Second Floor* – Frank Vosper	9M	4F	288	+ 64
Dec. 8	*The Young Idea* – Noel Coward	7M	7F	243	+ 27
Dec. 15	*Good Morning, Bill* – P. G. Wodehouse	4M	3F	259	+ 31
Dec. 22	*The School for Scandal* – R. B. Sheridan	12M	6F★	224	– 8

1935 Producer: Bladon Peake

Date	Play	Author	M	F	Freda Jackson as	Box Office Income £	Profit/Loss £
July 29/	*Hollywood Holiday*	Benn W. Levy and John van Druten	14M	10F	May Z. Pardee	154	− 86
Aug. 5						68	−170
Aug. 12	*Payment Deferred*	Jeffrey Dell	7M	3F	Madame Collins	—	
Aug. 19	*Someone at the Door*	Dorothy and Campbell Christie	6M	1F	Gwendolyn Tupman	197	− 19
Aug. 26	*Distinguished Villa*	Kate O'Brien	3M	3F	Lady Marian Mainwaring	312	+ 89
Sept. 2	*Tilly of Bloomsbury*	Ian Hay	6M	7F		227	+ 10
Sept. 9	*The Second Man*	S. N. Behrman	2M	2F		228	+ 55
Sept. 16	*Marriage à la Mode*	John Dryden	8M	7F	Melantha	302	+ 79
Sept. 23	*Thark*	Ben Travers	6M	5F	Mrs. Frush	338	+ 97
Sept. 30	*Escape Me Never*	Margaret Kennedy	11M	7F	First Spinster / Another Passer-by		
P Oct. 7	*The Wasp's Nest*	Adelaide Eden Phillpotts and Jan Stewart	10M	3F	Ellen	206	− 17
Oct. 14	*Hobson's Choice*	Harold Brighouse	7M	5F	Maggie Hobson	255	+ 16
Oct. 21	*Charmeuse*	E. Temple Thurston	3M	4F	Mrs. Thorpe	193	− 25
Oct. 28	*Mid-Channel*	Arthur Pinero	6M	5F	Stella Kirby	225	+ 6
Nov. 4	*Eden End*	J. B. Priestley	4M	3F		282	+ 42
Nov. 11	*The White Chateau*	Reginald Berkeley	11M	5F		212	− 78
Nov. 18	*Bunty Pulls The Strings*	Graham Moffat	5M	5F		230	− 14
Nov. 25	*The Taming of the Shrew*	William Shakespeare	10M	6F		273	+ 48
Dec. 2	*Accent on Youth*	Samson Raphaelson	6M	3F		173	− 53
Dec. 9	*Barnet's Folly*	Jan Stewer	8M	7F		218	− 19
Dec. 16	*The Barretts of Wimpole Street*	Rudolf Besier	11M	5F		281	+ 8
Dec. 26	*Sinbad the Sailor*	Margaret Carter	10M	6F		344	+ 82
Jan. 2		,,				208	− 61

(shillings and pence omitted)

199

					Box Office Income £	Profit/ Loss £
1940	**Producer: William E. Brookfield**					
Sept. 16	*Dear Octopus* - Dodie Smith	5M	12F		339	+ 40
Sept. 23	*Musical Chairs* - Ronald Mackenzie	4M	4F		191	– 22
Sept. 30	*Pride and Prejudice* - Helen Jerome (from Jane Austen)	7M	10F		264	– 19
Oct. 7	*The High Road* - Frederick Lonsdale	8M	4F		216	– 20
Oct. 14	*Romance* - Edward Sheldon	9M	9F		297	+ 18
Oct. 21	*The Bishop Misbehaves* - G. Frederick Jackson	7M	3F		241	+ 8
Oct. 28	*The Best People* - David Grey and Avery Hopwood	7M	5F		271	+ 18
Nov. 4	*Indoor Fireworks* - Arthur Macrae	5M	5F		208	– 4
Nov. 11	*Little Ladyship* - Ian Hay	6M	16F		301	+ 49
Nov. 18	*Third Party Risk* - G. Lennox and G. Ashley	7M	4F		176	– 18
Nov. 25	*Rebecca* - Daphne du Maurier	8M	10F		270	+ 6
Dec. 2	*Rebecca* - Daphne du Maurier				254	+ 3
Dec. 9	*Trelawny of the 'Wells'* - A. W. Pinero	9M	10F		193	– 57
Dec. 16	*The Light of Heart* - Emlyn Williams	4M	4F		208	– 21
Dec. 26	*The Middle Watch* - Ian Hay and Stephen King-Hall	6M	7F		211	– 3
1945	**Producer: Alex Reeve**					
July 12	*Dear Octopus* - Dodie Smith	5M	2F		168	–217
July 16	*Dear Octopus* - Dodie Smith				374	– 24
July 23	*The Amazing Dr. Clitterhouse* - Barrie Lyndon	10M	2F		386	+ 8
July 30	*The Barretts of Wimpole Street* - Rudolf Besier	12M	5F		404	– 11
Aug. 6	*The Family Upstairs* - Harry Delf	4M	5F		449	+ 70
Aug. 13	*The Wind and the Rain* - Merton Hodge	6M	3F		376	+ 16
Aug. 20	*Blithe Spirit* - Noel Coward	2M	5F		441	+ 71
Aug. 27	*Winterset* - Maxwell Anderson	17M	5F		292	–105
Sept. 3	*Acacia Avenue* - Mabel and Denis Constanduros	4M	5F		364	– 1
Sept. 10	*Carnival* - H. C. M. Hardinge	16M	6F		387	– 30
Sept. 17	*Without the Prince* - Philip King	6M	4F		386	+ 7
Sept. 24	*The Banbury Nose* - Peter Ustinov	9M	4F		330	– 79
Oct. 1	*Hay Fever* - Noel Coward	4M	5F		423	+ 51
Oct. 8	*Jane Eyre* - Helen Jerome (from Charlotte Brontë)	6M	8F		467	+ 73

Oct. 15	*The Green Pack* – Edgar Wallace	7M	2F	412	+ 42
Oct. 22	*The Simpleton of the Unexpected Isles*				
	– Bernard Shaw	9M	5F	320	– 65
Oct. 29 P	*Murder Out of Tune* – Falkland L. Cary	4M	5F	438	+ 61
Nov. 5	*Jane Steps Out* – Kenneth Horne	3M	5F	477	+102
Nov. 12	*Quinneys* – Horace Annesley Vachell	5M	3F	379	+ 24
Nov. 19	*How Are They At Home* – J. B. Priestley	7M	6F	440	+ 26
Nov. 26	*An Enemy of the People* – Henrik Ibsen	7M	2F	300	– 92
Dec. 3	*The First Mrs. Fraser* – St. John Ervine	4M	4F	392	+ 3
Dec. 10	*I Lived with You* – Ivor Novello	4M	10F	384	Neither
Dec. 17	*I Lived with You* – Ivor Novello			112	–275
Dec. 26 P	*Command Performance* – Alex Reeve and				
	Osborne Robinson	8M	10F⋆	393	–105
Dec. 31	*Command Performance*			383	–108
Jan. 7	*Command Performance*			406	– 93

(Figures for 1940 and 1945 are exclusive of remission of entertainment tax)

1950   Producer: Alex Reeve

Date		Title – Author		Cast			Northampton Gross Receipts £	Profit/Loss £	Kettering Gross Receipts £	Profit/Loss £
July 24		French Without Tears – Terence Rattigan		7M	3F	(LH)	684	+ 24	342	+ 2
July 31		The Foolish Gentlewoman – Margery Sharp		2M	6F	(AR)	711	+ 31	295	– 41
Aug. 7		The Damask Cheek – John van Druten and Lloyd Morris		3M	6F	(LH)	770	+ 30	239	– 76
Aug. 14		Master of Arts – William Douglas Home		6M	4F	(AR)	736	+ 44	293	– 46
Aug. 21		The Years Between – Daphne du Maurier		6M	4F	(LH)	749	+ 71	300	– 45
Aug. 28		The Mill on the Floss – David Tearle (from George Eliot)		8M	6F	(AR)	771	+ 23	267	– 55
Sept. 4		Young Wives' Tale – Ronald Jeans		3M	6F	(LH)	773	+ 92	303	– 30
Sept. 11		Top Secret – Alan Melville		6M	3F	(AR)	728	+ 64	281	– 29
Sept. 18		Max – Denis Cannan		5M	3F	(LH)	609	– 43	250	– 64
Sept. 25	P	The River and the Sea – Noel Scott		4M	4F	(AR)	523	–107	197	–104
Oct. 2		Don't Listen Ladies – Stephen Powys and Guy Bolton		5M	4F	(LH)	681	+ 24	272	– 47
Oct. 9		Devonshire Cream – Eden Phillpotts		5M	3F	(AR)	689	+ 38	256	– 96
Oct. 16		Mr. Gillie – James Bridie		6M	2F	(LH)	666	+ 7	168	–114
Oct. 23		Mansfield Park – Constance Cox (from Jane Austen)		5M	6F	(AR)	771	+ 52	387	+ 45
Oct. 30		If This Be Error – Rachel Grieve		3M	4F	(LH)	656	– 10	198	–103
Nov. 6		A Wind on the Heath – Ronald Adam		7M	6F	(AR)	619	– 67	234	– 57
Nov. 13		The Perfect Woman – Wallace Geoffrey and Basil Mitchell		8M	2F	(LH)	667	– 61	273	– 65
Nov. 20		The Eleventh Hour – Heath MacGregor		5M	3F	(AR)	603	– 96	187	– 90
Nov. 27		Summer In December – James Liggat		6M	6F	(LH)	638	– 60	153	–127
Dec. 4		Background – Warren Chetham-Strode		4M	4F	(AR)	506	–197	106	–152
Dec. 11		Wishing Well – E. Eynon Evans		6M	5F	(LH)	492	–163	n.a.	n.a.
Dec. 26	P	The Snow Princess – Alex Reeve and Dorothy Carr		9M	6F *	(AR)	934	– 81	1,347	+230
Jan. 2		Babes in the Wood (Kettering)					991	+ 60	1,028	+ 58
Jan. 9							1,058	+117	918	+ 22

These productions played a second week in Kettering. There were effectively two acting companies – one produced by Alex Reeve (AR), the other by Lionel Hamilton (LH), though there was some mobility between them.

1955   Producer: Alex Reeve

Date		Title	Author	Nigel Hawthorne as			Box Office Income £	Profit/ Loss £
July 25	P	*The Lady of the Camellias*	Phyllis Hartnoll (from Alexandre Dumas)		10M	6F	552	–142
Aug. 1							467	–217
Aug. 8		*Witness for the Prosecution*	Agatha Christie	Leonard Vole	13M	6F	757	+203
Aug. 15		*Come Back Peter*	A. P. Dearsley	George	6M	4F	586	+ 97
Aug. 22		*Manor of Northstead*	William Douglas Home	Lord Pym	5M	4F	440	+ 79
Aug. 29		*Meet Mr. Callaghan*	Peter Cheyney & Gerald Verner	Bellamy Meraulto	8M	3F	531	+ 4
Sept. 5		*Daddy Long Legs*	Emile Littler & Jean Webster		8M	11F	767	+181
Sept. 12		*The Cat and the Canary*	John Willard	Paul Jones	6M	4F	625	+ 80
Sept. 19		*The Book of the Month*	Basil Thomas	Nicholas Barnes	4M	4F	641	+121
Sept. 26		*The Widow's Mite*	Cyril Campion		7M	9F	570	+ 43
Oct. 3		*It's Never Too Late*	Felicity Douglas	Chris Martyn	3M	5F	589	+ 64
Oct. 10		*The Secret Tent*	Elizabeth Addyman		8M	4F	598	+ 66
Oct. 18		*The Rivals*	R. B. Sheridan	Captain Absolute	6M	4F	701	+167
Oct. 24		*Both Ends Meet*	Arthur Macrae	Mr. Wilson	5M	2F	619	+ 96
Oct. 31		*Serious Charge*	Philip King		4M	4F	477	– 60
Nov. 7		*The Heiress of Rosings*	Cedric Wallis	Marquess of Chippenham	9M	6F	637	+ 88
Nov. 14		*Seagulls Over Sorrento*	Hugh Hastings	McIntosh	3M	4F	716	+151
Nov. 21		*I am a Camera*	John van Druten	Fritz Wendel	5M	5F	725	+129
Nov. 28		*Come on Jeeves*	P. G. Wodehouse & Guy Bolton	Colonel Meredith	7M	3F	521	+ 1
Dec. 5		*The Running Man*	Anthony Armstrong & Arnold Ridley	Frank			534	+ 1
Dec. 12		*The Moon is Blue*	F. Hugh Herbert	Donald Gresham	3M	1F	537	+ 29
Dec. 26	P	*Babes in the Wood*	Alex Reeve	Will Scarlet	11M	6F*	1,260	+467
Jan. 3							1,084	+348
Jan. 10							1,051	+323
Jan. 17							1,018	+389

1960 Producer: Lionel Hamilton

Date	Title	Author	M	F	Gross Receipts £	Profit/Loss £	Total Admissions
Sept. 6	This Happy Breed	Noel Coward	5M	7F	761	+108	3,234
Sept. 12	The Unexpected Guest	Agatha Christie	8M	3F	917	+273	3,941
Sept. 19	The Constant Wife	Somerset Maugham	4M	5F	770	+166	3,246
Sept. 26	Five Finger Exercise	Peter Shaffer	3M	2F	750	+145	3,182
Oct. 3	The Complaisant Lover	Graham Greene	6M	3M	759	+132	3,181
Oct. 10	The Grass in Greener	Hugh and Margaret Williams	3M	2F	829	+203	
Oct. 17	A Shred of Evidence	R. C. Sherriff	6M	3F	760	+122	
Oct. 24	And Suddenly It's Spring	Jack Popplewell	4M	3F	794	+163	
Nov. 8	The School for Scandal	R. B. Sheridan	10M	4F	801	+126	
Nov. 14	The School for Scandal	R. B. Sheridan			997	+306	
Nov. 21	A Taste of Honey	Shelagh Delaney	3M	2F	917	+171	
Nov. 28	The Aspern Papers	Michael Redgrave (from Henry James)	2M	4F	634	− 54	
Dec. 5	Roar Like a Dove	Lesley Storm	5M	4F	709	+ 12	
Dec. 12	Roar Like a Dove	Lesley Storm			766	+107	
Dec. 26 P	Puss in Boots	Alan Brown	12M	5F*	(Box Office) 1,743	n.a.	
Jan. 2	Puss in Boots	Alan Brown		"	1,797		
Jan. 9	Puss in Boots	Alan Brown		"	1,232		
Jan. 16	Puss in Boots	Alan Brown		"	1,071		
Jan. 23	Puss in Boots	Alan Brown		"	1,067		

204

1965   Producer: Alan Vaughan Williams

				Gross Receipts £	Profit/ Loss £	Total Admis- sions
July 31	*Doctor in the House* – Richard Gordon	5M	4F	2,377	–211	8,546
Aug. 17	*Busman's Honeymoon* – Dorothy L. Sayers & M. St. Clare Byrne	8M	3F	1,534	– 59	5,482
Aug. 30	*Roar Like a Dove* – Lesley Storm	5M	4F	1,538	+ 47	5,535
Sept. 14	*Death of a Salesman* – Arthur Miller	9M	5F	1,134	–484	4,146
Sept. 28	*One for the Pot* – Ray Cooney & Tony Hilton	6M	3F	1,411	–145	5,214
Oct. 12	*Design for Living* – Noel Coward	6M	3F	1,270	–277	4,623
Oct. 26	*The Hostage* – Brendan Behan	9M	4F	1,591	–562	3,707
Nov. 16	*Jane Eyre* – Helen Jerome (from Charlotte Brontë)	6M	7F	3,294	+530	12,413
Dec. 7	*Old Tyme Music Hall*	5M	5F	1,524	–441	5,460
Dec. 27 to Jan. 29	*Dick Whittington* – V. C. Clinton-Baddeley	10M	7F★	8,433	+801	24,267

205

1970   Producer: Willard Stoker

Date	Play	Author	Cast	Box Office Income £	Profit/ Loss £	Admissions	%
Aug. 1	The House on the Cliff	George Batson	2M 4F	266		649	
Aug. 3				840	-904	2,572	
Aug. 10	The Man Most Likely To	Joyce Rayburn	3M 2F	814		2,168	
Aug. 18				826	+ 38	2,479	
Aug. 25	The Daughter-in-Law	D. H. Lawrence	2M 3F	1,056		2,936	
Sept. 1				580	-738	1,817	
Sept. 8	Plaza Suite	Neil Simon	4M 3F	753		2,106	
Sept. 15				635	-711	1,933	47%
Sept. 21	The School for Wives	Molière (trans. Miles Malleson)	6M 2F	705		1,966	46%
Sept. 29				653	-641	2,017	
Oct. 5	The Italian Girl	James Saunders (from Iris Murdoch)	3M 4F	698		1,971	
Oct. 13				480	-1,054	1,487	
Oct. 19	A Clean Kill	Michael Gilbert	4M 3F	582		1,599	
Oct. 27				757	- 44	2,326	
Nov. 2	The Happy Apple	Jack Pulman	7M 2F	801		2,167	
Nov. 10				615	-845	1,930	47%
Nov. 16	Not Now Darling	Ray Cooney & John Chapman	5M 5F	686		1,910	45%
Nov. 24				730	-732	2,232	
Nov. 30				1,068		3,133	
Dec. 7				785		2,066	
Dec. 26	Cinderella	Jill Fenton	11M 4F*	484		966	80%
Dec. 28				2,827	-484	6,272	86%
Jan. 4				1,552		3,888	80%
Jan. 11				1,623		3,988	82%
Jan. 18				1,697		4,304	89%

1975   Artistic Director: Christopher Denys

Date	Title	Author	Cast	Box Office Income £	Profit/ Loss £	Total Admissions
Aug. 2	*The Lion in Winter*	James Goldman	5M 2F	2,081	-1,992	2,797
Aug. 12	*The Gentle Hook*	Francis Durbridge	6M 3F	3,279	+ 525	4,354
Sept. 2	*A Tailor for the Ladies*	George Feydeau (trans. Christopher Denys)	6M 4F	2,197	-1,941	3,058
Sept. 23	*Lock Up Your Daughters*	Bernard Miles	12M 6F	5,504	-1,247	6,426
Oct. 14	*A Midsummer Night's Dream*	William Shakespeare	12M 5F	2,417	-1,436	3,447
Oct. 28 P	*The Great Northampton Fire and After*	Christopher Denys	6M 3F	1,670	-1,153	2,532
Nov. 11	*Loot*	Joe Orton	5M 1F	2,573	- 455	3,596
Nov. 26	*A Christmas Carol*	John Downing (from Charles Dickens)	16M 4F*	6,860	+ 813	9,569
Dec. 18 to Jan. 24	*Joseph and the Amazing Technicolor Dreamcoat*	Andrew Lloyd Webber & Tim Rice	12M 2F*	16,348	- 934	20,066

1980 Artistic Director: David Kelsey

						Box Office	Capacity
Aug. 2		On Approval	Frederick Lonsdale	2M	2F	51.3%	
Aug. 20		Bodies	James Saunders	2M	2F	44.6%	
Sept. 10		The Odd Couple	Neil Simon	6M	2F	53.7%	
Oct. 2	P	Wuthering Heights	Donald Cotton (from Emily Brontë)	7M	4F	70.5%	
Oct. 29		The Seagull	Anton Chekhov (trans. Ronald Hingley)	7M	5F	35%	
Nov. 19	P	Quartet to Murder	Lionel Hamilton	2M	3F	47.4%	
Dec. 20	P	Mother Goose	Donald Cotton	8M	6F*	78.6%	

1985 Artistic Director: Michael Napier Brown

						Box Office	Capacity
Aug. 23		Annie	Thomas Meehan	8M	6F*	71%	77%
Oct. 9		When the Wind Blows	Raymond Briggs	1M	1F	68%	75%
Oct. 23		Blood Brothers	Willy Russell	6M	5F	87%	94%
Nov. 13		Season's Greetings	Alan Ayckbourn	5M	4F	82%	90%
Dec. 9	P	The Sleeping Beauty	Vilma Hollingbery	6M	5F*	74%	78%

1990   Artistic Director: Michael Napier Brown

						Box Office	Capacity
Aug. 30	P	*How Green Was My Valley*	Shaun McKenna (from Richard Llewellyn)	10M	5F	59%	60%
Oct. 4		*Separation*	Tom Kempinski	1M	1F	26%	30%
Nov. 1		*Hay Fever*	Noel Coward	4M	4F	61%	64%
Nov. 7–25 STUDIO		*Hard Times*	Stephen Jeffreys (from Charles Dickens)	2M	2F	66%	77%
Dec. 10	P	*Robin Hood*	Vilma Hollingbery	7M	4F*	63%	68%

The Royal Theatre's seating capacity after the 1983 renovations is 439 in the stalls and dress circle, plus 144 in the gallery. The large proportion of cheap gallery seats distorts the percentage attendance. Show reports now give both percentage of capacity and percentage of box office.

209

Shakespearean Productions

Date	Play	Director	Designer
24.12.1927	A Midsummer Night's Dream	Rupert Harvey	Charles Maynard
26. 5.1930	Scene from King John	Herbert Prentice	Herbert Prentice & Osborne Robinson
27. 2.1933	Twelfth Night	Robert Young	Osborne Robinson
3. 4.1933	The Merchant of Venice	Robert Young	Osborne Robinson
5. 3.1934	Othello	Robert Young	Osborne Robinson
25.11.1935	The Taming of the Shrew	Bladon Peake	Osborne Robinson
16. 3.1936	Macbeth	Bladon Peake	Osborne Robinson
23. 5.1938	Romeo and Juliet	William Sherwood	Osborne Robinson
2.10.1939	Romeo and Juliet	William Sherwood	Osborne Robinson
8. 3.1948	Twelfth Night	Alex Reeve	Osborne Robinson
23. 3.1954	Much Ado About Nothing	Joseph E. Wright	Osborne Robinson
15. 3.1955	As You Like It	Alex Reeve	Osborne Robinson
13. 3.1956	A Midsummer Night's Dream	Alex Reeve	Osborne Robinson
12. 3.1957	The Merchant of Venice	Lionel Hamilton	Osborne Robinson
11. 3.1958	Hamlet	Lionel Hamilton	Osborne Robinson
5. 5.1959	Twelfth Night	Lionel Hamilton	Osborne Robinson
14. 3.1961	The Merry Wives of Windsor	Lionel Hamilton	Osborne Robinson
6. 5.1964	King John	Keith Andrews	Osborne Robinson
9. 3.1965	King Lear	Keith Andrews	Osborne Robinson
2. 5.1967	The Tempest	Willard Stoker	Osborne Robinson
19. 3.1968	The Merchant of Venice	Willard Stoker	Osborne Robinson
4. 3.1969	Othello	Willard Stoker	Osborne Robinson
3. 3.1970	Twelfth Night	Willard Stoker	Alan Miller Bunford
26.10.1971	Romeo and Juliet	Willard Stoker	Osborne Robinson
27. 2.1973	Much Ado About Nothing	Willard Stoker	Osborne Robinson
15. 4.1975	As You Like It	Willard Stoker	Osborne Robinson

210

14.10.1975	A Midsummer Night's Dream	Christopher Denys	Helen Wilkinson
11. 5.1976	Macbeth	Christopher Denys	Ray Lett
6. 4.1977	Twelfth Night	David Kelsey	Ray Lett
21. 3.1979	Hamlet	David Kelsey	Ray Lett
7.10.1982	Romeo and Juliet	Michael Napier Brown	Ray Lett
17. 9.1987	Macbeth	Michael Napier Brown	Ray Lett

Grants received by Northampton Repertory Players

	Arts Council of Great Britain		Northampton County Borough (Theatre rental in brackets)	Northamptonshire County Council
1950-1	£50	(1)		
1951-2	£1,000 (to Kettering Repertory Theatre Ltd.)			
1952-3	£1,000 (to Kettering Repertory Theatre Ltd.)			
1953-4	£68.10s. (incl. grant for repairs)			
	£686.11s.	*		
1954-5	£375	*		
1955-6	£274.6s.	*		
1956-7	£581.10s.	*		
1957-8	£707.19s.	*		
1958-9	£1,551.4s.	+ (2)		
1959-60	£2,300	+	£2,500 (£825)	
1960-1	£3,632.9s.6d.	+	,, ,,	
1961-2	£4,250	+ (3)	,,	
1962-3	£6,099.11s.5d.	+	,,	
1963-4	£7,300	+ (4)		
1964-5	£6,550	+	£829 (£850)	

211

Year			
1965-6	£9,050	£2,687 (£3,000)	
1966-7	£16,102	£2,150	
1967-8	£18,882	£2,650	
1968-9	£18,750	£2,150	
1969-70	£18,700	£3,650	
1970-1	£19,475	£2,150	
1971-2	£21,500	£2,150	
1972-3	£23,000	£3,000	
1973-4	£23,650		
1974-5	£28,500	£15,350	£1,750
1975-6	£32,000	£15,000	£15,662 (capital grant)
1976-7	£45,000	£20,000	£11,150
1977-8	£47,500	£20,000	£20,000
1978-79	£63,000	£22,000	£20,000
1979-80	£64,000	£25,000	£22,000
1980-1	£72,750	£28,786	£22,000
1981-2	£80,000	£35,850	£22,300
1982-3	£86,000	£37,000	£24,000
1983-4	£81,180 (+£70,000 Housing the Arts)	£34,458 (£5,500)	£26,000
1984-5	£95,500	£34,750	£30,000

+ (5)

East Midlands Arts

Year			
1985-6	£115,500	£44,500	£38,500
1986-7	£137,731	£46,800 (£12,000)	£57,000
1987-8	£144,731	£53,500	£63,074
1988-9	£138,427	£53,500	£62,334
1989-90	£140,426	£66,000	£66,000
1990-91	£153,050	£73,570	£73,712
1991-92	£165,290	£76,960	£78,006

(6)

(7)

212

* Grants in respect of transport subsidy.

+ Including grants in respect of transport subsidy.

The borough council also charges rent on 15 and 34 Guildhall Road. Currently £17,250.

Figures from Arts Council Annual Reports and N.B.C. and N.C.C. records.

Notes

1. "A consolation award of £50 was made to Northampton for the production of Constance Cox's adaptation of *Mansfield Park*". This was part of a new play competition. Four prizes of £100 were offered, but only two awarded to a field of seven entries.

2. Incl. transport subsidy of £751 which brought £3,077 to the box office.

3. Incl. transport subsidy of £750 which brought £3,123.7s.6d. to the box office (13,041 people). A.C.G.B. AR listed the performance of sixteen theatres.

4. Made up of £5,500 grant, £1,000 capital expenditure, £800 transport subsidy.

5. Made up of £7,500 grant, £750 capital expenditure, £800 transport subsidy.

6. Additional grants for specific activities were paid in several years.

7. E.M.A. grant to Derby Playhouse £258,970. A.C.G.B. grant to Leicester Haymarket Theatre and the Nottingham Playhouse were £720,500 and £507,600 respectively in 1990-1 (AR).

Income and Expenditure Accounts 1954 and 1991

	27.3.54						30.3.91	
INCOME	£	s	d	£	s	d	£	£
Box office receipts	29,146.	0.	5				490,238	
Sponsorship							23,500	
less Agency and								
card commis.							(838)	
Discount							(1,364)	
				29,146.	0.	5		511,536
THEATRE-IN-EDUCATION FEES								8,382
MISCELLANEOUS PROFITS								
Catering	956.	8.	10				18,583	
Bar	1,002.	9.	0				24,480	
Cigarettes	54.	19.	11					
Programme	1,012.	0.	6				11,932	
Puritan Maid	80.	8.	3					
less commis. on sales	(170.	11.	10)					
				2,935.	14.	8		
Hire of costumes etc.							18,637	
Royalties Cafe							6,335	
Sundry sales							716	
								80,683
SUNDRY RECEIPTS								
Donations	135.	17.	1				2,656	
Interest received	380.	0.	0				7,496	
Development Trust/								
investment income	4.	5.	2				10,600	
Curtain advert receipts	203.	19.	3					
				723.	19.	3		20,752
GRANTS RECEIVED								
East Midlands Arts							164,679	
Northampton Borough								
Council							73,570	
Northamptonshire								
County Council							73,712	
Other grants							6,333	
								318,294
TOTAL INCOME				32,805.	14.	4		939,647

214

	27.3.54						30.3.91	
EXPENSES	£	s	d	£	s	d	£	£

SALARIES AND WAGES

Executive directors	2,140.	0.	0					
Artistes	9,760.	2.	6				149,984	
Additional artistes	500.	0.	0				24,304	
Stage staff	2,846.	13.	8				173,861	
Front of house staff	4,564.	11.	8				48,417	
Casual labour	153.	19.	7				35,039	
Administration							97,352	
Catering staff							7,544	
				19,965.	7.	5		536,501

PREMISES

Rent of theatre & stores	1,667.	9.	6				30,018	
Rates of theatre	808.	18.	1				1,755	
Heat and light	839.	9.	1				23,344	
Repairs and renewals	801.	7.	7				16,306	
Capital expenditure written off							34,281	
Cleaning contract							16,795	
				4,117.	4.	3		122,499

ADVERTISING & PUBLICITY

				2,077.	9.	0		44,359

PRINTING & STATIONERY

Box office stationery	335.	7.	2					
General stationery & postage	133.	1.	0					15,857
				468.	8	2		
Royalties and levies				2,256.	8.	0		
Authors' royalties								45,077

STAGE EXPENSES

Stage disbursements	431.	14.	3					
Costumes, wigs & props	867.	17.	4				31,721	
Scenery	190.	16.	2				24,269	
Piano hire, records, etc	32.	14.	11					
Play scripts	38.	3.	3					
Sundry licences	25.	8.	9					

	27.3.54	30.3.91

Electrics 6,483
Rehearsal rooms 452
Theatre licences &
subscriptions 327
1,586. 14. 8 63,252

Travelling,
entertainment &
general expenses 559. 7. 1 38,332

Carried forward 31,030. 18. 7 865,877

	27.3.54						30.3.91	
EXPENSES	£	s	d	£	s	d	£	£

Brought forward 31,030. 18. 7 865,877

MISCELLANEOUS EXPENSES

Professional services 167. 10. 9 8,200
Telephone 78. 16. 7 7,161
Bank charges 167. 18. 6 668
Party bookings 45
Subscription scheme 6,760
Training 1,518
Re-charged to
co-productions (13,408)
Production 25,448
Pension scheme 310
Derngate box office 24,000
Bad debts (1,395)
Audience survey 3,620
Education development 4,300
Cleaning materials etc. 88. 7. 2
Sundries 108. 17. 2 10,646
611. 10. 2 77,873

INSURANCES

National Insurance 538. 11. 7 35,431
Other insurance 302. 11. 1 5,065
841. 2. 8 40,496

216

DEPRECIATION

Stage furniture	104. 16. 3	
Fixtures & fittings	35. 9. 6	
Stage electrical installation	217. 5. 0	
		357. 10. 9
TOTAL EXPENSES	32,841. 2. 2	984,246
NET LOSS	(35. 7.10)	(44,599)

Select Bibliography

Arts Council.
  Annual Reports.
  The Theatre Today in England and Wales, London, 1970.
  The Glory of the Garden. The Development of the Arts in England. A Strategy for a Decade, London, 1984

Beauman, Sally. *The Royal Shakespeare Company A History of Ten Decades,* London, 1982.
Bird, Henry. *The Sipario Dipinto,* Northampton, 1978.
Brown, Cynthia. *Northampton 1835-1985 Shoe Town, New Town,* Chichester, 1990.

Cary, Falkland L. *Practical Playwriting,* London n.d.
Cave, Richard. *Theatre in Focus Terence Gray and the Cambridge Festival Theatre,* Cambridge, 1980.
Chisholm, Cecil. *Repertory: An Outline of the Modern Theatre Movement,* London, 1934.

The Dictionary of National Bibliography (D.N.B.), London.
Dyas, Aubrey. *Adventure in Repertory. Northampton Repertory Theatre 1927-48,* Northampton, 1948. (Abbreviated reference *Adventure. . . .*)

East Midlands Arts. *Annual Reports.*
Elsom, John.
  Theatre Outside London, London, 1971.
  Postwar British Theatre, London, 1979.
Elsom, John, and Tomlin, Nicholas. *The History of the National Theatre,* London, 1978.
Ervine, St. John. *The Organised Theatre A Plea in Civics,* London, 1924.

Flynn, Errol. *My Wicked, Wicked Ways,* London, 1960; repr. 1969.
Fothergill, John. *Confessions of An Innkeeper,* London, 1938.
Foulkes, Richard, ed. *The Northampton Repertory Theatre Some Questions and Suggestions,* Northampton, 1977.
Fuller, Roland. *The Bassett-Lowke Story,* London, 1984.

Goldie, Grace Wyndham. *The Liverpool Repertory Theatre 1911-1934,* Liverpool and London, 1935.
Green, Michael. *Nobody Hurt in Small Earthquake,* London, 1990.

Greenall, R. L.
A History of Northamptonshire and The Soke of Peterborough, Chichester, 1979.
ed. *Life in Old Northampton*, Northampton, 1975.
Northamptonshire Life 1914–39. A Photographic Survey, Northampton, 1979.

Harris, P. J. and Hartop, P. W.
Northamptonshire – its Land and People, Northampton 1950.
Hayman, Ronald.
The Set-up: An Anatomy of British Theatre, London, 1973.
British Theatre Since 1955, London, 1979.
Higham, Charles. *Errol Flynn The Untold Story*, London, 1980.
Holloway, Roland. *Roland Holloway's Northamptonshire Fifty years of photographs 1924–1974*, Northampton, 1985.
Hunt, Hugh. *The Abbey. Ireland's National Theatre 1904–78*, Dublin, 1979.

Jerrams, Richard. *Weekly Rep – a theatrical phenomenon*, Droitwich, 1991.

Kemp, Thomas C. *Birmingham Repertory Theatre The Playhouse and the Man*, Birmingham, 1944.

Landstone, Charles. *Off-Stage A Personal Record of the First Twelve Years of State Sponsored Drama in Great Britain*, London, 1953.
Leacroft, Richard, and Helen. *The Theatre in Leicestershire*, Leicester, 1986.

Macleod, Joseph. *The Actor's Right to Act*, London, 1981.
Macqueen-Pope, W. *The Footlights Flickered. The Story of the Theatre of the 1920s*, London, 1959.
Marshall, Norman. *The Other Theatre*, London, 1948.
Matthews, Bache. *A History of the Birmingham Repertory Company*, London, 1924.
Morley, Sheridan. *A Talent to Amuse*, London, 1974.

Parker, Anthony. *Pageants Their Presentation and Production*, London, 1954.
Parker, Louis N. *Several of My Lives*, London, 1928.
Pick, John. *The Theatre Industry*, Eastbourne, 1985.
Pogson, Rex. *Miss Horniman and the Gaiety Theatre, Manchester*, London, 1952.
Priestley, J. B. *Theatre Outlook*, London, 1947.

The Repertory Movement in Great Britain, Council of Repertory Theatres (C.O.R.T.), London, c. 1969.
Reynolds, Ernest.
Modern English Drama A Survey of the Theatre from 1900, London, 1949.
Northampton Repertory Theatre, Northampton, 1976.
Ridge, Harold C. *Stage-Lighting for 'Little' Theatres*, Cambridge, 1925.
Robinson, Colin. *Thomas Osborne Robinson OBE Beginnings*, Northampton, 1977; see also *Patron Extraordinaire. A Tribute to Osborne Robinson OBE*, Northampton, 1976.
Rowell, George, and Jackson, Anthony. *The Repertory Movement. A History of Regional Theatre in Britain*, Cambridge, 1984.

Saintsbury, George, ed. *John Dryden Three Plays*, repr. New York, 1957.

Seed, T. Alec. *The Sheffield Repertory Theatre A History*, Sheffield, 1959.

Simmons, Dawn Langley. *Margaret Rutherford A Blithe Spirit*, London, 1983.

Sixty Years of Northampton Repertory Players, Northampton, 1987.

Trewin, J. C. *The Birmingham Repertory Theatre 1913-63*, London, 1963.

Walmsley, David (compiler).
  An Ever-Rolling Stream. The Ongoing Story of the Development of Higher Education in Northampton and Northamptonshire, London, 1989.

Warwick, Lou.
  Death of a Theatre A History of the New Theatre, Northampton, Northampton, 1960.
  Theatre Un-Royal, Northampton, 1974.
  Drama That Smelled, Northampton, 1975.
  The Mackenzies Called Compton, Northampton, 1977.

Whitworth, Geoffrey. *The Making of a National Theatre*, London, 1951.

Wilding, Richard. *Supporting The Arts A Review of the Structure of Arts Funding*, London, 1989.

Williams, W. Emrys. *The Arts in Northampton*, Northampton, 1966.

Journals, newspapers and magazines

Bedfordshire on Sunday
Birmingham Mail
Birmingham Post and Journal
Birmingham Weekly Post

Cinema Theatres' Association Bulletin
Chronicle and Echo (C&E)

Daily Mirror
Drama

[Northamptonshire] Evening Telegraph (ET)

Financial Times

Independent on Sunday

Mercury and Herald (M&H)
Morning Post

New Statesman

Northampton Daily Chronicle (NDL)
Northampton Echo
Northampton Independent (NI)
Northants Herald and Post (NH&P)
Northants Post (NP)
Northamptonshire Image
Northamptonshire Past and Present

Observer

Plays and Players

Spectator
Stage
Sunday Times

Theatre Research International
Theatrephile
Theatre World
Time and Tide
The Times

Notes on Sources

Royal Theatre and Opera House (Northampton Repertory Players)

Accounts book 1920–3
Minute books of the board of directors 1927 to 1966 (BM).
Account books.
Wages payment books.
Theatre programmes from 1927 to the present (with some gaps in 1940s).
Alphabetical logbook of all plays produced from 1927 to the present.
Press cuttings book from 1978 – ongoing.
Budgets, show reports etc.
Photographs.

Northampton Borough Council

Financial data from 1960 to the present.

Northamptonshire County Council

Minutes of board of directors (BM) and attendant papers from 1966 onwards.
Financial data, annual reports (AR) and accounts from 1976 onwards.
Register of board members.

Northamptonshire County Record Office (N.C.R.O.)

Files on the Northampton Theatre Syndicate and the Royal Theatre.
Lady Henley's papers.

Local History Library, Central Library, Northampton

Theatre programmes from 1927 to the present.
Photographic collection.
Miscellaneous papers.
Local newspapers (including *Northampton Independent, NI*).

Chronicle and Echo Library

Press cuttings and photographic file.

University (of Leicester) Centre, Northampton

Miscellaneous programmes

Arts Council of Great Britain Library

Annual reports for A.C.G.B. and East Midlands Arts.

Personal Collections

Author's collection.
The late Lawrence Baskcomb (N.C.R.O.).
Family of the late Sir John Brown – papers related to the Northampton Theatre Syndicate (N.C.R.O.).
Bryan Douglas – photographs.
Lionel Hamilton – photographs.
Mrs. Irene Peake – press cuttings.
The late Aubrey Dyas Perkins (N.C.R.O.).

Items marked N.C.R.O. – to be deposited in the Northamptonshire County Record Office.

Index

List of Subscribers

ADAMS	Jonathon
ADDINGTON	Geoffrey & Betty
ALLEN	Melanie J.
ATTERBURY	Gladys L.
AYRES	Robert J.
BAILEY)	Councillor Trevor R.
WARD)	Miss Diane
BARKER	Kathleen
BENHAM	Hilda M.
BETTAM	Catherine A. M.
BLAND WOOD	W.
BOTTLE	Ted
BOWLES	Agnes & Alan
BRAILEY	Michael R.
BREWSTER	P.
BROWN	Alan
BROWN C.B.E.	John Francis
BROWN T. D.	Lt Col Kenneth Charles
BULLARD	H.
CARLSBERG BREWERY	
CARTER	Brian R.
CHARLTON	Philip
CHESHIRE	David F.
CHOWN	Trevor M.
CHRONICLE & ECHO	
CHUDLEY	Michael & Diana
CHURCH	William C.
CLARIDGE	Alan
CLAY	David H.
COLES	Dr. & Mrs. R. B.
COLES	Robert
COOPER	Anthony
CORIN	J. B.
COUTTS SMITH	J. R.
CURTIS	L. & A. B.
DANIELS	Paul

DAVID	Joanna
DAVID ABBOTT PUBLICITY	
DAWES	Prof Edwin A.
DAWSON	John
DAY	Geoff & Eileen
DICKENS	T.
DOBLE	Keith & Catherine
DOLBY	J. E.
DOUGLAS	Bryan
DOUGLAS	Peter
DUNMORE	Maurice & Alison
DUTTON	A. C.
DUTTON	Derek & Winifred
ECCLES	Anthony R.
ELLAM	E. B.
FALCON MANOR SCHOOL LIBRARY	
FLETCHER)	Nick
JAMES)	Max
FORD	John
FORD	Mary
GALLIMORE	Donald Edwin
GEE	W. Gordon
GOULD	Jack
GREEN	David M.
GREEN	Diana
HACKETT	Sylvia
HALL	Brian
HALLIWELL	Ron & Pam
HAMILTON	Lionel
HARCOURT MEADOWS (R T Williams)	
HARGRAVE	Alwyn J.
HAWTHORNE C.B.E.	Nigel
HESKETH	Lady Christian
HIGHGATE HOUSE	
HOBLEY	R. J. & B.
HOLLINGBERY	Vilma
HOOPER	Edwin
HOUGHTON	Derek
HUGHES	Robert
HULMES	Mr. & Mrs. Peter
IRESON	Tony
JAMESON	Anne
JONES	Ray E.
KIMBELL	Roger
KING	Christine A.

KINGSTHORPE BOOKSHOP
KNIGHT — Colin
KNIGHT — Mrs. Elizabeth
LANDER — P.
LATTAWAY — Julie M.
LEE — John & Joyce
LEES — Charles (In Memory)
LEWIS — Eric
LINES — David
LINNELL — Richard
MACKENZIE — Charles W.
MAIN — Gerald
MARCH — Glenn
MARKHAM-DOWDY — Doreen
MARTELL — Julie
MASKELL — Maria
MASUMOTO — Masahiko
MATTHEW FRASER LTD
MICHEL O.B.E. — David O.
MILBOURNE — Olive
MONK — Stan C.
MORGAN — Joe
MORRIS M.A. — R. J. B.
NAPIER BROWN — Michael
NIGHTINGALE — Frank
NORTHAMPTON REPERTORY THEATRE PLAYGOERS CLUB
NORTHAMPTONSHIRE RECORD OFFICE
OAKENFULL — Charles Aisne
PALMER — Bruce
PARRY — Mr. & Mrs. H.
PETERS — Arnold
PRICE — Donald
PRICE — Matthew
PRONTAPRINT
PURNELL — Robert Maurice
ROBERTS — Eric & Margaret
ROMOSE — Jorgen R.
ROSE — Bud
ROTARY CLUB OF NORTHAMPTON WEST
ROWAN MITCHELL — W.
SAVAGE — Diana
SAVAGE — Ken
SAVAGE — Peter & Doris
SAVAGE — Richard
SCHANSCHIEFF — Simon
STUPPLE — Richard

STURGESS   Stella
STUTLEY   Ray
SUTCLIFFE   Kenneth
THE GARRICK CLUB
THOMAS   Phil
THOMPSON   Andrew
TOLLER & COMPANY
TOMLINSON   Glenda & Peter
TOYER   Meg
TRAVIS   Constance
TRAVIS   E. R. A.
TRAVIS   Valerie
TUCKLEY   Fred (In Memory)
UNITED NEWSPAPERS SYNDICATION DEPT.
VICKERY   P. O. Robert J.
WARWICK   Nigel
WEISS   A. M.
WEST O.B.E.   Timothy
WILLIAMSON   Robert J. R.
WILSON   Ron

Lou Warwick.

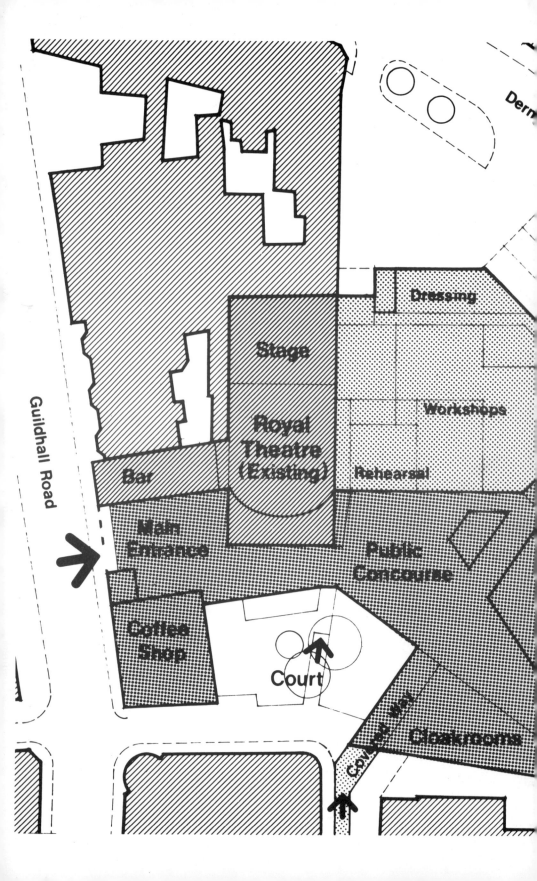